Riot and Great Anger

Irish Studies in Literature and Culture

MICHAEL PATRICK GILLESPIE

SERIES EDITOR

Riot and Great Anger

Stage Censorship in Twentieth-Century Ireland

Joan FitzPatrick Dean

THE UNIVERSITY OF WISCONSIN PRESS

The University of Wisconsin Press
1930 Monroe Street, 3rd Floor
Madison, Wisconsin 53711-2059
uwpress.wisc.edu

3 Henrietta Street
London WC2E 8LU, England
eurospanbookstore.com

3   5   4   2

Printed in the United States of America

Library of Congress Cataloging-in-Publication Data
Dean, Joan FitzPatrick.
Riot and great anger: stage censorship in twentieth-century Ireland /
Joan FitzPatrick Dean.
p.   cm.—(Irish studies in literature and culture)
Includes bibliographical references and index.
ISBN 0-299-19660-7 (cloth: alk. paper)
1. Theater—Censorship—Ireland—History—20th century.
I. Title.   II. Series.
PN2044.I73D43   2004
363.31′09417′0904—dc22   2003022354

ISBN 978-0-299-19664-6 (pbk.: alk. paper)

FOR JACK

As an Irishwoman, I desire to enter a most emphatic protest against Mr. J. M. Synge's new comedy, "The Playboy of the Western World."

—A Western Girl 2

Freeman's Journal, 28 January 1907

I am an 18-year-old UCD student who was shocked and disappointed to discover that the play *Barbaric Comedies* is staged in our National Theatre.

—Aisling Murray

Irish Times, 20 October 2000

Table of Contents

Acknowledgments

Earlier versions of chapters 4, 6, and 8 appeared in the *New Hibernia Review,* the *South Carolina Review,* and *Theatre Survey.* Thanks to the editors for their guidance and encouragement.

I am grateful to the librarians at the University of Missouri–Kansas City; the National University of Ireland, Galway; Trinity College, Dublin; the National Library of Ireland; the National Archives in Dublin; the Berg Collection of the New York Public Library; the Special Collections at Northwestern University; and the Theatre Museum Archives in London. David Sheehy at the Dublin Diocesan Archives and Ophelia Byrne at the Theatre Archive of the Linen Hall Library in Belfast were particularly helpful. I enjoyed the very generous assistance of the librarians at the Spencer Research Library at Kansas University, which houses the P. S. O'Hegarty Collection, especially L. E. James Helyar, Alexandra Mason, Ann Hyde, and Richard Clement.

I am happy to acknowledge the support of the University of Missouri Research Board and the School of Graduate Studies at the University of Missouri-Kansas City to travel to Ireland and Britain. The Missouri London Program provided the opportunity to conduct research in London over several months. Among my colleagues in Kansas City, my enduring debt is to Linda Voigts, but I also want to thank Tom Stroik and Tom Poe. I am especially grateful to Karen Vorst of the Department of Economics.

The faculty at University College Galway and then National University of Ireland, Galway—Kevin Barry, Hubert McDermott, Riana O'Dwyer, the late Pat Sheeran, Seán Ryder, Maire-Louise Coolahan, Catherine La Farge, Tom Bartlett, Daíbhí Ó Croínín, and Niall Ó Ciosáin—extended warm, unfailing hospitality. To Pat Collins, Sharon Wholley, and everyone at Charlie Byrne's Bookshop, many thanks. I am grateful to Rod Hall (Martin McDonagh's agent) and Carolyn Swift for their careful and patient responses.

Acknowledgments

I also want to thank Lane Butler, Christopher Murray, John Harrington, Jim Rogers and Tom Redshaw at the *New Hibernia Review,* Ben Novick, Wayne Chapman at the *South Carolina Review,* and Michael Gillespie. Mary Magray did a wonderful job in copyediting the manuscript. Charlotte Headricks, Marianne Wells, and Karen Vandevelde read sections of the manuscript; for their helpful suggestions I am very grateful, although any errors are mine alone.

My greatest debts are to my family: Joan the Greater, my brother Christopher, my sister Margaret, and in-laws who defy all stereotypes. My immediate family was always tolerant, often encouraging, and never complained about take-out. My daughter Flannery, she of the nimblest fingers, helped in typing and proofing the manuscript. By her and her sister Margaret I have been much amused.

Abbreviations

ACNI	Arts Council of Northern Ireland
BBC	British Broadcasting Corporation
Berg	Berg Collection, New York Public Library
BTA/LHL	British Theatre Archive, Linen Hall Library, Belfast
CEMA	Council for the Encouragement of Music and the Arts (Northern Ireland)
DDA	Dublin Diocesan Archives
GTA/NWU	Gate Theatre Archive, Northwestern University, Evanston, Illinois
INLA	Irish National Liberation Army
ILT	Irish Literary Theatre
IRA	Irish Republican Army
LCP	Lord Chamberlain's Papers, British Library
LCP Corr	Lord Chamberlain's Correspondence, British Library
LTOA/NUIG	Lyric Theatre-O'Malley Archive, National University of Ireland, Galway
MP	Member of (British) Parliament
NA	National Archives, Dublin
NLI	National Library of Ireland
NTS	National Theatre Society
O'H/KU	P. S. O'Hegarty Collection, Kansas University
PAC	Project Arts Centre
PEN	Poets, Essayists, Novelists
RIC	Royal Irish Constabulary
RUC	Royal Ulster Constabulary
TCD	Trinity College, Dublin
TMA	Theatre Museum Archives, London

Ajax Yeats Defies the Censor, from *Weekly Independent,* 29 August 1909. Yeats brandishes the sword of "The Shewing Up of Blanco Posnet" and uses the shield of George Bernard Shaw to protect the Abbey Theatre and *The Playboy* from censorship.

Riot and Great Anger

Introduction

There is no stage censorship in Ireland.

On 24 September 1819 Reverend W. C. Armstrong, then Provost of Sligo, suspended performances of *The Hypocrite,* Isaac Bickerstaffe's 1768 adaptation of Molière's *Tartuffe.* A touring company, under the management of a Mr. Clarke, staged in Sligo what Armstrong thought to be an unacceptable calumny on certain of its citizens. Clarke's company would continue its tour, apparently without incident elsewhere in the country, but Armstrong, who described himself as acting "from conscientious motives alone," banned *The Hypocrite* as a direct attack on devout Christians in his community. That neither Bickerstaffe nor Molière, both long dead, could have known anything of Sligo's inhabitants in 1819 mattered not at all. Armstrong banned the play as blasphemous and as a direct satire of living personages he believed were held up to mockery on the stage.

This was not the first time that Provost Armstrong had found stage plays objectionable. In his eighteen-year ministry in Sligo, Reverend Armstrong had established an association "with a view of ameliorating the condition of unfortunate females confined in our

3

prison." Only a month earlier Armstrong objected that a performance of John Gay's *The Beggar's Opera* "had most indecently slandered" the association.[1] Like many of his twentieth-century counterparts, Armstrong blended a deep suspicion about the stage with the anxiety that he personally was being traduced. Armstrong's fellow citizens, however, were not amused and protested vigorously against this ad hoc imposition of stage censorship. As provost, Armstrong presumed the powers of a magistrate, powers that others did not believe he had. "I must entertain a doubt of your powers as Provost to close the doors of the Theatre against the unanimous wish of the wealthy and respectable part of the population of the town," said Owen Wynne, owner of nearly thirteen thousand acres in County Sligo. "No such power has ever been called into action in any town in the kingdom. . . . [T]o adopt the proceedings you have taken, upon evidence which you did not choose to reveal, was not only inquisitorial, but incompatible with that 'Christian-like feeling' you profess."[2]

Armstrong was not the first to attempt to censor stage plays in Ireland; he certainly wasn't the last. His action against *The Hypocrite*, unusual only because it occurred in Sligo, touched issues that were central to theatre controversies in the twentieth century: a perceived slight or insult to religion, the counterprotest that argued for the right to hear the performance, and the charge that the would-be censor had no authority to ban a play. There was, as many have claimed, no stage censorship in Ireland. And like other would-be censors, Armstrong acted not on a careful reading of the text or attendance at the performance but on hearsay, on the reports of, and responses to, the play. Whereas Britain's Lord Chamberlain evaluated a fixed script, Irish censors, would-be censors, protesters, and picketers often were less than familiar with the plays they condemned. Moreover, published texts were often at variance with their performance; some have never been published. Cautioning Catholics against William Butler Yeats's *The Countess Cathleen* in 1899, Cardinal Michael Logue relied exclusively on extracts from an earlier version of the play compiled by one of Yeats's enemies. Lady Augusta Gregory noted that J. M. Synge's *The Playboy of the Western World* was never published as performed at the Abbey in 1907. In 1998 MPs wanted to withdraw Arts Council funding because of a localized audience response to an unpublished play. In all of these efforts to impose censorship, the very nature of what the theatre audience and the public "received," what it knew or, like Cardinal Logue, thought it knew, can hardly be limited to a text.

Theatre has often been a hotly contested cultural site and such contention is hardly unique to Ireland. In the fifth century B.C. Aristophanes' *Lysistrata* attacked the core values of his society—its patriarchy, militarism, and nationalism—to create a play that endured the millennia. He could do so only because of the privileged place that theatre enjoyed in his society. At least since the Renaissance, when private aristocratic performances and the suppressed (at least in Britain) mystery cycles yielded to for-profit productions, theatre has been where art meets commerce. The purchase of a ticket to a stage performance raises essential questions about what rights come with that ticket. Throughout the twentieth century art frequently sought to offend, disturb, and outrage the audience. Periodically, the audience, duly offended, disturbed, or outraged, expressed its objection and asserted a claim to its own freedom of expression. Audience disruptions of stage productions pitted protestors' rights against those of the producers and actors as well as other audience members. In the disruption of Sean O'Casey's *The Plough and the Stars,* Hanna Sheehy-Skeffington argued that theatregoers had purchased the right to express their disapproval. When she squared off against O'Casey in a public debate following the disruptions she led, she asserted her freedom to protest what offended her. Before 1940, it was more often an Irish audience that presumed its right to disrupt a performance rather than an established power, church or state, that asserted its prerogative to control the stage.

Irish censorship of the stage is unlike its control of any other form or medium—literary, electronic, or visual. The standards for stage censorship, among the most sensitive measures of a culture's sense of itself, map the boundaries of public discourse. Yet these boundaries are invariably localized in both time and space. What was vilified and condemned at the Abbey Theatre in 1907 as "un-Irish" was within a few years celebrated as characteristically Irish. What was censored in Britain was sometimes welcomed on the Irish stage. The interplay between the playwright and society in these theatre controversies indicates not only an evolving cultural identity but also a vertiginous horizon of expectations.

Most accounts of censorship in twentieth-century Ireland focus, quite rightly, on restrictions on printed materials (periodicals as well as novels and "health manuals") and cinema. The rigorous censorship of print and film owes much to Ireland's identity as a Catholic country, but, especially at the beginning of the century, Catholics may have been more at ease with theatre than many Protestants. Stage censorship in Ireland or the absence thereof mirrors the currents of Irish intellectual history: the relationship between church and state; the freedom of the individual; the individual's relationship to the community; the understanding of a collective past. In the twentieth century, theatre served as the site of these cultural confrontations not only because it was a public space, but also because the stage Irish had sensitized native as well as diasporic audiences. As Roy Foster suggests in *The Irish Story: Telling Tales and Making It Up in Ireland,* the nature of what was or is Irish has been contested throughout the century.[3] There are, of course, as many hues of Irish nationalism as there are images of Ireland. Yeats's *The Countess Cathleen* advanced one and was challenged by another. Even before the Irish Literary Theatre (ILT), Irish audiences found their own freedom of the theatre in the patriotic melodramas at the Queen's, which were neither sanctioned by British authority nor performed by foreign "artistes." The phenomenal growth of Irish theatre in the early twentieth century owes much to the nationalistic inspiration that was outside and in some ways antithetical to the well-documented work of Yeats, Gregory, and Synge. But in asserting his claim to freedom of the theatre, Yeats may be credited with investing the Irish stage with prerogatives unique in public discourse. The controversies surrounding Yeats, Synge, and George Bernard Shaw are not only among the best known, they are illustrative of attitudes toward censorship that figured prominently after Independence.

Throughout the century, but especially before 1922, the most serious censorship crises responded to comic plays by non-Catholic playwrights who employed an often contemporaneous, expressly Irish setting. During this period, which includes World War I, Ireland experienced a far-reaching censorship that was principally but not exclusively political. The London stage remained under the heavy hand of the Lord Chamberlain until 1968, but the 1909 production of *The Shewing-up of Blanco Posnet* openly defied his authority. The production of Shaw's play, the Abbey directors asserted, was proof of Ireland's maturity, sophistication, and openness and, in no small measure, a celebration of its freedom from capricious and inflexible censorship. Since then many Irish writers have taken considerable pride in the fact that Ireland never imposed stage censorship. No less relevant than the efforts to censor individual theatrical productions were the calls for an institutional stage censor. Such demands, usually inspired by controversial productions, tended to appeal to either moral or nationalistic principles. Typically, protesters argued that a controversial production epitomized the migration of pernicious foreign influences.

After Independence, the Free State grappled with legislation to create an expressly Irish censorship. Film was first on the agenda; the new government rushed through film censorship in 1923. Over the next five years, extensive debates and investigations produced the *Report of the Committee on Evil Literature* that in turn informed the Censorship of Publications Act of 1929. By this time, however, the Irish stage had constructed a tradition of its own freedom of the theatre that flouted the Lord Chamberlain's authority. To adopt a preproduction licensing of stage plays would have mirrored a reviled British Chamberlain. Theatre was afforded a special privilege in its exclusion from even the legislative debates about censorship in the 1920s. In these debates, as throughout Irish discourse in the century, the likely prospective audience was key, especially if it might include children. As Richard Hayes, the film censor, observed in the 1940s: "The Abbey audiences are 100 per cent adult and the cinema audiences may conceivably be as much as 80 per cent children."[4]

During the period 1939–45, virtually all forms of public and private communications—post, telegrams, radio, newspapers, and even theatre—were censored to assure Ireland's neutrality under the sweeping powers of the Emergency legislation. Again, the official legislation overlooked, or at least failed to specify, theatre. After the lifting of Emergency censorship, its comptroller, Thomas J. Coyne, suggested that the omission of theatre was purely an oversight, the correction of which he recommended in any future legislation. When the state did intervene in censoring plays during the Emergency, it presumed ad hoc powers and the more menacing threat of punitive action against the theatres as well as the plays.

Throughout the century, Irish plays engendered not just controversy but also outrage and even violence. Sometimes playwrights expressed surprise at how controversial their works were, but more often they knew the likely response and were consciously provocative. As Gustave Le Bon observed in 1895, the understanding or reception of a text is inextricably bound to a specific time and place, to the "different mental constitution" of audience members.[5] The limitations of textual analysis are nowhere more evident than in the study of dramatic productions. With the exception of a few satirical playlets, the plays under consideration were all intended for public performance. Not only is their production tied to specific, well-studied movements and institutions—the Irish literary revival, the Abbey Theatre, An Tóstal, for instance—but to factors that frame the reception of the play. The theatre space, advanced publicity, seating arrangements, ticket prices, and actors' nationalities all shaped the audience's expectations of, and responses to, the play. To historicize the critical moments in Ireland's rejection of institutional stage censorship, the reception of individual plays as well as the broader thinking about censorship in Ireland are crucial. Roland Barthes's formulation of theatricality, "theater-minus-text,"[6] and Anne Ubersfeld's and Patrice Pavis's analyses of the relationship among text, *mise en scène,* and performance are particularly valuable in understanding the calls for and resistance to theatrical censorship.[7] By the time the Abbey Theatre opened, these signs and sensations—from the increasingly familiar set design of a rural cottage and the darkened auditorium to the audience's sense of its own theatricality and Yeats's own highly theatrical presentation of himself—shaped not only the reception, but also what was accepted or rejected as Irish drama. In some instances, protests responded to neither the text nor the production. After the first night, no one in the theatre heard much of *The Playboy.* To look to a static text alone for an explanation is to exclude the real genesis of theatrical disorder: the complex interplay of text, performance, publicity, memory, reputation, reviews, and rumor. As much as Annie Horniman wanted an Abbey repertory with "no politics,"[8] political and cultural aspirations have always found a home in Irish theatre. Indeed, the Irish stage serves as the site of ideological encounters that reflect subtle distinctions and submerged conflicts within and among the nationalist, Catholic, intellectual, and artistic communities in Ireland.

Many commentators approach Irish plays as outside or distinct from the development of modern English-speaking drama. Indeed, when it first spoke with an Irish accent, Irish drama defined itself in contradistinction to British drama and was seen as another medium for the incubation of various strains of cultural nationalism. Games were Gaelic. Popular advertisements for everything from matches to bicycles hailed their products as "Irish-made" or "all-Irish." Clothing, food, the most ordinary objects were inscribed as Irish or Celtic. Certainly one of the most damning invectives that the nationalistic press leveled against Synge was that he was the minion of foreign influences. Yet in bringing Shaw's *Blanco Posnet* to the stage, for instance, Irish drama responded to specific events in Britain, where its own vigilance committees and other fervidly censorious constituencies were active. In other cases, such as the controversies that surrounded Tennessee Williams's plays in the fifties, what happened in Ireland was not unrelated to what happened in Britain and the United States.

Censorship in Ireland has reached into all of the arts and even into everyday expression, but stage censorship has proved especially thorny because it exists only on an extralegal, ad hoc basis. The battles over stage censorship reveal a country that is more pluralistic, heterogeneous, and complex than one constructed on simplistic binary polarities of Catholic or Protestant, urban or rural, pro- or anti-Treaty. Each instance of attempted stage censorship is deeply rooted in a particular moment of time. Today the restrictions—especially those imposed on printed works in the 1930s, '40s, '50s, and '60s—are seen as harsh, puritanical, and repressive in comparison to those of other English-speaking or European countries. The workings of the censorship board, for instance, prompted Alec Craig to observe in 1977 that "so far as the control of literature was concerned [Irish censorship sought] to reverse the whole tradition of English-speaking peoples as regards the law of obscene publications."[9] But

Irish theatre was always accorded an anomalous freedom. Norman St. John-Stevas in *Obscenity and the Law* argued that since *The Playboy* riots in 1907, "Irish theatre has been considerably freer than the English."[10]

By mid-century, people who knew nothing else about *The Playboy of the Western World* and *The Plough and the Stars* knew that these plays occasioned riots. The very fact that there was no institutional stage censorship in Ireland facilitated the construction of a tradition of Irish theatrical disorder. In all of the instances here considered, a specific play or its author provoked either censorship or the call for it. In each instance, the play, whether seen in performance, read as a text, or known only by reputation, produced a visceral and sometimes violent reaction. Later productions of the same play might pass without a comparable reaction, but the most turbulent disorders are the best known. With few exceptions, attempts at Irish stage censorship were not only futile but, by generating publicity and notoriety, self-defeating and counterproductive. Why these plays were viewed as threatening, evil, or immoral and why some people, willing to abridge civil liberties through institutional stage censorship, were eager to proscribe them is the subject of this study.

Theatrical Censorship and Disorder in Ireland

This is bigger than Jurassic Park! Thanks to the protest you've put up, The Passion of St. Tibulus is breaking all box office records!

—*Father Ted*

Two striking anomalies foreground any analysis of Irish stage censorship: first, the Lord Chamberlain's authority did not extend to Ireland; second, despite strict, even draconian, regulation of print and film, Ireland as Free State and Republic never institutionalized stage censorship. Although many writers proudly proclaim, "There is no stage censorship in Ireland," de facto instances of censorship regularly occurred throughout the twentieth century. Before Independence, the prevailing standards for acceptable stage productions in Ireland drew heavily upon the British model, especially in restricting the representation of living or recently deceased people as stage characters and in prohibiting obscenity and blasphemy. The majority of plays performed in Ireland at the end of the nineteenth century were works licensed by the Lord Chamberlain that usually featured British actors. In the twentieth century, Irish plays and players came to dominate. Despite calls for an institutional dramatic censorship, Ireland never adopted a pre-production approval or licensing of plays. What was seen as incendiary or immoral by Irish audiences, such as bringing the Irish tricolor into a public house in O'Casey's *Plough,* posed no problem to the Lord Chamberlain and audiences outside Ireland. What was acceptable to and even beloved by Dublin audiences caused civil disorder in Westport. And on more than one occasion—most notably the 1909 production of Shaw's *The Shewing-up of Blanco Posnet* at the Abbey and the 1928 production of Oscar Wilde's *Salome* in the inaugural season of the Gate—Irish productions of plays banned elsewhere, especially in England, capitalized on the freedom afforded theatre in Ireland.

Laws Governing Censorship

Institutional stage censorship in England dates back to 1544 when Henry VIII appointed the first "Master of the Revels, an official under the Lord Chamberlain."[1] Beginning with Edmund Tilney in 1579, the Master of the Revels reviewed plays before their production. Plays previously performed, such as Colley Cibber's 1700 reworking of Shakespeare's *Richard III,* were sometimes suppressed on an ad hoc basis. Other legal mechanisms governed the licensing and safety not of the plays but of the venues where they were performed; still others, such as the vagrancy laws, applied to theatre companies and individual actors. The enforcement of these laws was selective; some fell into desuetude. By the early 1730s, "if a manager wished to operate a theatre without the sanction of letters patent, and even under the disapproval of Lord Chamberlain, there was no remedy at law available to the Crown or to others who opposed him."[2] The powers of the Master of the Revels and Lord Chamberlain waned and waxed, remaining ill-defined for more than a century.

After the Restoration, the Lord Chamberlain oversaw "the management of the theatres, particularly their relationships with actors and actresses," while the Master of the Revels dealt with licensing the plays.[3] As theatre in Britain reclaimed its popularity in the late seventeenth century, hostility to theatre and calls for censorship of the stage intensified. Jeremy Collier's 1698 diatribe, "A Short View of the Immorality and Profaneness of the English Stage," fully articulated the religious prejudice against theatre. Within forty years, the stage would come under strict regulation—not, however, in response to religious agitation or moralistic motive. Stung by scathing satires of John Gay and Henry Fielding, politicians enacted the Licensing Act of 1737 (Walpole's Act), which formalized theatre censorship by investing the Lord Chamberlain with the authority to censor or to ban plays. Thereafter, any manager who planned to present a new play in London was legally bound to submit it for licensing by the Lord Chamberlain, an obligation that continued until 1968. The specific prohibition against the stage depiction of living or recently deceased personages or of the Royal family was now entrenched as a, perhaps *the,* central tenet of British stage censorship. Those in power would be spared the humiliation of being traduced, usually comically, on the public stage. Importantly, the Lord Chamberlain licensed a specific script, fixed and committed to paper. The text, rather than a staged performance, received a permanently valid license. In rare instances, however, a license could be suspended, as was the case for W. S. Gilbert's *The Mikado* (1885) when Prince Fushimi of Japan visited London in 1907.[4] While the 1737 Licensing Act gave the Lord Chamberlain control over plays performed in London and British towns with royal residences, no commensurate powers or procedures were established for any authority in Ireland.

In 1832 a select committee of the House of Commons reviewed the Licensing Act of 1737, the decline of the British theatre, and the disadvantages to those who wrote for the stage. In considering the extent to which laws governing dramatic literature contributed to the obvious decline in the English stage, the hearings examined the ineffectiveness of the copyright laws and the disproportionately slim earnings of even the most successful playwrights. Among those interviewed by the committee were the Lord Chamberlain himself, his deputies, shareholders and managers of the "legitimate" theatres, actors (including Edmund Kean), magistrates, a few playwrights, and proprietors of nonpatent houses like the Adelphia Theatre. Testimony addressed the exact authority, practices, and activities of the Lord Chamberlain, the effects of greater tolerance of drama outside the legitimate theatres, and the economics of the theatres. Douglas Jerrold, author of the hugely popular *Black-Eyed Susan* (1829), reported that "[playwrights] received a double injury: in the first place, they are not paid for their pieces, and in the next place, they are represented by the skeletons [in abridged performances] of their drama; so that, as it was emphatically said by a sufferer, the author was not only robbed but murdered."[5] The 1832 hearings also considered the Lord Chamberlain's ineffectiveness in regulating the nonpatent theatres, especially music halls, which offered increasing competition to the legitimate theatres.

The 1832 report reaffirmed that the Lord Chamberlain's powers did not extend to Ireland. Both James Winston, then manager of the Haymarket Theatre, and George Colman (the Younger), the Examiner of Plays between 1824 and 1836, explicitly stated that Ireland was outside the Lord Chamberlain's authority. When asked "Is the Dublin theatre under your protection?" Colman replied: "No, there is a Lord Lieutenant there; it is under the control of his household. . . . [T]here is a sort of Master of the Revels appointed there; they are under control, dependent on the Lord Lieutenant's regime."[6] Colman was mistaken; there had been a Master of the Revels, but the position had degenerated into a sinecure and faded away. Nor was Colman aware of a further anomaly: whatever authority the Lord Lieutenant had over theatre was limited to Dublin.[7]

Parliament addressed the piracy question raised by Jerrold and others in the Dramatic Copyright Act of 1833 but was not quick to liberalize competition among theatres such as to end the patent monopoly on "straight" plays. The Theatres Act of 1843 did not only that but also extended the authority of the Lord Chamberlain to all plays in all theatres in England. Like the 1737 Licensing Act, the 1843 act did not apply to Ireland. The Theatres Regulation Act of 1843, which forbade public performances of any unlicensed play, contained two exceptions: performances that did not charge admission and those of a "bona fide society" did not require the Lord Chamberlain's approval. (Some of the most controversial London "theatre club" productions before 1968 circumvented the Lord Chamberlain's authority through the second of these loopholes.) In 1853 another select committee of the House of Commons considered the regulation of a burgeoning number of public entertainment alternatives: "publichouses, hotels, beershops, dancing saloons, coffeehouses, theatres, temperance hotels." In 1866 yet another parliamentary select committee, concerned with the licensing and regulation of theatres, as opposed to plays, again extended the Lord Chamberlain's powers, this time to places of entertainment other than theatres.

In the late nineteenth century the laws governing plays underwent epochal changes: the American Copyright Chace Act of 1891 assured the dramatist's rights and ended the trans-Atlantic piracy of printed dramatic works. It facilitated the simultaneous production and publication of plays, a phenomenon that became a distinctive feature of the Irish theatre movement early in the twentieth century when dramatists published their plays, especially in the nationalist press, before they were performed. Padraic Colum, for instance, published several plays, including the accepted-then-rejected *The Saxon Shillin'* before his first stage production in 1903. Because the public might read a play and claim to know it without, or before, attending a performance, the publication of Irish plays became a critical factor in several censorship controversies.

While the 1832 hearings professed an interest in nurturing and revitalizing the stage, the 1892 hearings, the final inquiry before 1909, were quite a different matter. By the end of the nineteenth century the British stage was again robust—too robust for the Lord Chamberlain's activities to escape criticism. Whereas writing for the stage had been disreputable and dangerous—disreputable because of the often salacious nature of successful plays and dangerous because of the myriad legal snares—by 1892 it was potentially lucrative if not always respectable. As Richard Findlater notes: "Organized opposition to the Lord Chamberlain began seriously only after it demonstrably became both respectable and profitable to write plays, and when it became clear that the more serious new drama was the kind that the Lord Chamberlain was most likely to mutilate or to suppress."[8] The Lord Chamberlain's attention, moreover, shifted away from the concerns that motivated the Licensing Act of 1737—satire, subversion, and sedition—and toward the nebulous questions of indecency and public morals. With few exceptions, and most of those during wartime, the Lord Chamberlain's censorship had become more often a "moral" than a political one by the end of the nineteenth century.

The opening salvo in the eighty-two-year campaign against institutional stage censorship in Britain came in William Archer's "The Censorship of the Stage" (1886). Archer denounced the entire process of play licensing and attacked the Lord Chamberlain for banning a centennial production of Shelley's *The Cenci* (1819) because it dealt with incest. Archer was joined by many playwrights, including Oscar Wilde, whose *Salome* had been in rehearsal with Sarah Bernhardt for three weeks in 1892 when it was banned because of its treatment of scriptural material.[9] But the need to convene another parliamentary investigation of the Lord Chamberlain's censorship had already been galvanized on 13 March 1891 when J. T. Grein's Independent Theatre Society presented a single private performance of Henrik Ibsen's unlicensed *Ghosts*. The 1892 hearings turned on the Lord Chamberlain's refusal to license a growing number of plays that were neither salacious nor offensively satirical but rather "literary" plays by well-respected writers.

Ibsen's translator and Shaw's close friend, Archer was the only witness invited to testify before the 1892 committee who condemned the censorship. The Lord Chamberlain drew strong support from the theatre community, mainly from managers and owners. Throughout the eighteenth, nineteenth, and twentieth centuries theatre managers coexisted in a symbiotic relationship with the Lord Chamberlain. The Lord Chamberlain's license indemnified owners, managers, and financial backers against legal prosecution and most protests. It provided a ready answer to objections that a production was indecent, immoral, or offensive. Since the preproduction censor worked from a text, there was always the possibility that an actor might depart from the approved script in performance or that the production might employ staging, props, or gestures to contravene the Lord Chamberlain's directions. In several instances, the officials from the Lord Chamberlain's office monitored productions and intervened after the licensing.[10] But managers were eager to accommodate the Lord Chamberlain's directives and unwilling to challenge his authority.

Archer's testimony detailed egregious inconsistencies in the Lord Chamberlain's licensing practices. As an exception to the supposedly inflexible rule against depicting living personages on the stage, Archer cited the fact that a year before Daniel O'Connell's death, Charles Mathews played the Irishman on the stage. Such a glaring exception to one of the Lord Chamberlain's bedrock principles was, of course, a political decision: if the personages were Irish, they might easily fall outside the hallowed interdiction on depicting living persons, especially politicians, on stage. For Archer, however, even more salient were the retrogressive and puritanical licensing standards.

The 1892 committee also heard from Michael Gunn, proprietor and manager of the Gaiety Theatre in Dublin. Although none of the theatres in Ireland fell under the jurisdiction of the Lord Chamberlain, Gunn reported that "conditions of a stringent character are inserted into the patents as to no plays being produced which shall be contrary to good morals or manners, indecent, subversive of law and order, or inimical to religion or the government of the country." Gunn also averred that "no plays hav[e] ever been produced [in Dublin] which have in any way offended public taste."[11] However naive Gunn's sweeping assertion, it provided yet another reason to leave Ireland out of England's theatre censorship.

Gunn's testimony pointed to the second important legal means of control over the stage in Ireland: the licensing of theatres through letters patent issued by Her Majesty's government through the Lord Lieutenant. Letters patent provided a number of conditions to assure public safety, to maintain order, and to prohibit immorality on the stage. The last Patent for the Theatre Royal, issued in 1909, contains the following clauses, which by the beginning of the twentieth century had become standard for theatres in both England and Ireland:

No profanity or impropriety of language to be permitted on the Stage.

No indecency of dress dance or gesture language to be permitted on the Stage.

No offensive personalities or representations of living person to be permitted on the Stage nor anything calculated to produce riot or breach of the peace.

No Exhibition of Wild Beasts or dangerous performances to be permitted on the Stage.

No Women or Children to be hang [sic] from the flies nor fixed in position from which they cannot release themselves. . . .

[N]o representations shall be admitted on the Stage by virtue or under cover of these Presents whereby the Christian religion may in any manner suffer reproach. And We hereby strictly prohibit all and every degree and abuse of misrepresentation of sacred characters which may in any degree tend to expose religion or bring it into contempt. And that no such characters be introduced or played in any other light than such as may increase the just esteem of those who answer the end of these sacred functions.[12]

In Dublin, then, the primary mechanism of legal control over theatre was in licensing the premises, the actual physical space, rather than the play. Gunn testified that theatres in Belfast were licensed by the mayor, in Cork by the corporation, and in Dublin by the recent Dublin Corporation Act of 1890.[13] Many of the provisions of this act, such as fire regulations, addressed public safety. The 1890 act reiterated that Irish theatres operated "under authority of letters patent from Her Majesty, Her heirs or successors or of licenses by any licensing authority."[14] In Dublin the theatre managers assumed responsibility for "expunging all such offensive expressions passages and gestures."[15] The 1890 Dublin Corporation Act also stipulated a penalty of fifty pounds per day for any person who offered "public performance of stage plays" in a venue that was without a license.[16] In Britain, the gravest penalty for performing an unlicensed play was that the license for the theatre would not be renewed.

An act passed by the Irish Parliament on 25 November 1786, the one that vexed Yeats and Gregory in 1898, created a monopoly by requiring letters patent in all Dublin venues performing plays. Noting that well-regulated theatres "tend to improve the morals of the people," An Act for Regulating the Stage in the City and County of Dublin put an end to the eighteenth-century aspirations for an Irish national theatre in Fishamble Street.[17] As a deterrent to any upstart companies or theatres, the law stipulated an exorbitant fine of three hundred pounds per performance ("one moiety to be paid to the governors or guardians of the [Rotunda] Lying-in-hospital"[18]) against Dublin theatre owners or managers performing in an unlicensed venue. The facilities at the Rotunda Hospital were a special exception, exempt from any form of licensing because, from its inception, the hospital envisioned dramatic entertainments as one of several funding sources for its charitable ventures.[19] Irish letters patent endowed the patentee and theatre with rights, but also, affirming the 1786 act, restricted competition from nonpatent theatres. Like their British counterparts, the patents were franchises, with their own "noncompete" clauses. The 1909 patent for the Theatre Royal in Dublin, for instance, "forb[ade] all persons during term time and space hereinbefore limited from presuming to erect build or keep open . . . any Theatre" within the city and county of Dublin.[20]

From the late seventeenth through the early nineteenth centuries, stage censorship in Ireland emulated the British model. The title for the Irish stage censor, Master of the Revels, was identical with that of his British counterpart; both were court appointments. Between 1661, beginning with James Ogilby, and 1830, ending with William Micke (or Meeke), control of Irish theatre was nominally in the hands of the Irish Master of the Revels. La Tourette Stockwell asserts that by 1720 the Deputy Master of the Revels, who actually carried out the functions of the office, had become synonymous with the manager of the Theatre Royal. By the end of the eighteenth century, both positions, Master and Deputy Master, had become sinecures and soon disappeared.[21]

Despite Gunn's testimony, the Irish stage figured only marginally in the final report of the 1892 select committee. Writing on behalf of Irish amateur companies, Francis R. Wolfe faulted the 1892 hearings for failing to properly investigate the theatres in Dublin.[22] He rightly charged that the committee took Gunn's self-interested word that all was well and moved on to local and more pressing questions. For the amateurs represented by Wolfe, these conditions constituted a threat that could destroy an amateur company overnight; the more successful an amateur company became, the greater the risk.

In 1909 another parliamentary committee took up the question of stage censorship (discussed in chapter 4). At the very time the 1909 committee was scrutinizing the Lord Chamberlain's powers, the Abbey defied his and the Lord Lieutenant's authority. Ireland had claimed freedom from British theatre censorship. Even after Independence, the Free State refused to qualify that freedom as the Irish stage remained sui generis.

Typology of Theatre Protest

Theatre protest has existed as long as theatre has. The conventions of audience response—cheering or clapping to show approval and booing, hissing, stamping, and whistling to express disapproval—have remained largely consistent over the past century in the

English-speaking world. Like all conventions, these are arbitrary sig-
nifiers that, as anyone who has ever heard what sounds like booing
at a Springsteen concert knows, take meaning from their context.
Unlike other literary forms, theatre elicits a physical response from
its audience, and its etiquette anticipates that response. Vaudeville,
music hall, and other variety entertainments exploited audience re-
actions by incorporating them into the performance, as banter and
heckling for instance. More typically, the audience applauds at the
end of scenes and acts (sometimes in response to impressive scenic or
costume design, musical performance, or individual speeches) and
during the formal, carefully planned curtain calls at the conclusion
of the performance. Modern English-speaking audiences are so polite that they can effectively register disapproval simply by withholding applause or leaving the theatre; more rarely, they may express im-
patience by rhythmic clapping and opprobrium by booing, hissing,
or stomping their feet. In episodes of extreme audience disapproval,
these physical responses have enormous potential for violence.

Despite modern amenities, even today's theatres can be constric-
tive and easily induce feelings of claustrophobia. Unlike most cinemas, theatre seating is usually preassigned and entry after the curtain
is often restricted if not prohibited. Perhaps for those very reasons,
certain decorum is expected in theatre. A single individual with a
bad cough or a mobile phone can unintentionally distract an entire
audience and even the performers. Simply leaving the theatre during
a performance is likely to inconvenience and disturb at least a portion of the audience. When more than one person deliberately plans
to disrupt a performance, they have chosen a conspicuous protest
with an excellent likelihood of success. And it will cost no more than
the price of admission.

The etiquette of playgoing is essential to the question of theatre
protest. What Hans Robert Jauss calls the horizon of expectations
is specific to both time and place. Not only in Ireland, but throughout Europe and America, a paradigmatic shift occurred in the late
nineteenth century that significantly accelerated the change from
Shakespeare's day to our own: some theatres for "straight" or "legitimate" plays became less democratic. The audience standards reflect a

more reverential view of the performance as art, not simply entertainment. (Chapter 3 addresses the changes in audience deportment that occurred early in the century.) Fundamental changes occurred again at the end of the century, when theatres cultivated nontraditional theatregoers. In both cases, the audience's horizon of expectations was destabilized and the likelihood of disorder increased.

In Britain and America theatre disturbances occasionally turned vicious and deadly. As defined by law, a riot is a public disturbance by a group (rather than by isolated individuals) whose lawless, or at least reckless, behavior carries the potential for violence and threatens the safety of others. The terms of the riot act enacted under George I called for a minimum of twelve people engaged in unlawful or riotous assembly who were, after the reading of the act, allotted an hour to disperse. Riots were an extreme manifestation of audience theatricality that endangered actors and other theatre personnel as well as other audience members. The idiomatic usage, that describes riots as "staged," underscores their theatricality. Theatre riots are very rarely spontaneous, not least because of the requirement of a quorum of a dozen demonstrators.

Institutional stage censorship never precluded theatrical disorder. Despite strict regulation of the stage in Britain, theatrical disorder was not uncommon. In 1679, two men set fire to the Lincoln's Inn Theatre in London to drive the Duchess of Portland from the theatre. In 1721, a patron in one of the stage seats crossed the stage at the Lincoln's Inn Theatre during a performance of *Macbeth* to speak with someone on the opposite side and set off a melee. When the theatre manager intervened, the intoxicated patron struck the manager in the face. Others in the stage seats came to the defense of their fellow patron, while the actors joined in on the side of the manager. Before the military arrived to quell the disturbance, the furniture, boxes, and scenery were so badly damaged that the theatre had to close for a week. In 1737 at the Haymarket Theatre, and in 1740 and again in 1754 at the Drury Lane Theater, the appearance of foreign, usually French, performers provoked violent disorder in English audiences. Like the most famous and bloodiest theatrical disorder, the Astor Place riot in New York City on 10 May 1849, the perceived insult of a foreign actor triggered audience violence. Attempts to reform theatre admission policies provoked major theatre disturbances in London on at least two occasions: in 1760, when David Garrick tried to abolish the half-price admission after the third act, and again in 1809, when the Old Price (OP) riots occupied the better part of four months at Covent Garden. All of these disturbances, which took place outside Ireland, point to the theatre as a public space shared by anyone with the price of a ticket.

Throughout the eighteenth and nineteenth centuries Ireland witnessed theatrical riots and disturbances, the best known occurring in 1712, 1747, 1754, and 1784. The tradition of student demonstrations in Irish theatres goes back at least to 1743 when Theophilus Cibber played his part and read that of Thomas Sheridan in a controversial performance of *Cato*. When theatre managers like Sheridan in Dublin and later Garrick in London attempted to insist on greater order and decorum in the mid-eighteenth century, violent displeasure greeted their reforms. The 1747 riots grew out of Sheridan's attempt to end stage sitting; many "gentlemen" felt theirs was the right to abuse and molest the actors and to gain admission to the greenroom and backstage areas. As in the 1721 disturbance at the Theatre Royal in London, a theatre manager intervened to stop disruptive behavior on the stage at Dublin's Smock-Alley (Theatre Royal) Theatre in 1747. Obstreperous and drunk, Mr. Kelly, climbed on the stage to attack George Ann Bellamy, who was appearing as Cleopatra in John Dryden's *All for Love,* and then came backstage to claim his "rights" as a "gentleman." Sheridan intervened, breaking Kelly's nose. A contemporary account records that "the theatre was converted into a battle-field, in which swords, cudgels, and other weapons were freely used. The undergraduates took several of the opposing faction prisoners and carried them off to the College where they inflicted condign punishment upon them, with, it is said, the approval of the provost."[23] The ensuing tumult, which lasted more than six weeks, spread from the theatre to Sheridan's supporters at Trinity College and eventually engulfed Dublin. The next season Sheridan attempted to end the practices of admitting latecomers (who were often drunk and disorderly), giving refunds, and honoring "silver tickets"—passes issued to "permanent free-riders—members of the viceregal court, theatre proprietors, their relatives and descendants, et cetera."[24] Riots again ensued. Here, as in the twentieth century, the circumstances of performance, the venue, the audience's rights, and the actors' vulnerability to physical assault, are critical factors.

Since "legitimate" theatre in Ireland was so closely identified with Dublin Castle in the early nineteenth century, theatrical protests were typically antiestablishment and in some ways anticipated the demonstrations and disorder of the twentieth century. The most celebrated instance of theatre disorder in Ireland in the nineteenth century, the Bottle Riot, occurred on 14 December 1822, when Lord Lieutenant the Marquess Wellesley attended a performance of *She Stoops to Conquer* and *Tom Thumb* at the recently opened Theatre Royal in Hawkins Street. Earlier that year, in July, on dates near the anniversary of the Battle of the Boyne, and again in November, around King William's birthday (4 November), Wellesley as well as Lord Mayor Flemming tried to prevent the traditional decoration of the statue of King William that stood before Parliament House. Incensed Orangemen saw this as Wellesley's traitorous, partisan interference in their ritual celebrations. Wellesley's announcement that he would attend the theatre "was call to riot": large blocks of tickets were purchased; Orangemen packed the galleries; placards were prepared; insulting handbills, dropped as confetti, were printed. As soon as Wellesley entered the theatre, demonstrations erupted on both sides: from the Orangemen and from those who, like Wellesley, supported Catholic Emancipation. Handbills denouncing popery, Lord Mayor Flemming, and Wellesley wafted down from the gallery. Nonetheless, the play went on. After the performance, during the playing of "God Save the King," Wellesley stepped forward in his box, so that for the first time those in the theatre could see him. Chaos erupted: whistles signaled the beginning of the riot; opponents of the Orangemen were beaten; the first missile, thought to be a bottle, struck the curtain; another missile, weighing either eight and a half ounces or more than two pounds (depending on your source), tore the upholstery on a chair in Wellesley's box. Four men were arrested, including one, James Forbes, who had been involved in the decoration of King William's statue the previous July. Three of the four were subsequently charged with conspiracy to murder the

Lord Lieutenant, a charge that was later dropped.[25] Like eighteenth-century Irish theatre disturbances, the Bottle Riot revealed Irish theatre as a very public space in which a socially and politically heterogeneous public staged political and cultural confrontations. And like many of the violent theatre disturbances and riots in Ireland before the twentieth century, and unlike all those in the twentieth century, the Bottle Riot had nothing to do with the play being performed on stage.

Censorship in Ireland

The most important studies on censorship in Ireland are Michael Adams's invaluable *Censorship: The Irish Experience,* Julia Carlson's interviews with authors who experienced censorship, *Banned in Ireland,* and Donal Ó Drisceoil's authoritative *Censorship in Ireland: 1939–1945.* All of them touch on theatre but focus on the censorship of other materials. Adams's survey of attitudes expressed in the popular press at critical junctures, especially when the legislation was under debate, remains unsurpassed in its assiduous research and dispassionate analysis.[26] Helen M. Burke's incisive analysis, *Riotous Performances: The Struggle for Hegemony in the Irish Theatre, 1712–1784,* describes the eighteenth-century Dublin stage as the site of a series of disturbances that reflected distinctly Irish concerns. Gerard Whelan's *Spiked: Church-State Intrigue and The Rose Tatoo,* written with Carolyn Swift, examines the efforts to shut down the Pike production of that play in light of recently released government documents.

After the Act of Union (1800), most British laws extended to Ireland, as did the Lord Chamberlain's standards for, although not his authority over, theatre. The censorship controversies surrounding plays by Yeats, Synge, Shaw, and George A. Birmingham reveal not only attitudes toward censorship but also about the stage, a national theatre, and the arts in general. Beyond the concern for indecency, the criteria for British stage censorship were remarkably dissimilar to those that would govern Irish censorship of film and printed material. In Ireland, vastly different standards, owing in large measure to the Catholic church, were at work. The dramatization of biblical episodes and the representation of Christ were taboo in England but commonplace in Ireland in religious dramas, mystery plays, and

24

nativity pageants. In the nineteenth century the Lord Chamberlain grew even more restrictive about the staging of material derived from Scripture. In Ireland, however, the freedom from these prohibitions would become especially significant in the late nineteenth and early twentieth centuries when Irish playwrights from Katharine Tynan and Oscar Wilde to Lady Gregory and Yeats turned to biblical episodes and revivified the miracle play. Similarly, the British stricture against representing historical and living persons was plainly subverted by Irish political melodrama.

Under British law the theatre manager applied to the Lord Chamberlain to license a play before its first performance. Before the 1930s, the dramatist rarely dealt directly with the office of the Lord Chamberlain. Instead, the theatre manager and, later, the writer's agent applied for the license, which indemnified those presenting the play against legal action and provided a convenient response to charges of immorality, obscenity, subversion, or blasphemy. Especially in the twentieth century, protracted correspondence between those representing the playwright or the theatre and the Lord Chamberlain's office negotiated the terms of a license. The Lord Chamberlain's papers include many complaints about licensed plays from groups and individuals. The Lord Chamberlain's file on J. P. Donleavy's *The Ginger Man,* for instance, includes letters of protest from private citizens and the (London) Public Morality Council, responses from the Lord Chamberlain to those protests, internal memoranda, as well as correspondence over excised or modified dialogue. When *The Ginger Man* appeared in Dublin, the production was not bound by any of the Lord Chamberlain's revisions. As the manager of the Gaiety Theatre came to realize, his contract with the writer and producer obligated him not to change the play. Just as the Lord Chamberlain's banning of Shaw's *The Shewing-up of Blanco Posnet* did not prevent the play's performance in Dublin, his cuts to *The Ginger Man* did not cross the Irish Sea.

The Irish Free State was quick to institute film censorship in 1923. Although Ireland never employed a prerelease or preperformance licensing of plays, it, like many countries, still does for films. Under such a licensing or certification scheme, cinema managers as well as film distributors, producers, and directors often work directly with the licensing authority to assure the widest commercial possibilities. This is also the case in the United States, for example, as filmmakers negotiate cuts to assure an R (Restricted) rating and to avoid the commercial kibosh of an NC-17 (No Children under 17) designation.[27] The R rating, like the Lord Chamberlain's license, provides protection from charges of indecency and indemnifies the theatre against prosecution. In Ireland, this was the model for the censoring authority in film, although until recently the British certification process preceded the work of the Irish film censor.

The Censorship of Publications Act of 1929 sought to protect the young, vulnerable, and innocent, although neither the report of the Irish Committee on Evil Literature nor *The Problem of Undesirable Printed Matter: Some Suggested Remedies* recommended that the state ban books solely because they might corrupt children. Even the Catholic Truth Society argued "the censorship which should protect the young from literary influences pernicious to the immature is the censorship exercised in the home and the school and through the spiritual director."[28] Because "most of the books and periodicals on sale [in Ireland] were published in countries outside the legislation" and most publishers were beyond the reach of Irish law, the Free State adopted a procedure of banning books only after publication.[29] In effect, the censorship of printed material was a ban against distribution (including sales and public circulation through libraries), although, curiously, not against possession. Given the enormous amount of potentially censurable material, the 1929 legislation provided a means for individuals or groups to call material to the Censorship Board's attention and request that the work be suppressed. This procedure catered to the well-established vigilance societies, such as the Catholic Truth Society and later the League of Decency, whose express purpose was to purify Ireland of what they found offensive. In practice, marked passages rather than "the general tendency of the work" formed the basis for banning books. As capricious as the Lord Chamberlain's licensing was, it was less arbitrary than the smut hunting that exploited this censoring mechanism. Famously, a literary work like Kate O'Brien's *The Land of Spices* (1941) was banned on the basis of a single sentence.

Between 1939 and 1945, virtually all forms of public and private communications—post, telegrams, radio, newspapers, and even theatre—were censored under the sweeping powers of the Emergency legislation to assure Ireland's neutrality. Again, theatre was anomalous: remarkably, it was overlooked in the official legislation. A decade after the Censorship of Publications Act, the Emergency Power Order of 1939 identified three criteria for censoring films: those that would be "prejudicial to the maintenance of law and order or to the preservation of the State or would be likely to lead to a breach of the peace or to cause offense to the people of a friendly foreign nation."[30] The film censor directly echoed these principles: "In order to avoid demonstrations prejudicial to the maintenance of law and order, or the creation of scenes likely to lead to a breach of the peace, films showing pictures of rulers, statesmen, warriors and flags of the belligerents must not be shown."[31] In at least two instances, these standards would be applied to silence or significantly abridge stage plays. When the Emergency censorship did need to deal with objectionable productions, it presumed ad hoc powers and the more menacing threat of making life difficult, if not impossible, for theatres.

Battles to censor theatrical productions were waged on many fronts in the late 1950s. There was one unequivocal instance of censorship when *The Ginger Man* was closed. In other instances, plays were interfered with, but the larger campaign for control of the stage was decisively lost. The popular determination to claim freedom of the theatre in the 1960s and beyond triumphed in the hugely popular productions of plays that had previously been the targets of censorship.

Taxonomy of Theatre Censorship

Any taxonomy of censorship is complex. With reference to books, Seán O'Faoláin identified seven censorships operating in Ireland in the 1950s: censorship by fear; by the bookseller; by librarians; by library users; by library committees; by the Censorship Board; and by the public exercised on bookshops.[32] Still other potential censors might influence a play's performance and, like several of those identified by O'Faoláin, those operated without legal basis. Censorship by fear and intimidation is not only the most difficult to document, it is also among the most pernicious.

Stage censorship can come from many sources and take many forms. It can be institutionalized as in England. It can cause or be caused by the withdrawal of funding. It can be imposed by a state agency. At times, theatre reviewers and journalists have been accused of acting as censors by virtue of their privileged access to public opinion. What some would describe as censorship exists whenever certain plays are chosen for performance while others are rejected. As Synge and Sean O'Casey discovered during the rehearsals at the Abbey, censorship can come from actors who refuse to say certain lines or to play certain roles. Theatre censorship involves not only the creative process and the means of production, distribution, and consumption, but legal statutes regulating those means. Theatres in Ireland, as elsewhere, were and are governed by building codes, fire and public safety regulations, as well as statutes restricting indecency, public disorder, hate speech, and incitement to riot. Perhaps the most revealing instances of censorship are also the most minatory because they operate outside the rule of law.

There is, first, the realm of authorial censorship, a term used here to refer, despite the inherently collaborative nature of theatre, to the self-censorship of the person who creates the "text." Authorial censorship involves both the self-censorship that is informed by the writer's artistic judgment, superego, conscience, or propriety as well as the editorial revisions, deletions, and emendations that are intrinsic to the creative process. There are, of course, fascinating examples of this phenomenon in which time and power are crucial factors. Francis Ford Coppola, for instance, revised the final sequences of *Apocalypse Now* and changed the ending of the film as it was originally released in 1979. Today audiences see Willard and Lance drift away from Kurtz's compound in the boat that has brought them upstream, whereas in the 1970s the film ended with the spectacular "purgative air strike" that Willard radioed in to "Almighty" to fulfill Kurtz's imperative, "Exterminate the brutes." Coppola's ownership and control of the film, the abiding American anxiety over Vietnam, and the highly collaborative nature of the medium all interact in extremely convoluted ways to allow for a new ending that is fundamentally at odds with, if not antithetical to, what audiences saw in 1979. Analogous and no less convoluted reworkings appear in Yeats's multiple revisions of *The Countess Cathleen*. In exploring the hermeneutics of censorship, Annabel Patterson describes another variant of authorial censorship as "the cultural code . . . by which matters of intense social and political concern continue to be discussed in the face of extensive political censorship [through] a highly sophisticated system of oblique communication, of unwritten rules."[33] But unlike early modern England, where offensive authors were tortured, dismembered, and executed, twentieth-century Ireland reveled in its "freedom of the theatre"; its theatrical disorders rarely emanated from authors pursuing obliqueness or what Patterson calls "the strategies of indirection." On the modern Irish stage playwrights were, like Yeats in 1899, insensitive to, or unaware of, how audiences would receive their works (and in the case of *The Countess Cathleen,* willing to make whatever changes would avert censure) or, like Synge in 1907, willing to challenge the censorious impulses of their audience. Authorial censorship, although intensified by the panoptic internalization of external standards, is universal (although also localized) and beyond the concern of this study.[34]

Similarly, collegial censorship, a second category, involves a reader, advisor, publisher, or editor who is usually sympathetic to the author if not the text. Here another person enters the creative process and influences the text by offering suggestions or making demands. The choice of the adjective "collegial" indicates that the author retains the freedom to accept or reject the recommendations. This, too, might well be included in the broadest definition of censorship, but it likewise falls outside the scope of this study.[35]

The third tier of potential censorship, where this study begins its concern, is in the means of distribution and consumption of the text, its transformation from text to performance. Theatre is not only the most collaborative of the literary arts, it is also the most public. As the text moves toward performance, it is commodified—valued for its artistic, political, or financial worth. During this process, the potential for censorship increases exponentially. In bringing a play to the stage, forces and individuals increasingly participate in the collaboration that will produce, distribute, and facilitate the consumption or reception of a stage performance. In the case of a play, this third level of censorship involves an expanded array of possible interference: directors, producers, stage managers, theatre owners, patent holders, actors, or technical personnel can affect the work even before it is ever made available to the public. To distribute the theatrical production involves securing the resources and a theatrical space in which to perform the play, navigating a tangle of legal statutes, and generating publicity to attract an audience. Typically, this demands an organization—a theatrical company, a school, or an association—to undertake the play's production and to assume the financial and legal liabilities as well as the possibility of profit. Once produced, the play is presented to an audience typically composed of the paying public and media reviewers. Either before or after performance, one of the most potent sources of censorship may intervene: the money. Throughout the twentieth century, patrons, backers, and funding agencies have played a pivotal role in censorship controversies. Patrons include private individuals, corporate sponsors, the state, organizations, businesses, and, through lowered or no wages, artistic personnel. When a patron or funding agency disapproves of a performance, the threat of the withdrawal of support brings yet another potential censor to bear.

The fourth level of censorship involves those who respond to the work, those who "consume" the work as performance. For most literary works, including plays, the text is now subject to an even wider range of would-be censors, who have had no role prior to their experience of the play: reviewers, booksellers, the ticketed public, and society's institutions, including its legal and religious hierarchies. In Ireland the demand for censorship typically came from the insurgent press or religious organizations, usually the Catholic church. Although politically revolutionary, the advanced nationalist press was socially conservative, overtly moralistic, and eager to see an expressly Irish control imposed on theatre and, indeed, all the arts. By the end of the twentieth century, very different standards than those that prevailed at the end of the nineteenth, both in Ireland and in Britain, governed what could and could not be performed. Previously taboo themes, such as homosexuality, abortion, and incest, are not infrequently staged. The virulent but casual anti-Semitism and racism of earlier works are today proscribed under hate speech legislation in many countries, including Ireland.

The interplay between the playwright and society and between the actors and their audiences in these attempts at theatrical censorship maps an evolving cultural identity. The very decision to mount a public stage production is hardly a democratic procedure and rarely a purely artistic one. Typically, producers must be persuaded that the play has value. In the commercial theatre that means that the play will succeed in attracting a paying audience. The surest way to kill a stage performance is an empty theatre. If neither patron nor audience will support a play, it will not endure; it will rarely even debut. Conversely, the best way to sustain a theatrical production is to attract audiences, especially those who would typically not attend a play or those who might revisit a production to watch not only the play but the audience. And controversy is one of the surest ways to reach that expanded audience base.

Most of these controversial productions were staged in Dublin, but audiences in Belfast and occasionally in Sligo or Westport also chose the theatre as the site to air their grievances. In many cases, demonstrations in the theatre or on the streets were not spontaneous but deliberately planned, often as much to cultivate media attention as to put an end to the performance. By drawing the public's attention to a play as offensive and creating disorder that was in itself newsworthy, protesters inevitably risked creating a *succès de scandale,* especially in the case of the Irish productions of plays banned by Britain's Lord Chamberlain.

Some of these protests involved overt displays of civil disobedience; most were symbolic protests that offered little threat of violence; still others were intentionally clamant, unruly, and violent. Picket lines attempted to deter or to intimidate potential audience members from the theatre. Occasionally a small group hoped to incite a much larger public outrage. Often the protesters had neither seen nor read what they decried. After 1929 some drew upon the unusual model established by the Censorship of Publications Act by appealing directly to government agencies or the Gardai. In the two most unambiguous instances of stage censorship, the church (in the case of *The Ginger Man*) and the state (in the case of *Roly*

Poly) coerced the withdrawal of a running production from a theatre. Attempts at theatre censorship, however, rarely came from above.
And with few exceptions, efforts at stage censorship failed: not only
were the runs of the plays completed, but the would-be censors were
hoist with their own petard, creating a *cause célèbre* that enlarged the
audience.

The press reports of attempted stage censorship include "official"
comment from the author, stage management, and authorities (often
police or judicial reports). Typically, the press also carried correspondence that debated the merits of the play, its reception, and outrage
that located new protests in the context of previous ones. As Yeats
told his Irish audience in 1926, they didn't just disgrace themselves,
they disgraced themselves again. A chronological approach to the
struggles for and against stage censorship reveals the emergence of a
constructed tradition intrinsically linking theatre and animated, occasionally violent, protest. Early in the century, reviews almost invariably commented on the audience—its composition, size, response,
and mood. Audiences were regularly described as appreciative, unruly, or disappointed. Moreover, some papers listed the names of
well-known individuals in attendance. Audience response was sometimes as much of the "story" as the play or the actors' performances.
The papers thereby heightened the audience's theatricality by reporting on performances not only onstage but also off. In this regard,
they were not unlike their counterparts in London or New York at
the end of the nineteenth century. But Dublin audiences had unique
priorities, not least because of their consciousness of the stage Irishman. A history of implicit or overt theatrical attacks on their religion, ancestors, and beliefs loomed large for Irish audiences.

Several critics allege that Irish audiences show a proclivity toward
unruliness and link theatrical disruptions with larger anxieties about
civil disorder in Ireland. In *Thomas Sheridan of Smock-Alley*, Esther K.
Sheldon, for instance, situates theatrical disturbances in an overarch-
ing pattern of cultural activity: "Eighteenth-century Dublin was
prone to civil disturbances: destructive wars between rival street
gangs, Trinity demonstrations and high jinks, mobs of citizens
besieging government buildings in some protest or other.[36] In *Culture
and Anarchy in Ireland, 1890–1939*, F. S. L. Lyons catalogues a series of

riots in Belfast in the nineteenth century that "if anything, increased in frequency and intensity as time went on."[37] Despite Sheridan's attempts to reform the behavior of Dublin audiences by barring stage sitting and repeatedly raising the price of admission to "the gods," Irish theatre witnessed "nightly display of the grossest and most indecorous and often very ruffianly conduct,"[38] at least according to the *Dramatic Argus* in 1824. Similar allegations about audience behavior surface throughout the twentieth century. Andrew Davies remarked that "Irish audiences had always been noted for their volatility."[39] Thomas J. Coyne, assistant controller (1939–45) and then controller (1941–45) of the censorship during the Emergency, repeatedly raised questions about the excitability and demonstrativeness of Irish audiences. In reference to a play submitted to him in October 1944, Coyne wrote that a better play "might provoke a violent, emotional reaction in the audience."[40] Reviewing *The Bishop's Bonfire* in 1955, J. C. Trewin described audience unruliness at plays as an Irish birthright: "I know the reputation of these Irish playgoers when their blood is up. This time there was no Yeats . . . to stride on indignantly, with waving mane, to denounce the booers. Otherwise, I gather, it was the usual pattern."[41] The unruliness of an audience, let alone a city or culture, is a relative judgment. In the twentieth century, no one was ever killed during a theatrical disturbance in Ireland; only one person, a Westport Royal Irish Constabulary (RIC) officer, was seriously physically injured. Irish theatre censorship, nevertheless, was particularly threatening because it was, with few exceptions, outside the rule of law.

2

Theatre, Art, and Censorship

Nothing can be worse for an intellectual movement than a chorus of approval.

—AE (George Russell), "The Abbey Theatre"

Between 1897 and 1907 issues of stage censorship were at the core of the emergence of modern Irish drama. What would and would not be accepted on stage were questions that resurfaced in the most celebrated instances of theatrical disorder in the first decade of the century. There were, in fact, very few instances at any time during the twentieth century when institutional forces succeeded in censoring a play in Ireland and even fewer instances when Irish audiences rioted. Far more often, cries against a specific play, and typically only against isolated features of that play, formed the locus for resentment, sometimes expressed as physical violence.

In Ireland an abiding ambiguity about theatre conflated elements of puritanism, anti–intellectualism, and nationalism. Reaching back at least to Jeremy Collier, the suspicions about the respectability and morality of the stage and those associated with it were perhaps stronger in England but not unknown in Ireland. Until the 1980s, many Irish theatres closed their doors during Holy Week so as not to distract from the penitential run-up to Easter (and the Easter pantomimes). At end of the nineteenth century the Irish hybrid of prejudice against theatre may have been more intense among Protestants than Catholics. For Protestants, and Ulster Protestants in particular, the theatre smacked of sin. In his book on British stage censorship John Palmer writes that the "Nonconformist view of the theatre as the Gate of Hell was at one time almost universally held, and is held to this day [1912] by large sections of the British middle class."[1] Irish Protestants were no less familiar with the moral stigma surrounding the theatre. It was, after all, an opera house, not a theatre, that opened in Belfast in 1895. St. John Ervine recalls the apprehension of "eternal damnation" attached to the theatre by Belfast Protestants in his youth:

> The pleasure I drew from my visits to the play in my aunt's company . . . was marred by the panic into which she occasionally fell when she thought of what would be the state of her immortal soul if God should call her home while she was in the theatre. . . . I mention this matter because the belief that the pit of the theatre was only another name for the pit of hell was prevalent at that time [1880s], and has not yet [1930s] died out.[2]

Ervine attributes the theatrical stigma to "the conviction that the mummer violates the commandment that we shall not make unto ourselves graven images."[3] Although his reminiscence has an ironic grounding, the prejudice against theatre, seen in Belfast as late as 1974, was both intense and persistent.

Catholics may have been more comfortable with the spectacle, costumes, and lighting as well as the notion of theatrical performance as situated in a hieratic realm removed from the mundane. The spectacles familiar to Irish nationalists—monster meetings, siamsa, pageants, funerals, patriotic recitals and concerts, the feisanna—constitute a tradition alternate and antithetical to that of the patent theatres (although not unrelated to the Green Nights at the Star of Erin).[4] Moreover, rural Catholics in particular were familiar with drama as allied with religious festivals and liturgical celebrations, often presented within the confines of the parish hall. Whereas John Wesley had in 1764 seen theatre as inherently pernicious, Father Theobald Mathew saw such spectacles as a diverting and uplifting community activity that could serve the temperance movement and the Catholic church.[5]

The Catholic anxiety about theatre concerned itself more with the sixth and ninth commandments than the first. Nowhere is Catholic suspicion about the public, commercial theatre in nineteenth-century Ireland more clearly seen than in the prohibition against priests attending public performances issued at the Synod of Thurles in 1850. In the mid-nineteenth century, theatre in Ireland, as elsewhere, had forfeited much of its intellectual and artistic, let alone moral, pretenses. As part of the effort to professionalize the Catholic clergy, the Synod's prohibition linked theatregoing with other secular activities such as horse racing, card playing, and fox hunting.[6] The strictures on clerical theatre attendance were, however, flexible and apparently inapplicable to productions in Irish. James Cousins recalls that for the Irish language production of Hyde's *Casadh an tSugain* in 1901, "Catholic priests and Protestant parsons sat under the same roof."[7]

Throughout the late nineteenth century priests and nuns were, in fact, often involved in the forms of theatre best known outside of major cities. Recitations, pageants—sometimes epic in scale—sketches, as well as plays were regular features of the feis, many of which were sponsored or organized by members of the Catholic clergy. In 1898 Yeats enthusiastically wrote to Gregory about the possibility of recruiting a priest from Erris, Father John Hegarty, who had written a passion play for his parishioners.[8] That same year Father Eugene O'Growney wrote *The Passing of Conall*, which was performed at Aonach Tirconaill in Letterkenny, and Sister Mary Gertrude coauthored the operetta *Finola* and a prelude to Father O'Growney's play, *The Coming of Conall*.[9] Better known and conspicuously praised by Yeats in *Samhain* were two Catholic priests writing plays in Irish: Father Peter O'Leary, who wrote *An Sprid* (*The Ghost*, 1902), *Tadg Saor* (*Free Man* or *Tadg the Smith*, which was produced in Macroom in 1900), and *La an Amadan* and Father Dineen, whose contributions included *An Tobar Draoidheachta* (*The Enchanted Well*, 1902) and *Creideamh agus Gorta* (*Faith and Famine*, 1905). Beyond the authorship of plays, the receptivity of the Catholic clergy can also be glimpsed in the invitation Father O'Donovan of Loughrea extended to the Irish National Theatre Society (INTS) for their first performances outside Dublin. At least one priest, a Father

Conlon, is remembered for founding a theatre group, the Pioneer Dramatic Society.[10] In 1903 John Denvir testified to "the part taken in the dramatic revival by the priesthood."[11]

At the other end of the spectrum of Catholic clergy were two Irish Jesuits in Dublin, both frequent contributors to contemporary periodicals. Perhaps in deference to the Synod of Thurles restriction, they occasionally wrote simply under their given names, George O'Neill and Thomas A. Finlay, but other times they were identified as "Rev." and "S. J." Finlay, a founding member of the National Literary Society and an editor of *New Ireland Review,* was one of the two "Catholic divines" who vetted and approved *The Countess Cathleen* to assuage Edward Martyn's fears only weeks before its Irish public premiere. The commentaries of Finlay and O'Neill on the emergence of Irish drama as well as the original works of other Catholic clergy helped to diminish what vestiges of antitheatrical prejudice existed in Catholic Ireland.

During the second half of the nineteenth century, the appetite for theatrical entertainment increased with expanded leisure and disposal income. The 1890s remain unrivaled as a decade of theatrical building and renovation in Ireland. Seating 2,500 and designed by Frank Matcham, the Grand Opera House and Cirque opened in Belfast on 23 December 1895. In a single year, 1897, no fewer than four other new or refurbished theatres opened: the Everyman Palace in Cork, with a capacity of 530 (constructed and managed by Dan Lowery); the former Leinster Hall, now remodeled (also by Matcham) as the (Second) Theatre Royal, accommodating more than 2,000 patrons; Dan Lowery's Star of Erin, "completely redesigned" and renamed the Empire Palace (now the Olympia Theatre); and the Grand Lyric Hall, which soon became the Lyric Theatre of Varieties. The Theatre Royal, along with the Queen's Royal Theatre (seating 2,000; 1844–1969) and the Gaiety Theatre (seating 1,300; built in 1871 and still in operation today), were Dublin's only three patent theatres. Its music-hall venues ranged from the Empire Palace, the Lyric, the Tivoli Variety Theatre, and Mechanics' Institute[12] to smaller and less reputable houses. In addition to the purpose-built Dublin theatres, there were a number of venues that occasionally hosted dramatic performances: the Antient Concert Rooms (now the Palace Cinema), Molesworth Hall, and the Dublin Coffee Palace. There were other potential venues for plays such as the Round Room at the Rotunda Hospital, which alone was exempt from the onerous 1786 legislation. Still others, church halls and commercial spaces, would be claimed, but by law only the patent theatres could present conventional multiact plays. Theatre was booming. It was a raw, capitalistic, often profitable, but always risky, business.

Owners and managers, like Michael Gunn at the Gaiety, J. W. Whitbread at the Queen's, and a consortium headed by Frederick Mouillot at the Theatre Royal,[13] had good reason to fear increased competition. Indeed, several of the music halls were attracting a more respectable, and hence larger, clientele that demanded and financed greater comforts. Worse, the music halls were poaching on the patent theatres' dramatic fare as well as audiences. Lowery, for instance, featured the likes of Charles Godfrey and his "'potted Legit,' a melodramatic narrative sung, acted and monologued as a one-man Play."[14] In response to the frenzy of theatre openings and reopenings in 1897, the three patent theatres moved to consolidate their monopoly on the presentation of stage plays in order to recoup their substantial capital investments. So stiff was competition for the Dublin audiences that in January 1898 the patent theatres gave public warning against any illegal theatrical performance: "Notice is given that any person or persons, who shall for hire, gain, or any kind of reward whatsoever, act, represent, or perform, or cause to be performed"[15] would be prosecuted under An Act for Regulating the Stage in the City and County of Dublin, that specified "the penalty of forfeiting the sum of three hundred pounds sterling for every such offense."[16] Only circuses, puppet shows, and entertainments at the Rotunda were spared.[17]

In 1898 the patent theatres won a judgment against a Mr. McNally for performing plays at the unlicensed Mechanics' Institute. A Mr. Gaffney and a Mrs. Glenville took over from McNally, and on 6 April 1901 J. B. Carrickford and Louise Grafton followed them. Renaming the establishment the National Theatre, they recruited a company "composed mostly of old English stock actors" and a young man, Dawson Byrne. Byrne, who became a priest and wrote one of the first histories of the Abbey Theatre, recalled "a period of two years, 1901–03, during which over three hundred plays were produced, ranging from the Elizabethan period to the modern drama of those days."[18] In 1903 Carrickford and Grafton were threatened with fines totaling £270,000 (£300 for each of nine hundred performances as stipulated by the 1786 act). Faced with such an exorbitant fine and the additional threat of life imprisonment, they abruptly ceased operation.

Later that year, under the auspices of the Amateur Dramatic Defence Association, Francis R. Wolfe's *Theatres in Ireland* spelled out the impossible situation in which Dublin amateurs found themselves. They could not perform in an unlicensed hall or theatre, yet the Lord Lieutenant declined to license their venues. Wolfe charged that Gunn and other patent theatre managers abused the law by threatening prosecutions under the 1786 law. He also accused Gunn of inflating the price of tickets, pandering to the masses, and offering only a "choice between vulgar goodness and polished badness — errors of the age." The license Gunn secured for the Gaiety on 28 April 1871, Wolfe further argued, "forbids altogether the acting of tragedy, the ground for such prohibition being that the Lord Lieutenant had already granted the right to act tragedy to the Theatre Royal."[19] Although that genre restriction was subsequently modified, it demonstrates how the patent's exclusive franchise inhibited and restricted competition. In practice, some exceptions were tolerated. Dramatic sketches were performed by both amateurs and professionals in a wide variety of circumstances, ranging from the "potted" or condensed plays performed without intermission to the tableaux vivants at the original nights of the Irish Literary Society.[20] The very existence of the Amateur Dramatic Defence Association and the publication of two editions of Wolfe's pamphlet suggest a strong level of interest in amateur theatrics. While the occasional charity or benefit performance might escape notice, in her diaries Lady Gregory saw the 1786 law as an insuperable obstacle to the plans for an Irish theatre.[21] In such a highly competitive market, both patent and nonpatent theatres sought to cultivate a secure audience base with a fixed horizon of expectations. The solution came in 1898 in an amendment to the Local Government Bill that empowered the Lord Lieutenant to issue temporary licenses.[22]

There was a seasonal cycle for theatre that survived into the second half of the twentieth century. Theatres sometimes closed during Advent or shortly before Christmas and opened their most profitable shows, the pantomimes, just after Christmas. These holiday pantomimes, attracting large, family audiences, might run for as long as three months. All the theatres and music halls closed during Holy Week. Late summer brought the Dublin Horse Show and an increased tourist demand for entertainments. Decades later festivals, such as An Tóstal, held in spring in the 1950s, and the West Belfast Festival, held in the first week of August, provided different rhythms for the Irish theatre season.

Although Dublin theatres had their own specialties to attract different audiences, theatregoing in the 1890s was among the more democratic experiences in Irish cultural life. As in England and America, theatre had, by the end of the nineteenth century, become a place where high culture met popular culture. The introduction of stalls privileged wealthy patrons with comfort and exclusivity and drove the "pittites" to the outer edges of the auditorium. Nonetheless, rarely would a group of Irish people as diverse as one attending, say, a Shakespeare play at the Gaiety or Theatre Royal, find themselves in a similarly enclosed public space. Certainly not in a church, a shopping establishment, a hotel, nor a civic arena. Only sporting activities would have attracted crowds as diverse in religion, class, formal education, and political conviction as those that would gather in a large Dublin theatre—and many of those sporting events would have been in open-air venues rather than in enclosed, densely packed theatres.

Architecturally, Dublin theatres were not the great monumental theatres of other European capitals, but several were purpose-built and dedicated exclusively to theatrical or musical performances. Other cultural institutions had already begun the remarkable transformations that would shape a distinctly Irish identity, and between the late 1880s and the first decade of the new century, these and other theatres saw turbulent political and social confrontations. In undertaking to amend the existing laws, Yeats and others opened the possibility that theatre would become the best-known cultural site of the Irish Literary Revival. Gaelic games, the Fianna Eireann, and Irish language would remain indigenous nationalist phenomena, but Irish theatre quickly became a celebrated and often profitable export.

Irish theatre, however, meant different things to different people. One of the most egregious examples of caricature of the Irish was also one that overtly situated a cultural confrontation on the stage. In the late 1860s and early 1870s the salacious presentation *The Confessional Unmasked,* featuring the rabidly anti-Catholic William Murphy and his female assistant, provoked riots by angry Catholics in Birmingham and Whitehaven, Cumbria.[23] The "performance" traded on anti-Irish and anti-Catholic bigotry, as many believed the stage Irishman did. Indeed, the stage Irishman not only appeared in the published works catalogued by G. C. Duggan[24] but also in skits outside the legitimate theatres. Outside full-length plays, "the Irish Comic . . . was the most enduring figure in the whole of English-speaking music hall."[25] Richard Allen Cave convincingly argues that the stage Irishman had, from the eighteenth century and even before, been evolving: "As Irish these figures were Other, but grounds were being found on which their Otherness might be deemed admissible. What is noticeable in this is that Irish Otherness is often character-ised by preserving features of the stereotype while redeeming them from pejorative judgment." In the nineteenth century, Dion Bouci-cault and Tyrone Power accelerated "this process of redemption."[26]

In the late nineteenth century J. W. Whitbread and Hubert O'Grady created a melodramatic and heroic strain of Irish histori-cal plays. An Englishman from Portsmouth, Whitbread had already begun to tap the audience potential of the emergent cultural na-tionalism of the age in his patriotic melodramas. By 1895 four of his plays demonstrated the viability of Irish nationalism on the Dublin stage; another eleven followed in the next ten years. At the Queen's, claimed by Séamus de Búrca and others as the "people's theatre,"[27] Whitbread, like Lowery in his Irish music halls, attracted audiences by drawing heavily and freely on Irish types. To some, Whitbread was authentically Irish, "truly racy of the soil," in the words of the *Irish Playgoer.*[28] Whitbread and Lowery attracted Irish audiences even if, perhaps because, their productions lacked all pretense of creating "art." In his populist way, Whitbread realized the potential of theatre to express nationalist views in commercially viable entertainment.

In the 1890s Irish critics grew more vocal about the caricatures of the Irish, especially in English drama. In August 1890 W. J. Lawrence published his essay "The Irish Character in English Dramatic Literature" in *Gentleman's Magazine.* Surveying stage representations of the Irish from Shakespeare to Boucicault, Lawrence documented the scurrilous as well as the sympathetic stage Irishman. He concluded that a sea change had occurred: "Remodelled [*sic*] from life, the conventional stage Irishman became idealised in the hands of Dion Boucicault, who endowed him with pathos as well as wit, poetry as well as humour. Let those sneer who like, we have reason to be thankful for the sturdy vitality of Irish melodrama."[29] Joseph Holloway's response to patriotic melodramas at the Queen's echoes these sentiments. Over the next decade, however, many Irish nationalists would share neither Lawrence's sanguine assurance nor his sense of Irish drama. For some, "the sturdy vitality of Irish melodrama" was an unfortunate link to the oft-vilified commercial theatre. As Cheryl Herr observes, "Irish playwrights made use of a theatrical discourse that was, for all intents and purposes, imposed, alien, a colonializing of popular consciousness, . . . [but] added differences . . . to resist the colonization of consciousness."[30]

In 1895 the *New Ireland Review* posed the question, "Have we ever had Irish drama?" and answered unambiguously, "No." Notwithstanding "the new literary note in Mr. Whitbread's latest drama 'Lord Edward; or, '98'" and Boucicault's *The Colleen Bawn,* William Barrett foresaw the emergence of an Irish drama that would supplant the stage Irishman and surpass patriotic melodrama.[31] Barrett's provocative essay was answered by three articles in the next issue of the *New Ireland Review,* including one by James J. Scanlan defending Boucicault and Whitbread that was nearly three times the length of the original essay.

W. A. Henderson, the future secretary of the National Theatre Society (NTS), pursued a very different line of argument in the same publication just two years later: "Perhaps in no other branch of art," wrote Henderson, and "certainly in no other branch of literature, have our achievements been at once so numerous and so brilliant."[32] Focusing neither on the stage Irishman nor on Irish themes, Henderson employed an expansive, inclusive sense of what made a playwright

Irish. The prerequisite was simply that he was Irish by birth. More than a century later, Richard Eyre echoed that criterion and sentiment: "After the Restoration, not one, single great play was written by an Englishman. Congreve, Goldsmith, Sheridan, Wilde, Shaw, Synge, O'Casey, Beckett were all great playwrights and they were all Irish."[33] In 1897, however, Henderson's claim, especially his inclusion of Wilde as an Irish playwright, was remarkable.

Even before the first season of the ILT in 1899, three distinct views had emerged: first, that the Irish had no drama to call their own and, for centuries, British drama deployed the stage Irishman to malign the Irish. That Irish playwrights, including James Shirley (sometimes identified as "the inventor of the stage Irishman"),[34] were complicit only exacerbated the injury of pandering to the prejudices of the London audiences. Although the ILT and other theatre groups, like Power and Boucicault before them, set out to drive a stake through his heart,[35] the stage Irishman was undead. Throughout the twentieth century critics would recognize his reincarnations in the plays of Synge, Birmingham, and Martin McDonagh. A second perspective held that Boucicault and Whitbread had already begun the revision and reclamation of Irish history and stage types from British bigotry. Their works proved enormously popular with the Irish public and might form a basis to develop a distinctly Irish drama. The revision of Irish character types would ultimately banish the stage Irishman, a view that echoes in the recent rehabilitation of Boucicault and Whitbread.[36] The effects of the Queen's melodramas can be regarded from two antithetical perspectives. On one hand, some judge that the heightened level of audience response was cathartic, purging the audience of potentially revolutionary tendencies. On the other hand, the plays may be seen as fostering a growing patriotic awareness of Irish history that audiences took with them when they left the theatre. Finally, a view more dismissive of the outrages of the stage Irishman took pride in recognizing that in Sheridan, Oliver Goldsmith, and perhaps even Wilde and Shaw, the Irish had a long tradition of disproportionate contribution to English-speaking drama. Each of these perspectives implied a definition of what Irish drama was and of what was Irish. In 1897, for instance, the *New Ireland Review* indignantly condemned Villiers Stanford's

Shamus O'Brien as "bogus Irish drama."[37] As seen in the controversy engendered by Martin McDonagh, debate over what is authentically Irish drama persists into the twenty-first century.

One common element among these perspectives was the desire to see what was distinctively and uniquely Irish, specifically episodes from Irish history, dramatized. W. A. Henderson noted "the lack of Irish historical subjects in Irish plays. . . . [G]lorious material for the future dramatist lies in the unworked quarries of Irish history."[38] William Barrett hoped that "our modern dramatist" would "discover something which is characteristic of Ireland and Irishmen, and of no other country or people. We must have some characteristics peculiar to ourselves; it will be the work and reward of our dramatist to discover them."[39] Implicitly defining Irish drama as social realism, Barrett lamented that the melodramas of Whitbread and others had not provided an Irish Ibsen to dramatize contemporary Irish life.

After 1899 Yeats, the nationalist press, George Moore, and others targeted the "Theatre of Commerce," the only established, enduring, viable theatrical enterprise at work in Ireland or, for that matter, in England or the United States. At the same time, every aspect of the theatre, even in the Theatre of Commerce, from set design and acting style to the possibilities for both realistic and nonrealistic dramaturgy, was undergoing an epochal reexamination. The centrality of the great actor-managers of the nineteenth century was usurped by the author or the repertory company or the producer/director or the designer. Histrionic bombast yielded to more naturalistic and, later, expressionistic acting. Spectacular sets gave way to familiar drawing rooms, larger-than-life heroes to ordinary people, overt theatricality to realism, naturalism, and expressionism; stage lighting went from gas to electric. New theatres were smaller, pulling back from the gargantuan size of Covent Garden at well over three thousand seats as remodeled in 1809. The refurbishment of the Mechanics' Institute and the former Dublin morgue in 1904 produced an Abbey Theatre that accommodated a relatively modest 536.[40]

Throughout the twentieth century, theatre pursued its claim to artistic freedom of expression only by subverting the financial equation. To be sure, theatre has historically relied upon various forms of patronage, ranging from established religions or rulers and aristocrats to middle-class donors and multinational corporations. Between 1899 and 1929 in Ireland, the equation of revenue and expenses was broken by patrons, guarantors, subscribers, and, as is more commonly the case today, government subsidy. In the late twentieth century, the base sought to assure solvency and continuity expanded to include individual benefactors, club memberships, corporate sponsorship, and lottery profits. In 1899 Irish dramatic enterprises outside the commercial theatre played to even smaller houses and relied upon subsidy from patrons, sponsorship of clubs, or the dedication of unpaid actors and personnel.

For the ILT, the NTS, the Theatre of Ireland, and less well-known companies, dedicated amateurs assuaged the tyranny of the financial equation of the commercial theatre.[41] Overtly nationalistic motives inspired a passion for dramatic productions in many of these amateurs. Maire Nic Shiubhlaigh, for instance, "never thought of the National Theatre Society as a purely theatrical enterprise. It was merely part of a larger national movement."[42] As will be seen in chapter 3, such amateurs were inherently subversive because, without a contractual obligation, they maintained their independence. The theatres they created, however modest, were no less dangerous for undermining the hierarchical structures of the patent theatres. Moreover, the amateurs in question often described their overt political commitment as having a spiritual dimension.

The antagonism against the commercial theatre was shared by many in Ireland at the end of the nineteenth century. Yeats and others would use phrases like "Theatre of Commerce" to suggest a soulless, degenerate medium that had as its only objective financial profit. In *Beltaine* George Moore celebrated theatre as "the noblest form of art until it becomes a commercial enterprise. . . . There is probably nothing in life so low as a musical comedy, for in the musical comedy the meaning of life is expressed in eating, drinking, betting, and making presents to women."[43] For Moore, such superficial entertainments suited the English but not the Irish. In the nationalist press there was a steady stream of protest against not only the caricatures of the Irish but also what the *United Irishman* called "importing the immoral and unnatural ideas which underlie these plays"[44] at the commercial theatres. French plays, such as *La Poupée*, were ideally suited for such broadsides. Clearly what was on offer was alien and therefore, from a nationalist perspective, un-Irish and corrupting. This criticism would be more often expressed in the new century, but the week that the ILT performances opened in the Antient Concert Rooms, all three patent theatres advertised their plays by underscoring a single common credential: a London pedigree.

Beyond the patent theatres and the music halls, there was another dramatic tradition that sprang from the nationalist clubs. Arthur Griffith's Celtic Literary Society, founded in 1893, provided a more democratic and accessible alternative to the Contemporary Club (founded in 1885) and the National Literary Society (founded in 1892). As early as 1894, W. P. Ryan in *The Irish Literary Revival* offered the history of a movement that he dated from the 1880s, whose activities began outside of Ireland, on the south bank in London. There the Southwark Irish Literary Society featured Gaelic nights and, later, "Original Nights. Good Irish work in poem, story, sketch, and ballad."[45] For the Irish literary societies that sprang up both in and outside Ireland, "a system of 'original nights,' when the members are invited to contribute Irish sketches, anecdotes, legends, or the like" was in place by 1894.[46] At the same time nationalist clubs in Ireland, including Irish-speaking organizations large and small, quickly recognized the potential of plays to advance their aims, occupy their members, and publicize their existence.

The model Yeats followed to meet the financial demands of an Irish theatre and to create a base of support was typical of arts organizations in the late nineteenth century. His strategy for raising funds and support found its prototype in the transformation the Southwark Irish Literary Society into London's Irish Literary Society. There, titled aristocrats, degreed professionals, clergy, and anyone with letters after their names and a connection to Ireland, were recruited as Vice Presidents. The London organization's publication, the *Irish Literary Society Gazette,* conspicuously identified its supporters on its front cover. Yeats appealed not to the populist support of the Dublin public or even of the nationalist community but to an elite. Not only did Yeats need the guarantors' backing to break the financial equation but also to publicize the ILT. Even the recruitment of prestigious guarantors—editors, professors, aristocrats, and politicians—for the ILT received considerable press coverage. As Yeats wrote in 1897, "all the great names in Ireland are on our list" [of guarantors].[47] To publicize his fledgling organization and the impending public performance and to solidify the support of those great names, Yeats staged the tableaux performance of *The Countess Cathleen* in the bastion of the Ascendancy establishment: the Chief Secretary's lodge in Phoenix Park. Yeats himself knew he could not attend, but did advise the real countess who was playing the title role, Elizabeth, Countess of Fingall, "You can't look too thin or too miserable for this part!"[48]

None of the features of the tableaux performance—the private audience, the aristocrats, the Ascendancy venue, the stylized *mise en scène,* the rarified atmosphere—appealed to, or found favor with, the nationalist community. All these features, combined with the previously published version of the play, provided not only extensive preproduction publicity but also a target for nationalists and Yeats's enemies. By expanding the financial backing beyond the commitments of Edward Martyn, the guarantors of the ILT provided a base of support (that was, in fact, never tapped financially) across the lettered and literate upper class of Dublin society. With that support in place, Yeats recruited an English cast and an English director to implement a method of presentation and a style of acting that not only transgressed the custom of the commercial theatre but also, even today, seems stylized, inaccessible, and downright alien. Yeats justified importing professional English actors because "our company must be able to compete with travelling English companies,"[49] but there was not even the pretense of attempting an Irish, let alone a rural Irish, accent. Yeats, too, cultivated a highly stylized, presentational acting suited to symbolist drama with the lines chanted rather than spoken naturalistically. Even Martyn acknowledged that the ILT plays "are not expected to appeal to a popular audience."[50]

In early May 1899 there was a clear instance of censorship in Dublin that drew together the forces of clerical pressure, the concern with public morality, the latent suspicion about foreign works, and the law. Outside 16 Westmoreland Avenue, Benjamin Carter, a black man dressed in red knickers and exotic robes, distributed handbills for an exhibition. Gas jets illuminated advertisements announcing that the same display had been "Interdicted in Glasgow." A police superintendent and two clergymen testified to paying the admission fee (one shilling, or six pence after 6:00 P.M.) and walking down a long corridor displaying several dozen paintings before reaching a dimly lit inner sanctum where Distage's painting *The Slave Market at Cairo* (probably Maxime Dastugue's) was on show. The painting depicted nude men and women paraded before a mirror, so that both sides of their bodies were represented. The proprietors of this traveling exhibition provided seating before the painting for their patrons and offered souvenir photographs for sale. Carter and his two associates were arrested and brought before the Southern Police Court on 9 May 1899. Testimony against them touched on the obscenity of portraying male and female nudes in the same picture, the licentious atmosphere in which the painting was exhibited, and, not least, the postcards on sale. Although the testimony of Police Superintendent Lanktree, the Very Reverend Canon Fricker, and the Reverend Mr. Robinson withered under cross-examination for the defense, the exhibition was shut down. Within a week, the owners were reimbursed for the cost of their rental and left town; their legal prosecution was dropped.[51] This obscure proceeding, an unambiguous example of censorship, coincidentally occurred the same week as the controversy over Yeats's *The Countess Cathleen,* a putative example of censorship. But whereas the exhibition of this painting was quickly shut down, *The Countess Cathleen,* despite catcalls and clerical warnings, completed its run.

The 1892 Cameo edition of *The Countess Kathleen and Various Legends and Lyrics* was followed by the revisions to *The Countess Cathleen* that appeared in *Poems* (1895). Neither of these versions was what the Dublin audience heard in May 1899. The ILT not only needed to attract but also prepare an audience by modifying its horizon of expectations. From its beginning, the ILT announced its intent to "train" an audience. Essential to this strategy was a range of publications, unprecedented in its day. *Beltaine,* "The Organ of the Irish Literary Theatre," appeared in May 1899, just before the first ILT performances. Its premiere issue included essays by Lionel Johnson and George Moore, two lyrics from *The Countess Cathleen,* and other writings to prepare audiences for a theatrical experience quite unlike one at the Gaiety, Queen's, or Theatre Royal. No less importantly, like other Irish periodicals, *Beltaine* published plays, sometimes before they were performed. As select as the theatre audience may have been, enthusiasts and detractors alike would have access to many of the plays in print. The first performance of *The Countess Cathleen* was not the tableaux version at the Chief Secretary's lodge but a copyright performance of the earlier version, *The Countess Kathleen,* at the Atheneum Theatre in Shepherd's Bush, London, in 1892.[52] In licensing it on 5 May 1892 for public performance, the Lord Chamberlain found nothing objectionable, despite his strictures against blasphemy, one of the principal charges leveled against the play in Ireland. The students who protested the play referred to the availability of earlier published versions in the Kildare Street Library.

In 1892, Yeats described the play "as an attempt to mingle personal thought and feeling with the beliefs and customs of Christian Ireland, . . . an attempt to unite a more ample method to feeling not less national, Celtic, and distinctive."[53] Yeats later retreated from the assertion that the play was a realistic depiction of Irish customs and declared that it was actually symbolic, the product of his "fancy" rather than fact. From Yeats's published text, a fixed version that was unlike both the tableaux version and the May public performances, F. Hugh O'Donnell cobbled together and distributed in April 1899 his pamphlet *Souls for Gold! A Pseudo-Celtic Drama in Dublin.*[54] In response to O'Donnell's attack and in addition to the revisions and emendations that took place in rehearsals,[55] Yeats adapted a dubious cosmetic subtitle, "A Miracle Play in Four Acts." As Michael J. Sidnell points out, the subtitle appears in no printed version of the play: "The generic description was adduced only when the pressure of religious controversy made it strategically useful and not utterly preposterous for the play that actually emerged."[56] Many of the resultant incongruities mirrored those implicit in Yeats's writing. In 1894 the *New Ireland Review* commented that in *The Countess Kathleen,* as it was then known, Yeats had not "realised and expressed the great spiritual significance of some of the situations."[57] Indeed, even after the revisions that eliminated the scene of Shemus Rua battering and kicking the Marian shrine, the spiritual and theological significance of key episodes engendered controversy. When Edward Martyn balked over the play's theology, Yeats was willing to do whatever had to be done to assure Martyn's continuing support. In "offer[ing] to alter or omit any passages that a theologian of so much literary culture as your self may object to,"[58] Yeats demonstrated a cultural malleability that sustained him until the end of his life.[59]

The theatricality of the Dublin audience had been building throughout the decade. The larger theatres demanded a scale of gesture, scenery, and costume that could reach audiences of two thousand and intensified the audience's sense of its theatricality. The Queen's had a large and loyal Dublin audience for its repertory of popular, long-running, frequently revived plays, which would be seen time and time again. Especially at the Queen's, sing-song intervals, demonstrative responses to the heroes and villains of melodrama, and cathartic emotional displays interpolated the audience's participation with the displays of Irish patriotism enacted on stage. Cheryl Herr notes that many of the characters in these patriotic melodramas were themselves creatures of theatricality who relied upon disguise, declamation, and duplicity in consciously playing parts to survive.[60] The element of theatricality enveloped the audience and imbricated the playhouse's democracy, insurgent nationalism, and audience performativity.

Dublin audiences may well have been even more demonstrative than their London counterparts at the end of the nineteenth century. The editors of Yeats's letters flatly state, "Of course, Dublin audiences were far more vigorous and aggressive, even in the patent theatres, than any comparable London audience."[61] The patrons of the gods, in Ireland as in London, were also frequently associated with unruly behavior: "They were, it appears, given to pelting the occupants of the circle with orange peel and other equally objectionable missiles from the safety of their top gallery."[62] Vociferous responses at theatrical performances—booing, foot stamping, and catcalls—were not uncommon. Theatre disturbances reinforced a heightened sense of theatricality from within the audience itself. As Marc Baer demonstrates in *Theatrical Disorder in Late Georgian England,* the element of performativity can cross the fourth wall created by the proscenium arch and be adopted by the audience. The Irish theatre disturbances clearly lacked the epic scale of the OP riots analyzed by Baer (sustained rioting over the courses of sixty-seven performances in a theatre that accommodated over three thousand patrons),[63] but the intimacy of Dublin and the relatively small capacity of the Antient Concert Rooms and later the Abbey Theatre created an equally intense element of spectacle.

In the larger Dublin theatres intermissions often featured impromptu songs and recitals from patrons in the gallery. As Mary Colum recalls, "when the curtain fell on an act and the rather dreary commercial orchestra ceased its sounds, someone would call up to the 'gods,' 'Raise us a harmony,' and the harmony would start, sometimes several voices together singing a patriotic ballad or an old come-all-ye, sometimes a solo singer would give an aria from an opera."[64] Her future husband, Padraic Colum, noted that at the turn of the century, "the Gaiety Theatre was crowded with young men and women from the Gaelic League branches—the gallery, anyway. They sang national songs in the intervals (in those days there was always someone in the gallery who could sing, and sing very well, and his songs would be taken up by others)."[65] A number of rituals, including several not limited to Ireland—the call for the author to appear on stage and address the audience, the presentation of flowers from the management to the actors—sustained the theatrics beyond the performance of the play. Moreover, theatrical reporting in the Dublin press in the 1890s paid particular attention to the audience and the level of their demonstrativeness. The centennial celebrations commemorating the 1798 Rebellion intensified the audience's awareness of its theatricality and transformative powers. The commemorations turned defeat into a moment of historical sacrifice that implied that what had been attempted in 1798 would one day, possibly soon, be realized.

Reports of the ILT premiere consistently emphasized the sense of anticipation that attended not only the play but also the audience's coming to the theatre. Yeats's own highly theatrical presentation of himself appears throughout accounts of the ILT. James Cousins recalls growing "accustomed to his Oscar Wildean rig-out and forelock."[66] Declan Kiberd suggests that Yeats's flamboyant public image was a response to his meeting Oscar Wilde in London in 1888: "Rejecting the mask of the professional Irishman which London publishers eagerly proffered to him, Yeats created instead his own mask of the anti-self."[67] In time, Gregory also acquired a distinctive style of dress and self-presentation.

The reviews of *The Countess Cathleen* reveal as much about the intricacies of Dublin journalism at the time as about the quality of Yeats's play or the Irish reception of the ILT.[68] The pitched rivalries among the dailies and weekly journals responded as much to what competitors printed as to what Yeats published or the ILT performed. Two days before the public premiere of *The Countess Cathleen,* the *Daily Nation* asked that "those Irish Catholics, who may form a portion of the audience, will so give expression to their disapproval as to effectually discourage any further ventures of a similar kind."[69] As Robert Hogan and James Kilroy rightly judged, "Quite clearly, this was incitement to riot."[70] The initial reviews of Yeats's play ran true to form. The *Irish Times,* which at the beginning of the year ran articles on "Literature in 1898" and "Drama in 1898" with London bylines, dismissed it as "neither a play nor a presentment of either the ideals or actions or motives of Irish men and women." The average Irish playgoer, warned the *Irish Times,* would take offense at the transaction that valued the Countess's soul far above that of any peasant, but no less important is the criticism, thrice repeated, that *The Countess Cathleen* was "not a play. It is without action, without definiteness in the characterisation, without consistency in the dramatic development, without truth in its reflection of Celtic temperament or life, and like all inferior plays, that it fails to excite the smallest genuine interest."[71] Ironically, the *Irish Times* was one of the few Dublin papers that was not openly partisan in the controversy over the founding of the ILT and its inaugural production. T. P. Gill, the editor of the *Daily Express,* would host a banquet, famously recalled by George Moore in *Hail and Farewell,* for many of the central figures in the ILT in May 1899. Gill's support for the ILT, not least as one of its financial guarantors, prompted an aggressive campaign against the Theatre of Commerce in the *Daily Express* throughout early 1899. Lamenting the gross immorality of the stage, the *Daily Express* took aim at plays like *Kitty Grey, Zaza,* and *The Geisha,* which had also roused London's vigilance organizations. The *Daily Express* railed against salacious, imported plays although it continued to advertise them. The weekly publication of the Gaelic

League, *An Claidheamh Soluis,* held little rancor against Yeats's work, but "absolutely den[ied] the right of the new venture to be called either 'Irish' or 'National.'" *An Claidheamh Soluis* was bemused that other papers denounced titillating stage plays:

> Night after night, week after week, month after month, the lowest Cockney comedies, abounding in what the *Daily Express* characterizes as "thinly-veiled obscenity" are produced before Dublin audiences, and the Dublin dailies, when they do not write favourable dramatic criticisms, hold their peace most judiciously. . . . Any attempt, therefore, to purify the stage in Dublin must be looked upon as a most necessary sanitary measure, and as a work worthy of Christian gentlemen.[72]

A decade later the *Leader* and other nationalist publications were still demanding such "sanitary measures." The Gaelic League was willing to concede that as "a literary vehicle for the national thought of Ireland, . . . [t]his thing is the perfect flower of the 'new movement' going on in Ireland," but its highest praise was reserved for "the manful protest of the Catholic University students, . . . clean, sane, cultured young Irishmen."[73]

The students who protested in the theatre and in the press were hardly the gallery boys or "slogging gangs"[74] of the London theatre. They were neither uneducated nor unruly. Nor were they very numerous. What the *Freeman's Journal* described as a "small, organised knot of less than a dozen disorderly boys,"[75] Joseph Holloway described as "twenty brainless, beardless, idiotic-looking youths."[76] Their letter of 8 May 1899, which appeared in the *Freeman's Journal* on 10 May 1899, reported "the results of our examination" of Yeats's play as available in the Kildare Street Library. They called for a response "from each of the Nationalist and Catholic leaders whose names have been lent to support this drama."[77] C. P. Curran, who soon followed these students at University College, Dublin, later observed that "the very scenes [the first two] and encumbrances to which the students had taken exception" were the ones Yeats revised. Curran chided Yeats for manipulating the students' protest and noted that "the deletions, restorations, revisions and emendations which the protean Yeats wrought in his texts are evidence certainly of his artistry but also of his insecurity."[78]

Cardinal Logue's letter, solicited by the *Daily Nation,* did not appear until 10 May 1899, that is, until after the first performance on 8 May and the initial reviews which appeared on 9 May. Despite the power of the Catholic church, his attempt at censorship was a comprehensive failure. Certainly, Logue's effort at clerical censorship was neither efficient nor efficacious. His letter of tentative condemnation appeared two days after the play opened and backfired conclusively. Rather than issuing a strict ban, he couched his warning in equivocal terms. Rather than diminishing or restricting the numbers who saw the play, he only intensified interest and, in all likelihood, increased attendance. Rather than objecting specifically to the production or the published play, Logue responded only to O'Donnell's parodic attack. Even Catholic priests like George O'Neill, who participated in the subsequent debate, could not endorse Logue's allegation that the play might be morally or theologically dangerous to Catholics. Logue's warning cannot even claim a measure of success in the protests by Catholic students in the theatre and in the press because those appeared before or on the same day as his letter. Although it may have envenomed the attack of Catholic nationalists like Patrick Pearse, Logue's caution was typically described in the press as "unfortunate." The *United Irishman* went further: "All Cardinal Logue's knowledge of *The Countess Cathleen* is derived, he admits, from the extracts published from it in Mr. O'Donnell's pamphlet and the *Daily Nation,* both publishers animated by hostile motives; nevertheless, his Eminence condemns the play and the audience who applauded it. The condemnation of the most obscure man who had read the play or of the most unlettered one who had witnessed it would weigh a hundredfold more with every intelligent man."[79] Yeats was hardly deferential to the Cardinal in defending his work in the London press when he claimed "victory" in the *Morning Leader* over Logue's "singular naivete, . . . carelessness and indifference."[80] Logue attempted to exert his influence over the Catholics of Ireland to proscribe *The Countess Cathleen,* but he failed miserably.

Debate continued long after the play concluded its brief run. Even moderate voices, however, such as that of George O'Neill in the *New Ireland Review,* were critical of the image of the Irish peasant in *The Countess:* "[I]t does seem cruel that a theatre professing to be above all things sympathetically national should at its first performance show them [the Irish peasants] forth as demoralized poltroons, starvelings in soul as well as in body."[81] On 20 May 1899 in *An Claidheamh Soluis* Patrick Pearse denounced the play as not Irish and the "'Irish' Literary Theatre" as more dangerous than Trinity College. "Let us," Pearse urged, "strangle it at its birth."[82] While not specifically a call for censorship, Pearse's plea is some measure of the vehemence with which the militant nationalists greeted *The Countess Cathleen* and the ILT.

No less revelatory is the volte-face that Arthur Griffith's *United Irishman* underwent in the first six months of 1899. In its first issues, in January 1899, the paper carried articles as well as announcements of lectures by O'Donnell, the pamphleteer whose *Souls for Gold!* fomented the clerical attack on *The Countess Cathleen.* Gradually, O'Donnell was phased out as a contributor and relegated to letters to the editor (one of which was derided as "mischievous nonsense" in a subsequent letter). Concurrently, Yeats, *The Countess Cathleen,* and the ILT gained increasing but not unqualified favor. Whereas in May 1899, the *United Irishman* protested that the ILT was "far above the people's heads," it soon reported that Yeats's play "has gained a vast amount of popularity." Yeats was praised for replying to his critics "sensibly." The Catholic students who condemned *The Countess Cathleen* mistook "a purely symbolic play for a pseudo-historical one." By July, in an article by Frank Fay, *The Countess Cathleen* had become "exquisite."[83]

The breadth of response to the play—the condescension of the *Irish Times,* the ambivalence of the *United Irishman,* the murderous wrath of Pearse, and the reservations expressed even by the *Daily Express*—exposed a spectrum of attitudes toward the play, its author, and the ILT. At one extreme were the backers and founders of the ILT and those like Joseph Holloway who responded to the play with fervent enthusiasm. At the other extreme (among those who condemned it) there was a wide range of objections expressed. Pearse thought the ILT "insidious" because it sought to capitalize on, without committing to, the emergent cultural nationalism. Many, including Cardinal Logue, responding only to O'Donnell's *Souls for Gold!* thought it must be blasphemous and anti-Catholic. Others, like *An Claidheamh Soluis,* saw it as neither Irish nor identifiably English. To still others, it may have been Irish in one regard or another, but it was clearly at odds with Irish nationalism. The unconventional production challenged even sophisticated theatregoers. The acting induced in Holloway "a spiritual, half-mystic, visionary sensation," but Holloway also acknowledged that "many of the artists failed to allow those in front to clearly understand what they spoke."[84] With only three years' hindsight, Moore recalled the production as a "ridiculous representation."[85] To Francis Bickley, writing in 1912, both ILT plays were "marred by every defect of staging."[86]

Cardinal Logue's warning or tentative condemnation certainly had precisely the effect that it sought to avoid: it drove people to, not away from, the play. Logue's comments and the protests were widely dismissed as many commentators recorded a victory for liberty, intellectual freedom, and the forces of anticensorship. James Cousins, who was present for one of the protests, remembered that "in the duel of hiss and cheer, cheer won."[87] For T. W. Rolleston, one of the guarantors of the ILT and, with Yeats, a cofounder of the Irish Literary Society in London, the run of *The Countess Cathleen* asserted both that "an audience or any members of it have a right to express disapproval as well as to applaud . . . an author's right to a fair hearing for his work."[88] For Yeats, however, Logue's letter was grist for the mill. After 1899 subsequent editions of "Poems" included *The Countess Cathleen* as well as Yeats's account of the play's reception. In that essay Logue's warning became a condemnation; the number of students who voiced their disapproval had grown from a dozen in the *Freeman's Journal* or twenty in Holloway's account to forty. For their letter to the Dublin press they were demonized as the thugs of obscurantism and the minions of clerical authority. Although Yeats vilified the students who protested his play, his revisions to *The Countess Cathleen* accommodated many of their objections.

James Joyce, who was present in the theatre for *The Countess Cathleen,* did not sign the letter that his classmates sent to the Irish press. His later response to the ILT came in 1901, in "The Day of the Rabblement." Joyce charged that despite the fact that "the censorship is powerless in Dublin," the ILT failed to make good on its plans to produce the European masterpieces. For him the aggressive pursuit of a uniquely Irish drama came at the expense of the possibilities that Ibsen explored. The rabblement was, of course, not Joyce's fellow students, but a vastly less demonstrative but still self-conscious audience: one "placid and intensely moral, . . . enthroned in boxes and galleries amid a hum of approval."[89]

The controversial production of *The Countess Cathleen* generated enormous publicity for the ILT at the very time that it was in competition with scores of clubs, organizations, and groups. Long after the brief run of the play, controversy and commentary continued. Independent of the dramatic merits of the play or its production, the ILT scored an auspicious debut—more specifically, *The Countess Cathleen* eclipsed Martyn's *The Heather Field* and became known, famously or infamously, out of all proportion to its literary merits because of its reception. Max Beerbohm commented in the *Saturday Review* that such enormous publicity must be an embarrassment to the ILT.[90] In the aftermath, Dublin observers were quick to note that "no one . . . will be other than pleased at the animated controversy which has raged round the *Countess Cathleen*."[91] Yeats and Gregory quickly absorbed the lessons of the value of such publicity. Theatre controversy, even negative, increased rather than decreased paid admissions. A year later Yeats wrote Gregory that "Maud Gonne has just passed through London (I saw her yesterday) on her way to Dublin, where a number of her newspaper [*United Irishman* of 6 April 1900 containing her essay "The Famine Queen"] has been suppressed to her great joy, as it will give a lift to the circulation."[92] The controversy that attended *The Countess Cathleen* may have paradoxically contributed to the initial success of the ILT as well as abetted embryonic rival theatre companies.

By May 1899 competing horizons of expectations for the ILT production of Yeats's and Martyn's plays made disappointment inevitable. From its inception, the ILT was fraught with what now seem to be incongruities, if not insuperable contradictions. The ILT defined itself as Irish but for all its productions except *Casadh an tSugain* imported directors and principal actors from England. It aspired to convey spiritual values, but ones that were hardly synonymous with Catholic teaching. It positioned itself as an alternative to the despised commercial theatre, but it was torn between a narrow appeal to "an uncorrupted and imaginative audience trained to listen by its passion for oratory"[93] and a wider appeal as a national theatre. It courted the Ascendancy, although Yeats dared not attend the tableaux vivants at the viceregal lodge. Its plays would be Irish, but in the first season neither in the Irish language nor performed with an Irish accent. It conflated the real and the ideal Ireland. Whatever the content of *The Countess Cathleen,* these nontextual elements—the professional English actors, the conspicuous absence of the native voice on stage, the antinaturalistic acting, the carefully cultivated, elite audience—informed the reception of the performance.

The May 1899 production by the ILT at the Antient Concert Rooms involved many features of stage censorship that recurred throughout the twentieth century. The playwright, producers, and public all appreciated the potentially incendiary nature of the production in advance of its performance. That the play was published before it was performed afforded O'Donnell and other detractors the opportunity to lampoon it and arrange for demonstrations. During rehearsal, the playwright made a number of changes, many of which sought to accommodate the sensibilities of the Dublin audience. The daily press played an aggressive role in covering and, in this instance, inciting the demonstrations of protest. Moreover, the publicity value of controversy was significant and appreciated as such at the time. As so often, the accusation that *The Countess Cathleen* was elitist, sacrilegious, and un-Irish in both source and spirit expanded to conclude that it was also immoral. The protestors were identified as young men—in this instance, Catholic university students. Counterdemonstrators, some of whom were Protestant university students, vocally answered the demonstrators. Neither group craved anonymity. Subsequently, the disruptions were described as pitting obscurantist against progressive constituencies. The question of whether the disturbances in the theatre were organized or preplanned was crucial because if they were, then the performance had not received a fair hearing. The presence of police in the theatre may well have done more to incite than deter disorder. Subsequent debate examined the corollary question of the audience's right to express its disapproval. Future protests self-referentially situated themselves in relation to this and other instances of theatre protest in

Ireland. As in all other instances, the target of the protest was the production itself and the objective was to silence it. Finally, and most importantly, the disruptions brought neither the performance nor the production to a halt. As the new century progressed, these features characterize the most celebrated attempts to censor theatre in Ireland, efforts that were overwhelmingly unsuccessful. Instead, these plays concluded their runs and assumed a place in theatre history out of all proportion to their literary qualities.

3

"The Evil Genius"

And as these vocal gladiators—
All of them—were stayers,
The stage became spectators
And the audience the players.
—*The Abbey Row*

In *Theatre Audiences,* Susan Bennett observes that "the refusal in much contemporary drama to take up either the issues or forms that are familiar to audiences 'trained' in the traditional experience of theatre (or, perhaps more significantly, theatre studies) begs that dramatic criticism adopts new discourses in questioning how plays engage audiences."[1] Although Bennett focuses on contemporary drama, Irish drama in the first decade of the twentieth century sought to redefine "the traditional experience of theatre" by deliberately reconditioning Dublin audiences and training new patrons. Positioning themselves as an alternative to the much-vilified Theatre of Commerce, Yeats and the ILT hoped to reinvent the experience of theatregoing in Dublin. Not only would the plays be different, so also would the audiences, acting, sets, and theatrical spaces. In their restrained acting style, shocking although native subject matter, recurrent and claustrophobic stage setting, and often abbreviated duration, these plays actively sought not only to reshape theatregoers' horizon of expectations. "Such plays will require," Yeats announced, changes "both in writers and audiences."[2] Those changes in audiences, acting, spaces, and theatre decorum—all material conditions that shaped the performance and its reception—are no less relevant than the published or unpublished texts to the question of stage censorship in the early years of the century.

In this context, the Dublin audience's self-consciousness—its theatricality, its role in enacting the national drama—flourished as the new century began. Not only did metaphors likening political events to stage plays proliferate in the popular press, but nationalist groups were also increasingly cognizant of the potential for drama as a medium for disseminating cultural values. For Padraic Colum, the new national drama was "an instrument in the national liberation."[3] In 1906 *Sinn Féin* claimed that "drama is the greatest nationalising force we have in our possession."[4] Then as now, there were important, improbable links between the stage and politics in Ireland. Several Irish reviewers were also political commentators or elected officials. Politicians wrote, acted in, and reviewed plays. Arthur Griffith, editor of the *United Irishman, Sinn Féin,* and *Nationality* and, later, the first president of the Dáil, authored several of the most vitriolic attacks on Synge. D. P. Moran wrote extensively on drama, as did P. S. O'Hegarty. As a youngster, Eamon de Valera himself had appeared on the Abbey stage on 28 November 1905 in *A Christmas Hamper.* As much as any playwright, these commentators, along with actor-activists like Maire Nic Shiubhlaigh and activist-actors like Maud Gonne, established the theatre as a staging area for politics.

The memoirs and recollections of those involved in dramatic groups provide alternative accounts to the development of Irish theatre at the beginning of the twentieth century and often do not accord primacy to Yeats. Many of those intimately associated with theatre describe the ILT as both a false step and a failure. In *The Splendid Years* Maire Nic Shiubhlaigh, for instance, repeatedly speaks of the "failure" and "death" of the ILT. Whereas Yeats in 1902 described a three-year experiment drawing to completion,[5] Nic Shiubhlaigh recalls that the ILT met with "loud protests, . . . bitter controversies—and then, what was worse, with a lack of interest."[6] W. G. Fay wrote that "the efforts of the Irish Literary Theatre closed with the failure of *Diarmuid and Grania.*"[7] Nic Shiubhlaigh identifies the Irish National Dramatic Company at the Camden Street

Theatre as "the first Irish theatre" and attributes the idea of a national theatre movement in Ireland not to Yeats but to W. G. Fay.[8] Seamus O'Sullivan writes that "the real beginning of a National Theatre came in the year 1902,"[9] referring again to the Irish National Dramatic Company under the Fays. For AE it was "a girl of genius, Alice Milligan, [who] began to have premonitions of a dramatic movement, and she wrote little plays to help the infant Gaelic League. . . . With Alice Milligan, with whom the brothers Fay were coworkers, were the infant beginnings of the Irish dramatic art."[10] In the 1940s Padraic Colum wrote that "without Inghinidhe Na h-Éireann [the Daughters of Erin] I do not think an Irish Theatre would have come into being" and described the Fay brothers as "two without whom the Irish Theatre would never have come into existence."[11] Acknowledging the importance of the ILT, James Cousins identified the Irish language production of Douglas Hyde's *The Twisting of the Rope (Casadh an tSugain)* as "the play that thus opened up the authentic drama of Ireland."[12] These various opinions, explored by scholars like Mary Trotter and Karen Vandevelde, illustrate how deeply contested, how pluralistic the origins of the Irish theatre movement were.

Unlike the ILT, the autochthonous nationalist theatre reclaimed humble, unlikely spaces for their theatrical ventures. In 1903, just as these small companies began to proliferate, when Mary Colum asserted that Dublin had grown "drama-mad,"[13] Joseph Holloway observed that there was "no public hall suitable for amateur theatricals."[14] Molesworth Hall was inadequate for theatre performance in many regards. Of the Hardwicke Street Hall that housed the Theatre of Ireland in 1911, the *Irish Times* wrote, "it would be hardly possible to imagine any barer, simpler place wherein to act; beside it, indeed, the Abbey Theatre is luxurious."[15] Many of these venues were leased by the evening, which obviated the possibility of rehearsing in the performance space. The space in Camden Street, the back of a butcher's shop, was "not wide enough to swing a cat in, well, not a good sized cat."[16] All the better to underscore the fact that these were grassroots, noncommercial ventures born of selfless commitment.

By the turn of the century, a "theatre" might refer not to a purpose-built structure, but to a church or school hall, a coffee "palace,"[17] a hole-in-the-wall space, or an open-air site. In such venues what Marvin Carlson calls "the articulation of space"[18] announced itself outside of and in opposition to the established theatre, in architecture as well as text and performance. Outdoor, public spaces were used for theatrical pageants, processions, and epics such as Pearse's at Saint Enda's. In *A Twelfth-Century Pageant Play* scenes depicting the founding of All Hallows Priory, the departure of the crusaders and the arrival of Dermot, and the marriage of Strongbow and Eva were enacted for four performances in late June 1907 in Saint Stephen's Green.[19] These epic, overtly theatrical productions, like their audiences, drew upon the traditions of great nationalist occasions—the monster rallies, commemorative celebrations, and parades. Even the burials of nationalist martyrs such as O'Donovan Rossa embraced their own theatricality: carefully blocked, fully scripted, elaborately costumed, they came with souvenir programs and full musical accompaniment.[20]

Small, typically nationalist, companies found themselves up against both the Scylla of the law and the Charybdis of a lack of suitable stages. With some success, Francis R. Wolfe and Yeats assailed the enduring monopoly of the patent theatres in 1898, but theatre patents continued to be issued—for the Abbey in 1905, for the Queen's in 1908—until, in fact, the improbably late date of 1951, when Eamon de Valera signed the last patent for the Queen's.[21] Letters patent, issued to individuals (rather than a theatre company or sponsoring organization), permitted specific types of productions at a single, dedicated venue. They charged the patentee, who was usually the manager or owner, with the responsibility of enforcing the terms of the patent, including the prohibitions of indecency, profanity, and incitement to riot, and thereby positioned the patentee as censor. Letters patent not only endowed the patentee and theatre with rights, but also restricted potential competition. Even in the twentieth century and even in Ireland, patents were neither cheaply nor easily obtained; patent holders tended to be conservative and certainly not above seeking recourse in the law against challenges from potential rivals. Like the Lord Chamberlain's license, the patent was a mechanism of state control, but, once obtained, it carried privilege and legal status.

Before the reforms of the Local Government (Ireland) Act for which Yeats lobbied so vigorously, the financial equation of the commercial theatre could not be broken. After 1899, however, numerous theatrical enterprises would rely not only on box office receipts but also upon the sponsorship of clubs, subsidy from patrons, and most importantly the dedication of unpaid actors, technicians, and enthusiasts. Another (temporary) loophole in the patent restriction was that abridged dramatic works could be performed as one-act plays. J. B. Carrickford and Louise Grafton performed over three hundred plays at the Mechanics' Institute as one-acts in hopes of evading legal prosecution, but in 1902 were run out of business.[22]

In 1905 the patent for the Abbey Theatre, issued to Gregory because neither Horniman nor Yeats spent enough time in Ireland to qualify as patentee, made it the fourth legally sanctioned theatre in Dublin. The Abbey's application for a patent was opposed by the three existing patent theatres, the Gaiety, the Queen's, and the Royal, largely on the basis that potential competition would, in fact, violate the patents already in place. Standing in favor of the patent was the prestige of "the best names," the description of the theatre as an anti-emigration incentive, and its relatively small seating capacity. Yeats reported to Gregory that the hearings in August 1904 presented "no difficulty about getting a patent for the plays of the Society."[23] The Abbey patent narrowly delineated the plays eligible for performance: "Plays in the Irish or English language written by Irish writers or on Irish subjects and such dramatic works of foreign authors as would tend to educate and interest the Irish public in the higher works of dramatic art."[24] Whereas the phrase "the higher works of dramatic art" today seems fraught with ambiguity, none existed in Dublin at the time. It meant plays that would not compete with the offerings at the three other patent theatres, those of the Theatre of Commerce. That the Abbey was a patent theatre may have only increased the vulnerability of smaller companies, especially those like the Theatre of Ireland. Even after a space was found, fitted, and equipped, that theatre still faced patent and licensing difficulties. In their shared commitment to "Irish" writing, overlapping personnel, common potential audience, and opposition to the commercial stage, groups such as Inghinidhe na hÉireann and Cumann na nGaedheal as well as the ILT sought to break the financial equation between revenue and expenses that governed commercial companies, dispose of the undead stage Irishman, and develop audiences with a new horizon of expectations.

All of these companies, described by Patrice Pavis as "minor theatre,"[25] can be grouped under an inclusive heading of cultural nationalism, but the willingness to confront political issues, the commitment to present (only) positive, uplifting images of the Irish and expressly didactic messages were crucial variables. Horniman's prohibition of political content at the Abbey alienated several of the most dedicated and talented enthusiasts.[26] Even beyond the various shades of nationalism espoused by these companies, their management and goals were profoundly dissimilar. While the Abbey relied upon a directorate, other groups were vastly more democratic and pursued antithetical means to achieve a similar purpose. Yeats gathered nominal support from a broad cross section of Irish (and Anglo-Irish) elites, whereas the other groups drew on long hours of labor from people who typically held another, often humble, job: W. G. Fay, an electrician; his brother Frank, an accountant. Aristocrats as well as the working class supported Inghinidhe na hÉireann's dramatic enterprises to advance an overtly political agenda. Nic Shiubhlaigh recalls that Inghinidhe na hÉireann "had a wide following amongst young girls all over the city." To her, "the revolt against the commercialism of the *professional* theatre" (emphasis added) demanded the commitment of amateurs and was her own reason for leaving the NTS. [27] The reliance upon external subsidy and insistence that the actors accept professional status soon proved decisive.

Amateurs like Nic Shiubhlaigh were profoundly subversive precisely because their refusal to accept wages for their work in theatre not only defied the privileged status of the commercial, especially patent, theatres, but also assured their independence. By definition, amateurs were outside the Theatre of Commerce; moreover, they were not contractually obligated to perform what offended their religious or political convictions. Amateurs challenged not only the financial equation of the commercial theatre but also the authoritarian hierarchies of theatre organizations, thereby subverting not only Dublin Castle and the Theatre Royal, but the Abbey directorate as well. Maire T. Quinn, secretary of Inghinidhe na hÉireann, annoyed Yeats and both Fays by using Maud Gonne's permission to claim the title role in *Cathleen ni Houlihan*, appearing in the Ulster Literary Theatre's production of Yeats' play in Belfast, and moonlighting in the National Literary Society's production of the Cousins's *The Sword of Dermot*. A week later, on 26 April 1903, the NTS banned actors from outside performances without prior permission. Actors like Quinn might, and often did, enact their own censorship by refusing to say a specific line or play a particular role.[28] Further, the very sites in which many of these performances were staged—shabby, makeshift spaces—suggested a renegade quality that undermined the licensing laws of the ruling government.

After 1899, questions of stage censorship in Ireland almost invariably recalled the ILT production of *The Countess Cathleen* as a precedent. When the debate over audience displeasure resurfaced in regard to Synge's plays, the issues accreted significance and meaning unique to Ireland. As the century progressed, those issues became consciously self-referential. Yeats's rhetoric in 1907 evoked his own experience eight years earlier. Then, T. W. Rolleston and others had insisted on the audience's right to express satisfaction as well as dissatisfaction, an insistence that reaffirmed the audience's participation and heightened its awareness of its own theatricality.

In November 1901, George Moore proposed a clerical censorship of drama in Ireland, asserting "the intelligent censorship of the Church will free the stage from the unintelligent and ignorant censorship of the public."[29] Moore had and would continue an intimate acquaintance with censorship spanning national borders and six decades. In the 1880s he did battle with Mudie's Select Library over the de facto banning of his novels, *A Modern Lover* and *A Mummer's Wife*. Many years later, in October 1930, the Lord Chamberlain refused to license his play *The Passing of the Essenes* for public performance because of its representation of Christ as an onstage character.[30] Only weeks before his call for clerical censorship in 1901, Moore sought but was denied Archbishop William Walsh's approval for *Diarmuid agus Grania*, Moore's theatrical collaboration with Yeats.[31] As Adrian Frazier points out, through this ploy "Moore was trying to outflank Edward Martyn, who had Archbishop Walsh's stated support for his efforts to clean up 'the present scandalous condition of the Dublin stage.'"[32] Extralegal, ad hoc efforts such as the archbishop's would continue to dog Irish theatre well into the second half of the century, and Moore, like Yeats, saw it coming. Moore's call for clerical censorship appealed to the idea of purity in theatre—"The theatre needs purification. I want to redeem it from the counting house and the various immorality that the counting house brings in its wake"[33]—but was motivated by fear of the mob.

Both Moore and Yeats abominated censorship, especially mob censorship, and recognized that it could threaten any fledging theatre venture as surely as could theatre licensing restrictions. Moreover, both appreciated how useful the support or involvement of clerics would be. In the first issue of *Samhain,* hot off the presses in the fall of 1901 when Moore proposed clerical control, Yeats promoted the dramatic accomplishments of Fathers O'Leary and Dineen.[34] The previous year, Moore cultivated a relationship with Father Thomas Finlay, the Jesuit editor and sometimes drama critic of the *New Ireland Review.* Certainly, clerical endorsement might assuage suspicions about their theatre enterprises, expand the potential audience, and perhaps even remove the threat of the hostile receptions that greeted *The Countess Cathleen.* A Catholic priest in particular might provide the theatre with an ally to placate those who felt that Yeats and Moore had little understanding of, let alone sympathy with, Catholic Ireland. In England, as Moore well knew, the Lord Chamberlain's censorship not only cut and banned plays, it also approved them. Because it provided the approval to face down critics who might attack plays on moral or other grounds, the Lord Chamberlain's licensing of plays had long enjoyed strong support from at least one quarter in the theatre community: the managers charged with enforcing the terms of the patent. Just as the Lord Chamberlain's approval indemnified productions against legal action and suppressed nearly all public protest, so might a clerical censorship diffuse the threat of nationalist or mob censorship.

Yeats's abiding anxieties over mob censorship, stoked by his reading of Nietzsche, resurfaced the next year in an article that appeared in the *United Irishman* in November 1902, "The Freedom of the Theatre." Recalling the attacks against *The Countess Cathleen,* Yeats argued that a moral judgment of drama was inherently dangerous: "The reign of the moralist is the reign of the mob."[35] Later that month, Thomas Kettle, one of those who had protested *The Countess Cathleen,* challenged Yeats. Kettle argued that he and his fellow students had attacked *The Countess Cathleen* as "artistically bad, and in relation to its audience, . . . quite unacceptable." "Drama," wrote Kettle, "is implicitly moral, for it deals with conduct, and conduct has for its very essence morality."[36] Throughout his life, Yeats would successfully bob and weave against the accusation that he condoned plays that were not moral or that were immoral. In 1903 he answered the charge by clarifying that his concern was with evocation of "morality" as an incitement to mob censorship: "My objection was to the rough and ready conscience of the newspaper and the pulpit in a matter so delicate and so difficult as literature. Every generation of men of letters has been called immoral by the pulpit or the newspaper."[37] Presciently, Yeats anticipated the problems he would face in the next five years.

At the beginning of the century, the ILT, the NTS, and other companies defined themselves not merely as intolerant of the stage Irishman, but also in contradistinction to what Yeats decried as vulgar and stupid, both the Theatre of Commerce and British theatre. In the mid-nineteenth century Dion Boucicault in *The Colleen Bawn* (1861), *Arrah-na-Pogue* (1864), and *The Shaughraun* (1874) undertook the deconstruction or inversion of the stage Irishman. In the first decade of the century, Irish drama came to be performed by Irish actors sometimes speaking Irish or, more often, with an Irish accent. And this insurgent native Irish drama, especially at the Abbey, would typically reject the formulas of the most popular British imports of the day and the reigning dramatic style in London, melodrama.

Melodrama was typically viewed, at least by intellectuals like Shaw, as an irredeemably degenerate form of drama. Like Aristotelian tragedy, melodrama evokes pity and fear, but, unlike tragedy, it appeals primarily, if not exclusively, to the emotions rather than the intellect. Characters, not of noble birth but of the middle or working class, typically had only slight involvement in public affairs (although nationalist heroes found a home at the Queen's Theatre). Melodrama relied upon the creation of suspense and sensation as surely as today's film thrillers. On stage, as Stephen Watt notes, this usually involved highly charged moments of discovery (and concealment), perilous rescues, and frenetic action.[38] Unlike tragedies, which in George Steiner's succinct formulation "end badly,"[39] melodramas did not always see the deaths of their heroes and heroines. Whitbread's *Wolfe Tone,* for instance, ends not with the eponymous character's suicide, but with his enemy's execution and Tone's pronouncement, "So perish all traitors!"[40] As such, the effect of melodrama, as Watt demonstrates, continues to be disputed. Does it result in catharsis and subsequent pacification or does it inspire the audience to reenact and renew the struggles depicted on stage. No less importantly, melodrama often divests the play—its characters, situation, and action— of ambiguity. Such ambiguities, evident in *The Countess Cathleen* and soon to figure conspicuously in Synge's plays, sometimes provoked the audience to display volubly their uneasiness, disapproval, and hostility and, in some instances, to demand stage censorship.

In stark contrast to the plays of the commercial theatre was the modest one-act, a sub-genre that claimed strong Irish precedents from the 1890s. The stage set for many of these "peasant plays" was to become the Abbey hallmark: the cottage with its hearth, which as represented on the Abbey stage, matched "the exact dimensions of an Irish cottage—12 feet high in front, sloping down to 8 feet at the back wall, 20 feet long and 12 feet wide."[41] With *The Countess Cathleen* and several of Synge's plays (although a shebeen in *The Playboy*), this became the familiar setting of peasant plays. Although Frank Fay had told an interviewer that "every country that wants a native drama must go to the country for it, it is not to be found in the city,"[42] the realities of those rural settings were often unpleasant: boredom, penury, gossip, enervation, despair, lovelessness, loss, death, drink, and misery. In *The Countess Cathleen* those realities, including famine, are emblematized in the opening scene when Seamus Rua hurls a dead wolf on the table.

In the early years of the new century, the Dublin public demonstrated a strong and consistent lack of interest in the Abbey. Although Yeats had solicited the nominal support of an Ascendancy elite for ILT, the Abbey repertory was an affront to its loyalist clientele. The Dublin working and lower classes found little to enjoy and less of themselves on the Abbey stage. A play in which Dublin audiences might have seen themselves won *United Irishman* competition for a new play. In January 1903 Padraic Colum's *The Saxon Shillin'* was slated for production by the NTS. W. G. Fay, fearful of the play's nationalist politics, asked Colum to modify its ending. When Colum declined, the production was withdrawn.[43] The stage representation of a human corpse, as Fay well knew, was disconcerting, and in the instance of *The Saxon Shillin'*, potentially incendiary. But the corpses were coming: one (alleged) in *In the Shadow of the Glen* and another in *Riders to the Sea*.

Like Gregory and to a lesser extent Yeats, Synge took as his subjects the lives of peasants. As Greene and Stephens observe: "When he did turn to Irish legendary material in his last play, *Deirdre of the Sorrows*, he changed the heroic characters with rare and royal names into western peasants."[44] In the Abbey repertory, the three directors systematically rejected not only melodrama as a genre, but also characters drawn from the sitting room, urban environments, and the ranks of the heroes and martyrs of Irish history, the very character types to which playwrights like Pearse, Milligan, and Martyn gravitated. For Gregory the familiar settings were the open-air market, the public space in a village, or the open road; for Synge, the peasant interior; for Yeats, a less realistic mythic space. The visual representation of these locales shocked (but then bored) theatregoers, not least because of their contrast with the often spectacular stage sets typically found on the legitimate stage. In *Staging Place: The Geography of Modern Drama*, Una Chaudhuri coins the term "geopathology" to refer to the problematic nature of place and home. Chaudhuri writes of the "victimage of location" and "the heroism of departure"[45]—terms that have immediate applicability to all of Synge's plays performed during his lifetime. As Thomas Kettle argued, the peasant plays forced the urban Irish audience to question its relationship to, and the existence of, an austere but remote and now often idealized life. When Irish geopathology was interrogated rather than idealized, especially through comedy, the cry for censorship went up.

Theatregoers also encountered an unfamiliar, subdued acting style appropriate to the typically smaller venues, with a greater emphasis on language rather than on flamboyant action and acting. Under W. G. Fay's guidance, the Abbey embraced a style of acting that was antithetical to the bombastic declamation suited to theatres that accommodated thousands. Several of the most telling accounts of the acting style can be found in the Scottish and English press coverage of the 1905 Irish Players on tour. In June 1906 the *Glasgow Observer* offered this account:

> It is no exaggeration to say that from the standpoint of histrionic art their visit to this city is the theatrical event of the season, if not, indeed, of our generation. This seems excessive praise, but it can be made good. Author, playwright, and actor unite in telling us that their mission in life is to hold the mirror up to nature; as to the acting it is not acting at all, it is simply the people we know, doing and saying the things we may see them do and hear them say in their native villages. There are no stage mannerisms, no playing to the gallery; no recognition of the audience in any shape or form. It is the highest form of art which effectually conceals its art.

In Cardiff, too, the company earned praise for its unaffected acting: "There was a strangeness over everything because all the customary tricks and trappings of the showman's art were absent."[46] Brenna Katz Clarke identifies two discrete acting styles, the decorative and the realistic, that emerged under the leadership of the Fays.[47] As acting styles evolved at the Abbey, more and more distance was put between the realistic style of the peasant plays and the decorative style appropriate to Yeats's experiments with chanting, psaltery, and a highly stylized presentation. The realistic, low-keyed acting style was ideally suited to the naturalistic language and dramaturgy of the peasant plays.

To accommodate this cultural nationalist self-definition in the available venues and with limited resources, the Irish national theatre movement gravitated toward the short, often one-act play requiring a single set.[48] Crafted for small casts, these short plays did not rely upon the resources of a large theatre, let alone expensive costumes, stage sets, and machinery. Many were written for performance by amateurs in "the halls and back streets."[49] At the Abbey and elsewhere, several short plays would typically be performed on a single bill. In 1903 John Denvir relished this development: "To give a short play in Irish . . . is now so much a matter of course that it is difficult to believe that the idea was a novelty a year or two ago. The

North, the South, the East, and the West are now represented in the band of our Irish play-writers."[50] Like the early works by many contemporary dramatists (Harold Pinter, David Mamet, Edward Albee), these plays employed a single set, required only a modest outlay for scenery, costumes, and lighting, and were written for performance outside traditional theatre spaces. Nonetheless, many were impatient with this dramatic fare. James Joyce and others looked for more full-length plays on the Ibsenite model. With specific reference to Lady Gregory's translations of four one-act plays by Douglas Hyde, Joyce contemptuously dismissed the subgenre as "dwarf-drama."[51] Joyce was hardly alone in his criticism. In 1906 the playwright Frank D'Alton lamented the preponderance of the "baby play . . . short and sketchy—single phrases."[52] After *The Playboy*, *Sinn Féin* described them as "not plays, but playlets"[53] performed not for the general public but the very few. W. G. Fay, however, judged that the ability to introduce a new short work teamed with established plays enabled the fledgling repertory system to work at all.

These plays, their sets, and their presentation were not the only radical departures in theatre formations at the turn of the century. Irish audiences were well accustomed to performing as well as hearing a play on a trip to the theatre. Jack B. Yeats's *Hellfire,* depicts an animated East End audience engaged in their own performances. Comparable singing taverns and free-and-easys catered to the entertainment needs of working-class Dublin audiences. Even in Dublin's patent theatres, "the music of the gods" featured singsongs or solo bravura performances, sometimes accompanied by portable pianos brought to the theatre and played by audience members. Helen M. Burke dates such "improvisational pléaráca, or revelry" in Dublin theatres from the 1730s.[54] The traditions of the audience's own performativity died hard. When Edward Martyn hired the Queen's for *A Doll's House* and *The Heather Field* "the audience was not the hushed assembly one might expect in a concert hall and hope for at an Ibsen production; they whistled, chirruped, chattered out loud, banged the doors going back and forth to the lobby bar, and sometimes, made rude remarks."[55]

Yeats and his Abbey directors imposed a very different decorum on proceedings at the Abbey, an imposition that embodied one of the many contradictory ideas endemic to the ILT and centered on the audience. There was, moreover, a decided difference in expectations for an Abbey audience than for a music hall or Gaiety Theatre one. Rather than undertaking any accommodation with the prevailing standard for behavior, a reverential silence and respectful decorum were expected. Open only one week per month and even then "sparsely attended," members of the Abbey audience arrayed themselves in carefully chosen nationalist garb. Yeats, of course, was selectively consistent in his highly theatrical wardrobe. Darrel Figgis, Thomas MacDonagh, and the Pearse brothers occasionally appeared in solid-color Gaelic kilts. Mary Colum recalls her own elaborate costumes for attending Abbey performances: "[they] had to be of Irish manufactured material. For dressy wear I had a white garment with blue and green embroidery, a blue brath, copper broaches [*sic*], and other archaeological adornments. For more ordinary wear, I had the Irish costume in blue green, a brath of the same colour with embroideries out of the *Book of Kells*." Colum, who with other members of the Twilight Literary Society attended every Abbey production, recalls that "the audience was so slender in those days that we [twelve students] visibly augmented it." [56] The singsongs and sing-alls from the larger theatres were not permitted at the Abbey; instead, the interaction of a costumed audience, respectfully silent yet participatory, created a rarified, intimate atmosphere. The theatricality of the audience spilled into the tearoom or lobby, as could be seen in the spectacle of leading nationalists, writers, editors, and Dublin celebrities during intermissions. Dawson Byrne alleges that before *The Playboy*, the only audience cultivated was a highbrow one prepared to sit "through a play in an attitude of stony indifference."[57] The theatre was now darkened before performances to underscore the divide between ordinary life and the realm of dramatic art. During the intervals, polite music, appropriate to the elevated aesthetic experience of the plays, was played by Arthur Darley. Silenced in the dark, the faithful still contrived a highly theatrical display of themselves *qua* audience.

Yeats's plans to reeducate his audience were extensive, multifaceted, unrelenting, and very public. As Marjorie Howes notes: "The beginning of Yeats's theatre was marked by a basic conflict: the desire to move 'the mass of the people,' and the recognition that in their current state the masses were not receptive to the kind of theatre he was creating. The masses needed to be transformed into a nation."[58] The masses also needed to be transformed into obedient audiences. Yeats lectured on the psaltery. He published essays by himself and his friends to condition audiences to appreciate something very unlike the theatre of commerce. He developed organizations to support the theatre. Theatre programs as well as in-house publications like *Beltaine* and *Samhain* charted the movement's progress. Plays were published in advance of, or contemporaneously with, their premiere staging. If there was any doubt about the reforms envisioned by Yeats, the NTS program on 14 March 1903 at Molesworth Hall (and reprinted early the next month in the *United Irishman*) made clear that theatre was not only a serious matter; it was art. In the interval between "The Hour-Glass" and "Twenty-Five," Yeats delivered his lecture on "The Reform of the Theatre," in which he instructed his audience that "when truth and beauty open their mouths to speak . . . all other mouths should be . . . silent."[59] As James W. Flannery points out, Yeats's plea was for "freedom from religious and political censorship,"[60] and with it went the audience's submission to the playwright's art. The audience may have been conditioned to accept poetic drama, chanted verse, even the psaltery, but nothing Yeats did could have prepared it for the playwright Holloway described as "the evil genius."[61]

Although *In the Shadow of the Glen,* unlike *Riders to the Sea* or *The Well of the Saints,* was not yet in print when it was first performed, actors thoroughly familiar with *The Playboy* spread word of its incendiary portrait of rural life. Before a word had been uttered in performance, the *Irish Daily Independent,* like the *Daily Nation* in 1899, raised a call to protest against Synge's play: "We hold that those who ambition the uprise of a dramatic art that shall be true, pure and National, should make their voices heard against the perversion of the Society's avowed aims."[62] Two important acting members of NTS, Dudley Digges and Maire Quinn, refused their roles in the play and resigned from the company to protest the production, as did Maud Gonne and Douglas Hyde. So distressed were Digges and Quinn over the decision to produce the play that they turned to the

Gaelic League and soon founded a company, the Cumann na nGaedheal Players, to compete with the NTS. As in other well-documented instances, the actors' dissatisfaction with policies and plays helped to create the rival companies that proliferated in the first decade of the century.[63] Moreover, Frazier argues that Synge's provocation was, unlike Yeats's in *The Countess Cathleen,* intentional, premeditated, and antagonistic: "Synge knew he was needling the Catholic Irish about their sexual 'squeamishness'; writing to his friend Stephen MacKenna, he as much as admits the play is, among other things, an attack on Irish marriage customs, in an anarchic celebration of 'volcanic force.'"[64]

At its premiere in October 1903, *In the Shadow of the Glen* was greeted with hissing and disturbances in the theatre as well as the highly theatrical departure of Gonne, Digges, and Quinn. Across the political spectrum, from the *Irish Times* through the *Freeman's Journal* to the *United Irishman,* the premiere "provoked a hurricane of abuse."[65] Lionel Pilkington notes that each member of the audience received a copy of the September *Samhain* "that underline[d] the theatre's aesthetic freedom,"[66] but the audience's freedom was another matter. Described as cynical, despairing, harsh, unsympathetic, unhealthy, *In the Shadow of the Glen* stunned even those sympathetic to the development of Irish theatre. Echoing a frequent charge against Synge, James Cousins "felt its humourless morbidity to be charged with disease."[67] The *Freeman's Journal* described Synge as "preoccupied with the sex problem" and found "touches of cynicism that make an ugly impression."[68] The most scathing attacks on *In the Shadow of the Glen* were directed at its un-Irish source, plot, and characters. Maud Gonne seized upon Yeats's catchphrase, "the freedom for [*sic*] the Theatre," to "ask for freedom for it from one thing more deadly than all else—freedom from the insidious and destructive tyranny of foreign influence."[69] The protracted wrangling between Griffith and a host of Synge's defenders over the origin of the story was still in full swing in early 1904, just before the 25 February premiere of *Riders to the Sea,* which was little better. Displaying Bartley's dead body on stage, an immediate reminder of Dan Burke's supposed corpse in *In the Shadow of the Glen,* proved particularly offensive to many. Although *Riders to the Sea* would acquire the approval of nationalists in later years, its premiere advanced suspicions about Synge as an unhealthy, morbid, decadent playwright under the sway of pernicious foreign influences. The most positive note came from a source accused of the same vices, George Moore.

While the actors' refusals, supporters' public walkouts, and nationalists' protests can be read as falling under the most inclusive definition of censorship, one Synge play was demonstrably censored: *The Tinker's Wedding*. Synge completed the play by early 1906, before *The Well of the Saints*. Early in 1904, he wrote John Masefield that, "The tinkers have been re-written since you heard them and are now twice as long (in two acts) and I think many times stronger and wickeder."[70] *Tinker's* was, he explained to Max Meyerfeld, "never played here because it was thought too immoral and anticlerical."[71] In 1909, during the furor over *Blanco Posnet*, Gregory quotes herself as telling the Lord Lieutenant: "We have refused plays that we thought would hurt Catholic religious feeling. We refused for instance to produce Synge's Tinkers much as we uphold his work, because a drunken Priest made ridiculous appears in it. That very play was asked for by [Herbert Beerbohm] Tree who you have been holding up to us, directly after Synge's death for production in London."[72] Yeats corroborated, perhaps inadvertently, that the Abbey acted as Synge's censor in refusing to produce *The Tinker's Wedding*: "There is a play of Mr. Synge's which we refused to produce at the Abbey, because we considered it might give offense to religious feeling in Ireland."[73]

Even without a performance of *The Tinker's Wedding*, by the time of the third Synge play performed by the Abbey, all concerned— Yeats, Gregory, Fay, and Synge himself—appreciated the need to rein in his colorful oaths and imprecations. On 17 June 1904, Holloway declared it "an unpleasant surprise."[74] Only days before the opening of *The Well of the Saints*, Holloway again wrote to the directors, "asking them to omit some of the expressions and soften down one or two of the situations."[75] Synge had deputized W. G. Fay, who judged *The Well of the Saints* Synge's best play, to make suitable emendations. Worthy of Synge's trust, Fay resisted Holloway's call for additional cuts.[76] The generally damning reviews for the premiere on 4 February 1905 reiterated now-familiar charges against Synge's work:

unhealthy, uninformed, un-Irish, unsympathetic, and "seriously marred by the squalor of the play's human nature."[77]

Those very charges were the subject of a discussion at the National Literary Society on 5 February 1906 of George Sigerson's "The Irish Peasantry and the Stage," published later that month in the *United Irishman*.[78] Like the "secessions" occasioned by, first, the production of *In the Shadow of the Glen* and, second, by the transformation of the Abbey into a limited liability company, the debate revealed the profound differences among those most supportive of the theatre movement. Yeats, *père and fils*, Sigerson, Holloway, Thomas Kettle, Padraic Colum, and Maurice Joy were all in attendance, as was one still smarting over *The Countess Cathleen:* George O'Neill. His account of the meeting, published in the *New Ireland Review* the next month, made plain his resentment: "We are unfairly represented by the persistent putting forward of types and traits not characteristic of our nation, and at the same time eminently injurious to its good name, while numerous types and traits which are genuinely characteristic and highly honorable are wholly and unduly kept in the back-ground."[79] As far as O'Neill was concerned, nothing had changed since the travesty of *The Countess Cathleen,* so he reprinted his thousand-word attack on Yeats's play as apposite to *In the Shadow of the Glen* and *The Well of the Saints.* O'Neill's essay demonstrates not only the rift within those who were supportive of the theatre movement, but also the way in which, in seven years, the movement had become self-referential. Yeats's outrages were now reiterated by Synge in more offensive language and under less defensible foreign influences. Once constructed, theatre history repeated itself. The significance of any single production was now seen in terms of a pattern in which meaning accreted in an emerging tradition.

As John P. Harrington notes, "discussion of *The Playboy* throughout [the twentieth] century consistently returns to the production history and Dublin origin. . . . [T]here is perhaps no other twentieth-century play that is so rigidly referred back to its opening nights."[80] The accounts of the scenes both in and outside the Abbey Theatre are well documented and the subject of extensive analysis. As Robert Hogan and James Kilroy observe: "There is one significant point which has never been made about *The Playboy* riots, and that is that they were caused by a rather small number of people."[81] Protests over *The Countess Cathleen* may very well have been organized in response to the incitement in the *Daily Nation* and, later, to Cardinal Logue's letter, but *The Playboy* appeared under very different circumstances. Although nothing in *An Claidheamh Soluis, United Irishman,* the *Republic,* or even the *Leader* targeted Synge's play, Holloway reported a rumor of organized opposition.

Variously read as a type of Christ, Parnell, Oedipus, Cuchulain, and perhaps Synge himself, Christy Mahon was originally played by W. G. Fay, who had played the male leads in Synge's three previously produced plays: the Tramp, Bartley, Martin Doul. Like *Riders to the Sea* and *In the Shadow of the Glen, The Playboy* dramatized profound ambiguities toward the community, the landscape, patriarchy, and the church. In *The Playboy,* further, and no less profound, ambiguities surrounded the hero and sexuality. Even after Gregory and Yeats had already "removed words and phrases from the acting text,"[82] Synge's *The Playboy* remained an affront because it is, by every definition, a comedy.

By 1907, just as fifty years later, playwrights were well aware of the likely flash points for a play in Ireland. In 1905 Dublin theatregoers knew what to expect from a Synge play with the result that they stayed away in droves, but *The Playboy* was, if nothing else, a huge box office success. Lady Gregory anticipated trouble with *Playboy* from an early date. Not only did she shield Yeats by arranging for an all-Synge evening, but later wrote that she knew that the skein of peculiar oaths and imprecations were provocative. Earlier protests, especially from nationalists, over *In the Shadow of the Glen* and the tepid reception of *Riders to the Sea* and *The Well of the Saints,* were not heeded. *Au contraire.* Fay asserted that not only was Synge fully cognizant of the incendiary nature of *The Playboy* but also that he wrote the play to provoke audiences and critics who opposed his earlier plays. As he was when he told Masefield that the *Tinker's* had grown "wickeder," Synge was fully conscious of the impact his plays were likely to have. As soon as he saw Synge's script, W. G. Fay "knew we were in for serious trouble unless he would consent to alter it drastically":

The temptation to hit back is strong, and among those who have yielded to it we find J. M. Synge. He could not forgive the crass ignorance, the fatuity, the malevolence with which *The Well of the Saints* had been received. He had given of his best in good faith, and offence had been taken where no offence had been intended. "Very well, then," he said to me bitterly one night, "the next play I write I will make sure will annoy them."[83]

If Fay's verbatim quotation of Synge contains even a modicum of accuracy—that is, if *The Playboy* was a response to the objections raised to *In the Shadow of the Glen* and *The Well of the Saints,* then the "oppositional theatre practice"[84] of *The Playboy* targeted a very narrow faction of the Dublin minority that actually supported the Abbey. Still smarting from the treatment of Colum's *The Saxon Shillin'* and Horniman's "No Politics" fiat, that faction was less detached from the subject on stage than was its creator. As seen in the 1906 debate over Sigerson's paper at the National Literary Society, contention about plays appropriate to an institution calling itself Irish and National ran very high. Synge would see "them" rise up from the darkened, silenced auditorium to play an unscripted role.

In regard to the question of stage censorship and *The Playboy,* three points have particular importance: whether the demonstrations were organized; what the oft-used phrase "the freedom of the theatre" meant; and whether the deployment of the police in the theatre was justified.[85] The debate over, and critical evaluation of, *The Playboy* employed a distinct vocabulary that had its own connotations and self-referential qualities. One of the key phrases was "organised opposition," which suggested an audience prepared to bushwhack the performance without giving it a fair hearing. The phrase had a provenance that reached back at least to the Astor Place riots in New York City in 1849, described by one pamphleteer as "the terrific and fatal riot" that left eleven dead and countless wounded.[86] "The freedom of the theatre," a phrase employed by Yeats five years earlier, was now claimed by both proponents and opponents of the play. To the former, the freedom of the theatre meant that the playwright and production should persevere in their artistic vision and maintain the integrity of the play. To the latter, the freedom of the theatre meant that audiences were at liberty to express both pleasure and displeasure.

To contextualize the performances that accompanied *The Playboy* is to recognize a number of unscripted players who took their place in the Abbey Theatre beginning on Monday, 28 January 1907, for the second performance of the play. By then the cast for the performance was far larger than the eleven characters in Synge's text. For the remainder of the run, groups and individuals responded no less to what they had read in the papers or heard on the street than to what they saw and heard on stage. In addition to the likely opponents of the play, students from Trinity College, recruited as "supporters" for the play, were primed to challenge those who expressed disapproval.

The Monday and Tuesday performances of *The Playboy* provide an extreme example of the gap between what semioticians identify as text and performance. In these rare instances, evidence concerning the exact nature of the latter is as strong as the exact language of the former. For both *The Playboy* and *The Countess Cathleen,* if not for all theatrical performances, it is impossible to assume that the author's text, itself often revised, edited, and altered, was acted exactly as written. Sara Allgood, who played the Widow Quin, recalled that on the Thursday evening performance, when "there was dead silence in the audience, we could not remember our lines."[87] The impossibility of knowing what was spoken that Augusta Gregory acknowledged in reference to *The Countess Cathleen* is even more pertinent to *The Playboy.* Gregory noted that in its original run *The Playboy* was never performed as printed.[88] Nic Shiubhlaigh says that "the play was never really heard on any night but the first."[89] Others who were in the theatre insist that the play could not be heard at all. With Synge's text fully submerged in the hue and cry and only the *mise en scène* of the Abbey peasant play surviving in the dumb show enacted, the most important actor in the theatre was the audience.

Demonstrating both for and against *The Playboy,* the audience asserted that it, too, had a role to play. That the protesters embraced their own theatricality was the most conspicuous feature of the performance, overwhelming and eclipsing the text. By Tuesday, the performance in the theatre was no longer one written by Synge. The cast had expanded to include policemen, Yeats, and numerous partisans both for and against the play. Many had, or took for themselves, speaking roles in which they addressed everyone in the theatre. Fay embellished Christy's scripted lines with a vigorous defense of Synge, reported as if verbatim in the press. Yeats's own script, denouncing the protestors from the stage, had been sent to the papers in advance so that his speech could likewise be quoted verbatim and at length.

Yeats stressed that the unruly spectators were "not part of their regular audience," although he, in fact, singled out for arrest two individuals who were not only part of the regular audience but also known as such by Yeats. Padraic Colum (Sr.) and Piaras Béaslaí were neither strangers to Dublin theatres nor hostile to the often enunciated if contradictory goals of the Abbey. Colum's son Padraic had already published several plays and had seen his *The Saxon Shillin'* accepted and then rejected by Yeats and W. G. Fay. Béaslaí, already a prizewinner in the Gaelic League's Oireachtas and president of the Irish language theatre society Na hAisterori, would in 1923 be one of the cofounders of An Comhar Dramaiochta. He wrote several plays in Irish, including *Cormac na Coille,* which was performed at the Rotunda by the Keating branch of the Gaelic League in May 1907. Yeats later said that he chose to single out these individuals specifically because of their public enthusiasm for the Abbey. Yeats's testimony against Béaslaí in court on Wednesday described "an obviously organised attempt" to disrupt the play. Both the organization of the dissidents and the disruption of the play were critical questions. Individual audience members spontaneously responding to the play by manifesting displeasure were, from one perspective, no different from individual audience members applauding, laughing, or otherwise expressing enjoyment or approval. On the other hand, if they were organized and predisposed to prevent the play's reception and went to the theatre as a group with that objective, then their response was neither independent nor spontaneous. Arguing that the Abbey faced an organized opposition to prevent the hearing of the play justified bringing in the law. Colum and Béaslaí, as well as others, wrote to the daily press where they vehemently denied being part of any organized disruption.[90] Arraigned that Wednesday, both asserted the authenticity and spontaneity of their response and their independence from any organized protest. Neither Colum nor Béaslaí relished the publicity that attended their arrest and conviction.

The Abbey quickly began advertising for patrons to support the play "against organized opposition," which advanced the notion that the disruptions were something other than a sincere, spontaneous response to the play. Ironically, the only obviously organized group was the Trinity students recruited to cheer the play. Those students were doubly privileged: not only were they from a privileged educational institution and class, but they were expressly invited to the performance, admitted without charge, and seated in the most expensive seats. The element of performativity is nowhere more clearly seen than in the Trinity student, variously described as the Galwegian or the man in the overcoat, who played the piano, was expelled, and returned to the theatre to sing "God Save the King."[91]

While condemning *The Playboy* as "indefensible" and describing Synge's four performed plays, including *Riders to the Sea,* as blasphemy less against Ireland than "against the moral order of the universe," the Gaelic League weekly, *An Claidheamh Soluis,* lamented the damage done to the Irish dramatic movement. "On both sides there have been mock-heroics and hysterics; on both a shameful lack of tolerance and broadmindedness; on both an even more painful want of that saving sense of humour which in his most tense and electric moments never deserts the genuine Gael."[92] In spring of 1907, *An Claidheamh Soluis* described the Abbey's claim to be a national theatre fizzling out, encouraged the Theatre of Ireland, and, like Yeats, recognized the need to reeducate the Irish theatre audience.

Yeats's principal strategy to defend his actions and *The Playboy* was to recall previous attacks on Synge, William Boyle (who withdrew his plays from the Abbey), and Padraic Colum. Like O'Neill, he reminded his readers that all this had happened before; past was indeed prologue. Yeats also reprinted his prepared remarks at the 4 February debate, in which he proudly announced the two-fold increase over the previous box office record. In comparison to the indifference with which *The Well of the Saints* had been met, *The Playboy* looked like good business, whatever hackles had been raised. Yeats claimed not only freedom of the theatre, but also victory. Sounding distinctly triumphal, Yeats said: "I am confident that I saw the rise in this country of a new thought, a new opinion, that we had long needed."[93] Similarly, Gregory spoke of "a victory in taking the Playboy to Belfast."[94] The commotion had barely died when the *Republic,* the Belfast Sinn

Féin paper, appreciated the inevitable backlash to protest: "All that the objectors to 'The Playboy' have accomplished so far is to encircle the head of Mr. Synge with an incongruous halo of martyrdom and give the Abbey Theatre the finest advertisement in its history."[95] Here the typical effects of attempts at stage censorship are evident: widespread press publicity created inordinate interest in the play; attendance soared; opponents and supporters both claimed moral high ground; revivals referred back to its initial reception.

Six months later, the Abbey took *The Playboy* on tour in Britain. Although under contract to a limited liability company, the cast refused to perform *The Playboy* outside Cambridge and London. When Synge's play reached London it experienced what it never had in Dublin: official censorship. When, on 22 May 1907, the obligatory license was sought for *The Playboy*, the Lord Chamberlain, Lord Althorpe, wrote the Examiner of Plays, G. A. Redford: "The words 'the loosed Kharki cutthroats' should be omitted, and on the license the words of the endorsement 'nor anything calculated to produce a breach of the peace' should be underlined. Subject to the above you may pass the piece for license."[96] The play was licensed for performance only after nineteen cuts. Gone were many oaths, two "bloodys," and "the scarlet-coated bishops of the courts of Rome."

Beginning on Monday, 10 June, *Spreading the News* and *The Playboy* opened for three performances at the Great Queen Street Theatre in London. In a very receptive review, the *Times* wrote: "Mr. Synge's play appeals to us primarily as a work of art, so delicate, so humourous, so 'strange' and individual, that we cannot force ourselves into caring whether it is, or will be, fair on Mayo or not. In construction, character, and dialogue this is the best play Mr. Synge has yet written."[97] Despite favorable reviews,[98] at least one article reported a near reenactment of what had happened in Dublin:

> A scene rarely witnessed in a London theatre took place . . . at the Great Queen Street at the performance for the second time of *The Playboy of the Western World,* practically the entire house fiercely protesting by booings and hissings against the play. Several gentlemen in the stalls rose to resent what they termed "the insult to Irish womanhood," and the angry confusion was naturally only increased by the ill-advised conduct of others, who by loud laughter

and cheers tried to drown the voices of the protestors. We have already expressed our opinion of the play, and while still holding that it is too poor and weak a phantasy to be accepted as an insult to the Irish, we certainly agree that if it is to be taken seriously its due fate is suppression, for it is an ugly and false idea convincingly and well told. The house, too, was displeased at the offence against good taste committed by the author in his description of the torture of a dog. The audience, by the way, were mannerly and quiet throughout, save at the moments of the offensive passages.[99]

Two years later, these questions of stage censorship would again surface when the Abbey asserted the right of Irish audiences to hear what the Lord Chamberlain censored by producing Shaw's *The Shewing-up of Blanco Posnet*. Two decades later, the disturbances over *The Plough and the Stars* would in many ways recapitulate the events surrounding the premiere of *The Playboy*. The initial reception was continually reimagined, re-evoked, always accreting significance for those favoring as well as those opposing the play. Ninety-three years after the fact, W. J. McCormack would note that "*The Playboy*, and its attendant rioters, had a prolonged influence on Irish public opinion, conditioning the tone in which Church and culture, bourgeois and bohemian, nationalist and non-political citizen spoke to each other."[100] How transient the trigger points for protest were can be seen in both Ireland and the United States. In both countries the premieres caused great uproar, yet within two years (1907/1909 for Dublin and 1911/1913 in the United States) *The Playboy* was performed to great acclaim. And in both cases there were very public conversions: fierce detractors became avid supporters.[101] That *The Playboy* quickly became the stuff of myth had as much to do with its reception as with the play itself. The Abbey management valorized their own courage and determination while demonizing their opponents. That was to become the principal marketing strategy when Synge's play toured. Seventy-eight years after the premiere of *The Playboy*, when Galway's Druid Theatre mounted a revival of Synge's play, it was still in the shadow of the 1907 disturbances as seen in a cartoon in *Punch* in which a placard announces "Riots at Abbey Theatre."[102]

In the emergent mythologizing of Irish freedom of the theatre and the attendant construction of a tradition of Irish theatrical disorder, the events in early 1907 took on disproportionate significance and meaning. In the midst of the chaotic run of *The Playboy,* James Murray, the critic for the *Irish Independent,* offered a brief survey of theatrical disturbances in Ireland. He began by claiming that "[a]s a rule, the Dublin theatregoer is one of the easiest and best tempered patrons of the drama."[103] It was the last time that such a claim would be made.

4

"The Boom of the Ban"

At the end of the first decade of the twentieth century the authority of the Lord Chamberlain was under greater challenge than at any time before the late 1960s when he was finally stripped of his power to censor and license plays. In 1909 as it had three times in the nineteenth century, Britain again undertook a review of the Lord Chamberlain's powers through a parliamentary inquiry. Although *The Playboy* was not a catalyst in this renewed protest over the licensing of plays, the intense scrutiny of the Lord Chamberlain in England soon offered the Abbey another opportunity to celebrate the freedom of the theatre in Ireland.

Between 1892 and 1909, the stage came under enormous pressure as the middle classes gained access to many more possibilities for entertainment and leisure. By the end of the nineteenth century, extended educational opportunities, organized sport leagues, expanded access to resorts and tourist destinations by train all provided alternatives to the popular stage and contributed to the demise of one of the most successful theatrical forms. "In such a changed context," writes Andrew Davies, "stage melodrama could not survive."[1] In both Ireland and Britain, the most obvious and enduring challenge to the popular theatre came from motion pictures. Many theatres, such as Dan Lowery's Star of Erin in Dublin in 1897, quickly made the transition from stage shows to cinema. Spectacular as the Victorian theatre was, it could not compete with the special effects, economic efficiencies, and star power of film. Concomitant with the decline in the commercial viability of spectacular melodrama was the rise of realistic drama that addressed contemporary social and, to a lesser extent, political issues. The number of plays licensed in Britain skyrocketed from an average of two hundred in the 1850s and 1860s, to four hundred in the 1890s, five hundred in the first decade of the century, and seven hundred in the 1910s.

After the 1892 hearings, the Lord Chamberlain continued to proscribe public performances of serious works that dealt with social problems such as prostitution, adultery, abortion, and sexually transmitted diseases. Not only did the Lord Chamberlain refuse to license contemporary plays like Maeterlinck's *Monna Vanna* for public performance (although the Maeterlinck Society did perform it in a private, "members only" meeting), but he also found other works disturbing, such as Sophocles's *Oedipus Rex*. While serious "straight" plays that were neither escapist nor sensationalistic, classics as well as new works, were burdened with the Lord Chamberlain's scrutiny, unlicensed plays flourished. As the playwright Henry Arthur Jones observed, "every music hall and variety theatre in the UK, even to the lowest, has been acting uncensored plays without a single [official] reproach."[2] When the Lord Chamberlain banned Harley Granville-Barker's *Waste* and Edward Garnett's *The Breaking Point* in 1907, he galvanized the wrath of prominent authors. In protest, a letter signed by seventy-one writers, including Synge, Shaw, and Yeats, appeared in the *Times* on 27 October 1907. Thirty-one years after launching his attack on the Lord Chamberlain, William Archer wrote that the "censorship fight is taking up all my time." Still, he enthused about the planned protests of the Dramatic Authors of England: "An effigy of [G. A.] Redford [the Examiner of Plays for the Lord Chamberlain], which is being prepared by the Savoy property-man, will be carried by Frederick Harrison and W. B. Yeats; and over its head will wave a banner, carried by Gilbert Murray, with the inscription 'Ecrasez l'Infâme!"'[3] A 1908 study ridiculed the Lord Chamberlain's licensing procedure by documenting centuries of capricious, ridiculous, and corrupt decisions and reprinted the writers' letter for the abolition of his authority.[4] After a meeting between a group of the letter's signatories and the home secretary, Herbert Gladstone, on 22 February 1908, the lengthy bureaucratic process of convening another hearing on stage censorship began. That parliamentary inquiry provided the background for the Abbey's defiant production of *The Shewing-up of Blanco Posnet* in 1909.

From late July through the end of August 1909, the committee heard evidence from prominent writers and theatre luminaries of the day: Archer, Shaw, Granville-Barker, Herbert Beerbohm Tree, Bram Stoker, Pinero, W. S. Gilbert, Gilbert Murray, J. M. Barrie. The 1909 hearings touched on every aspect of the regulation of the stage: the qualifications (or lack thereof) of G. A. Redford, a former bank manager, to serve as the examiner of plays, the history and criteria of stage censorship, the economic consequences of licensing, and what might happen if the Chamberlain lost his authority. Publications denouncing the Lord Chamberlain's censorship proliferated. In *The Censorship Muddle and a Way Out of It* (1909), Henry Arthur Jones advocated eliminating preproduction licensing in favor of an inspector general who "shall not meddle with problems of morality, but only with exhibitions of indecency."[5] The ten-thousand-word statement that Shaw was not permitted to read into the minutes of the 1909 hearings appeared as a pamphlet and then in the preface to *The Shewing-up of Blanco Posnet*.[6] That same year, John Galsworthy's barbed *Justification of Censorship* satirized the censorship as perpetuating mediocrity, as "a bulwark for the preservation of average thought and sensibility."[7] Perhaps the most damning indictment of the Lord Chamberlain's authority came from the Examiner of Plays, G. A. Redford. When asked what principles guided his work, he said, "Simply bringing to bear an official point of view and keeping up a standard. There are no principles that can be defined. I follow precedent."[8]

The most comprehensive and meticulous analysis of the hearings, John Palmer's *The Censor and the Theatres* (1912), took particular aim at the fact that the theatre had been singled out for such virulent censorship in ways that other forms of expression had not. Palmer focused on the secret practices unearthed by the hearings. Since the nineteenth century, there was a considerable element of negotiation in licensing a play as theatre managers and officials from the Lord Chamberlain's Office often thrashed out exactly what words and phrases would be changed or deleted. These "surreptitious negotiations," Palmer argued, not only were beyond the official procedures but also skewed the number of plays officially banned and suggested collusion between the managers and the Lord Chamberlain's officials. Moreover, managers used the license as "an affidavit of decency" that indemnified them against litigation, a particular threat to productions touring in the provinces. The managers welcomed the Lord Chamberlain's authority out of fear that they might have to seek licenses in every locality where a touring production played.[9]

The 1909 hearings also reexamined the Lord Chamberlain's ban on representing Christ on stage, interrogating religious issues, and depicting biblical characters. So adamant were these interdictions that W. Graham Robertson, the set designer for the aborted 1892 London production of *Salome,* lashed out at Wilde's "thoughtlessness" in allowing Sarah Bernhardt to enter rehearsals for a play everyone knew would be banned.[10] The aversion to religious representations on stage reached back to the mid-sixteenth century and the suppression of the mystery plays.[11] Within a year of Elizabeth I's ascension to the throne in 1558, "Mayors and Justices of the Peace were commanded to ensure that no plays with a religious or political theme be performed."[12] Throughout the eighteenth and nineteenth centuries, the horror of dramatic representations of sacred personages and themes became more deeply entrenched as tradition if not stated policy. So adamantine were the strictures against religion on stage that even overtly devout plays, including passion plays, moralities, and miracle plays—rooted in medieval Christianity and by 1909 one of the staples of the early film industry—were summarily denied licenses. Public performance of Laurence Houseman's *Bethlehem* (1902) was forbidden, as was the Oberammagau Passion Play. In refusing to license *Johannis* the Lord Chamberlain stated the ban categorically: "Scriptural plays, or plays founded on, or adapted from, the Scriptures, are *ineligible for licence* in Great Britain."[13] The

1909 hearings noted rare exceptions made for nativity plays, but exposed that the criteria for banning plays owed not to a concern for public morality or welfare, but to custom and convenience. The Lord Chamberlain followed precedent, not principle.

This hostility toward religious dramatizations extended to Ireland as well. A Protestant clergyman, for example, objected to the passion play presented by the boys of Saint Enda at the Abbey in 1911: "I write on behalf of many in our city who hope that the authorities will not permit such sacred scenes to be put on the stage of the theatre. It is surely unedifying and improper."[14] It was the frank, colloquial discussion of Christ by a gunslinger in the American West that provoked the denial of a license for *Blanco Posnet*. Shaw refused the cuts the Lord Chamberlain demanded, asserting that they included passages central to the play's meaning.

Since the 1892 hearings, the Lord Chamberlain banned three of Shaw's nineteen plays. He dismissed *Mrs. Warren's Profession* as "immoral and otherwise improper for the stage" in 1894. *Blanco Posnet* and *Press Cuttings* were inspired by, and challenged, two of the Lord Chamberlain's most rigid strictures: the former addressed religious subjects and was potentially blasphemous; the latter satirized living personages, specifically politicians. The "Irish" content of Shaw's plays strikingly affected the way in which the Lord Chamberlain evaluated them. Richard Findlater asserts that the licensed *John Bull's Other Island* (1904) "by the Chamberlain's own standards was ultimately far more subversive"[15] than the banned *Press Cuttings,* subtitled "a topical sketch compiled from the editorial and correspondence columns of the daily papers during the Women's War in 1909." In early 1900 Yeats informed the readers of *Beltaine* that "Mr. Bernard Shaw promises us [the ILT] a play which he describes as an Irish Rogue's Comedy."[16] Four years later Shaw offered the Abbey *John Bull's Other Island.* On 5 October 1904, Yeats wrote Shaw that although the play presented many difficulties and might cause a disturbance, "we can play it, and survive to play something else."[17] But once Yeats saw the play performed at the Court Theatre in London, he expressed quite a different opinion to Gregory: "I don't really like it. It is fundamentally ugly and shapeless."[18] Shaw believed that his hostility to what he called the "neo-Gaelic movement" prompted the rejection of a commissioned play. The formal explanation for declining to produce the play was echoed in 1911 when the Abbey rejected Birmingham's *Eleanor's Enterprise:* the play's casting requirements (especially its upper-class English characters) were beyond the scope of the Abbey acting company.

In the summer of 1909, the Abbey was still reaping the blowback of *The Playboy's* productions in Dublin and London: anemic attendance, insistent needling from the nationalist press, and challenges from upstart companies like the Theatre of Ireland. With a dull summer looming and the joint select committee preparing its hearings, *Blanco Posnet* was an inspired choice for Horse Show Week. Plainly a morality tale, *Blanco Posnet* is a fable fraught with references to the theatre. Among the charges leveled against Blanco is his predilection for dangerous pleasures: "Did your holidays leave your character unspoiled? Oh, no, no. It was theatres: it was gambling: it was evil company: it was reading vain romances."[19] A blackguard who quotes Scripture to serve his own purposes, Blanco lauds the Sheriff by quoting Shakespeare: "As the actor says in the play, 'a Daniel come to judgment.' A rotten actor he was, too" (393). The Sheriff's posse, headed by a man known by his religious title, Elder Daniel, is referred to as a "vigilance committee," although they police horse thieves rather than playwrights. Shaw knew it would be banned; he wrote it to be banned.

Blanco Posnet was not the first play banned by the Lord Chamberlain to be performed in Ireland. In 1739, only two years after the Licensing Act endowed the Lord Chamberlain with fresh powers, he banned Henry Brooke's historical tragedy *Gustavus Vasa*. Although performed without incident in Ireland, it was banned as a satire on the prime minister of England.[20] But whereas *Gustavus Vasa* had been performed in Ireland without a license that was subsequently denied in Britain, *Blanco Posnet* had already been denied a license. While the earlier controversies over *The Countess Cathleen* and Synge's plays were largely internecine affairs, the Abbey production of Shaw's *Blanco Posnet* pitted Irish rights against British law. Writing from a postcolonial perspective, Lucy McDiarmid positions the episode as a "drama of Irish cultural resistance."[21] From this perspective, Shaw, Yeats, and especially Gregory waged a heroic struggle in defying the Castle's threat to stop the production. From the perspective of the nationalist press, however, the controversy over *Blanco Posnet* was a conflict of a different stripe: one that pitted titled aristocrat against titled aristocrat.

Because Lord Lieutenant Aberdeen was in Scotland, much of the initial wrangling took place between Gregory and an official, unnamed in *Our Irish Theatre*. Despite his awareness of the joint select committee hearings in London, Aberdeen appears not to have read the play. As Lady Gregory explains, there was at least one cut that she chose to make and recommended to Shaw, who did, in fact, rewrite the objectionable passage. In a statement to the press published the Monday before the premiere, Gregory and Yeats catalogued the multitudes that might take offense:

> We were told that Mr. Redford had objected, that the Lord Chamberlain had objected, and that if produced it will certainly offend excited officials in London, and might offend officials in Dublin, or the Law Officers of the Crown, or the Lord Lieutenant, or Dublin Society, or Archbishop Walsh, or the Church of Ireland, or the rowdies up for the Horse Show, or newspaper editors, or the King.[22]

Gregory's account identifies three discrete Irish constituencies that any production, especially one as potentially explosive as *Blanco Posnet,* would have to accommodate, assuming, of course, that Shaw, the actors, and the other Abbey personnel were placated. The first was the Catholic hierarchy—both Cardinal Logue and Archbishop Walsh concerned Gregory and the Lord Lieutenant.[23] If either stirred up protest, then the terms of the patent, specifically those prohibiting incitement to riot, might be breached and the patent itself jeopardized. Gregory, however, argued that those most attentive to the prelate's edicts were not the theatre's regular patrons. Besides, the Irish Literary Theatre had endured Logue's denunciation of *The Countess Cathleen* a decade earlier and would take the risk.

The second constituency was the nationalists, whose power to inflame public protest against a play was a matter of record. *The Playboy* built on the Abbey's willingness to undertake a challenging play, even when they had every reason to suspect that it would be provocative and unpopular. There is ample evidence that an understanding was sought and realized to forestall a preproduction bashing of the play by nationalists.[24] On 21 August 1909, Griffith cautioned *Sinn Féin* readers to avoid any form of activity that Dublin Castle might use as a pretext for acting against the play and the Abbey:

> Writing with knowledge we may say that the Castle has decided that if a disturbance takes place in the Abbey Theatre on the occasion of the production of the play, it will use that disturbance to interdict the play, and thus reestablish in full working order a machine with which hereafter to crush national drama.
>
> Therefore any person who takes any part in disturbing this play is simply playing the Castle game, consciously or unconsciously. Any who think the play would be too much for their feelings should keep away. Anyone who goes to see the play and who disapproves of it should manifest his disapproval only by silence.[25]

The third threat was the authority of British law—as it migrated from the Lord Chamberlain's office to shape the de jure authority of Lord Aberdeen. The potential for disturbances, civil unrest, or riot was critical to both sides. As Gregory wrote Shaw:

> The worst thing that could happen to you, indeed the only real danger I see, is that there would be any demonstration against the play. This would justify Redmond, and enable the L.L. to warn us not to repeat it.[26]

The threat of a negative response from three constituencies was astutely and accurately gauged; the production went ahead.

In their negotiations with Dublin Castle over *Blanco Posnet*, Yeats and Gregory raised the ante by bruiting the possibility of an Abbey production of another banned play. As early as 13 August, Yeats raised the specter with Castle officials of an Abbey production of *Oedipus Rex,* banned in Britain only two years earlier.[27] This was one of the cards that Gregory and Yeats played most brilliantly. On 15 August, Gregory wrote Sir James Dougherty that if he served the Abbey with a threatening notice over *Blanco,* "we probably will postpone it till September 30, and produce it with the already promised 'Oedipus.'"[28] In that case, Gregory wrote Shaw a few days later, they could "have the fight over both plays."[29]

The preproduction publicity for *Blanco Posnet* is more easily measured in column feet than column inches. From early August, daily reporting in several papers, including *The Northern Whig* as well as the nationalist weeklies, provided blanket coverage. In the *Irish Times* the progress of the production was juxtaposed with a weekly Saturday feature on the testimony before the joint select committee in London, "How the Censor Works." To capitalize on the box office and to situate the production of *Blanco Posnet* in their construction of a heroic tradition of the freedom of the theatre in the Abbey, the directors scheduled a Tuesday performance of *The Playboy* and *The Rising of the Moon*. Although the Lord Lieutenant regaled Yeats and Gregory with a host of unpleasant scenarios if they persisted with *Blanco Posnet,* in the end he dithered and did nothing.

Press coverage, as well as the correspondence of Shaw, Gregory, and Yeats increasingly turned on arcane questions that had nothing to do with *Blanco Posnet:* Was Shaw Irish? Would Lady Lyttelton and her crowd attend the premiere? Could the Lord Lieutenant prohibit a play's production or was he obliged to respond only to disturbances? So desperate for news were the papers that they even ran articles reporting "no fresh developments." With the readership's appetite whetted, the papers served up several stories such as "'The Playboy' Recalled," in *The Evening Telegraph,* which also printed an unflattering sketch of Yeats giving evidence against protestors in the police courts in 1907. Shaw's preface to *Blanco Posnet* spoke of Yeats's and Gregory's production of *The Playboy* as "taking the field with every circumstance of defiance, and winning the battle with every trophy of victory" (372). Francis Sheehy-Skeffington's letter to the press recalled *The Playboy* and argued that "Mr. Yeats has no right to set himself up as censor" by requesting any changes in Shaw's play. *Sinn Féin,* ever ready for an opportunity to annoy Yeats, chided him for not producing *John Bull's Other Island* yet proceeding with *The Playboy.* Surprisingly, amid the numerous invocations of *The Playboy,* the presence of the police, positioned in the theatre in anticipation of disturbances, escaped attention.

The audience on Wednesday, 25 August, is variously described. The press duly noted a flock of correspondents covering the premiere for foreign papers. McDiarmid emphasizes the Ascendancy glitterati in attendance. Donal Dorcey, however, recalls an audience that reflected a broader cross section of the population:

It was perhaps the most mixed Abbey audience ever. The usual corps of first-nighters was reinforced by the fashionable set and the horsey set up for the Horse Show from England and the provinces, by those who wanted to see the Lord Lieutenant defied and those who wanted to see the Abbey humbled, by those who were always to be found where trouble promised, and even by a few who were interested in the dramatic art.[30]

The response of the reviewers was the feeling that they and the audience had been had. There was a tremendous sense of deflation, of being lured to the theatre under false pretenses. There were some positive reviews, but most critics were disappointed since this play hardly measured up to Shaw's other plays. The press's biggest complaint was how unscandalous Shaw's play was. Unanimously, the initial reviews put to rest any suspicions that the play was sacrilegious or that the production worthy of protest. No less important than the artistic merit of the play was the subsequent positioning of the successful staging of *Blanco Posnet*. As McDiarmid notes, Yeats and Gregory were eager to describe their victory, but the nationalist press was divided. Although *An Claidheamh Soluis* applauded the Abbey decision, others argued that *Blanco Posnet* jeopardized the independence of the Irish theatre and feared the possibility that British censorship might be extended to Ireland. The *Leader* saw the Abbey decision as a dangerous publicity stunt that threatened the autonomy of the Irish stage. D. P. Moran certainly did not see much Irish about the production, since Shaw would hardly have "counted" as an Irish playwright and *Blanco Posnet* was neither set in, nor about, Ireland. Although the *Leader* maintained neutral-to-happy relations with Gregory and always found space to praise her plays, Moran's contempt for Yeats was unqualified and unrelenting. After defending the police presence in the theatre during *The Playboy* disturbances, Yeats was often "Head Constable Yeats"; in 1910, he became "Pensioner Yeats." With the threat of unlawful disturbances over *Blanco Posnet* remote, the *Leader* availed of the opportunity to attack Yeats ad hominem:

In [an] incontinent scramble for notoriety, . . . [Yeats] rushed this Shaw play into Ireland, where it is foreign, and has no connections with the purposes of the Abbey Theatre; he rushed it as a piece of smart business for Horse Show Week, calculated to yield gate money and notoriety, and in so doing roused the sleeping dog of dramatic censorship in Ireland.[31]

For the *Leader*, the Abbey production of *Blanco Posnet* was yet another cheap ploy that confirmed its oft-expressed opinion about Yeats. On 11 September, the *Leader*'s regular satiric feature, "As Others See Us," used the voice of John Bull Jr.: "This is the country they want 'freedom' for, mark you. They have a pretty sight too much freedom, it strikes me, and the sooner things are tightened up all round this part of the Empire, the better, say I."[32] A separate article denounced Yeats "as Censor of audiences who protest at atrocities [*The Playboy*]" and accused him of "a piece of flagrant Britishism . . . to import this British quarrel over here," and allying the Abbey with the production of "filthy" foreign plays.[33] But not only did Yeats and Gregory claim victory in the press, they also claimed it at the box office. *Blanco Posnet* was revived at the Abbey in March, August, and December 1910, April and September 1911, December 1912, and January and November 1914, although by then the offensive nature of the play, Irish or not, was no longer in question. By then it was another trophy for the freedom of the theatre.

The Abbey production was also a gesture of solidarity with the opponents of the Lord Chamberlain, first among them Shaw, but certainly Yeats and Synge as well. The startling departure of the English language's most prolix playwright into the one-act genre in 1909 was hardly a coincidence. By intentionally incurring the Lord Chamberlain's wrath, Shaw provided textbook examples of how ludicrous the censorship had become. By exposing the Lord Chamberlain's ridiculous standards, the Abbey production of *Blanco Posnet* may have had even greater impact in London than in Dublin. The confrontation itself was carefully staged and highly theatrical, although Dublin Castle's threat to revoke the Abbey's patent was quite genuine.

In November 1909, the Joint Select Committee on Stage Plays (Censorship) presented its final report. Although the committee noted many recent changes in the theatre, it recommended nothing to diminish the Lord Chamberlain's power. The report was fraught with contradictions. Unlike earlier reports, it admitted the playwrights' vigorous opposition to licensing: "With rare exceptions all the dramatists of the day ask either for the abolition of the Censorship or for an appeal from its decision to some other authority. Not only playwrights belonging to a particular school of thought, but men of all schools, unite in this demand." The managers' as well as actors' organizations and theatre owners, on the other hand, favored retaining the Lord Chamberlain's licensing because the threat of numerous legal proceedings, which they saw as the inevitable alternative, would make their position "intolerable." Another contradiction concerned the number of plays censored. While stating that since 1895, only thirty out of more than seven thousand plays were refused a license, the report admitted that "almost every week plays are modified in greater or less degree to meet the objections of the Censorship; and we have been assured by playwrights that the fear of its intervention seriously hampers their work." In addition to a consulting committee that would work with the Lord Chamberlain's office, the report recommended dropping the ban on characters drawn from Scripture but continuing to ban "plays which touch upon religious subjects."[34] Some nativity and miracle plays might now be licensed, but only if their treatment of religion was anodyne.

In Ireland, the production of *Blanco Posnet* provoked many calls for an institutional, expressly Irish stage censorship. The *Dublin Evening Mail* argued that "surely, it would be better to have a censorship, with an appeal to arbitration against his decision, than to burden his Excellency with the thankless task of dramatic criticism."[35] Most aggressive in calling for censorship was the *Irish Catholic,* which was "reluctantly compelled to quote an example" of Posnet's blasphemy and argued: "To us what has occurred furnishes absolutely convincing proof that Ireland badly and sadly needs a competent and relevant Censorship."[36] The *Leader* was not opposed to censorship and had, on many occasions, railed against the English plays they described as "smutty," but it fiercely opposed the concept that an English or Castle official would have any control over Irish plays. In July, Avis (William Dawson) lamented the Hippodrome circus and variety act at the Theatre Royal as pandering to the masses, although its patrons were "far less offensive" than the music-hall customers. On 13 November 1909, the *Leader* again demanded theatre censorship of Charles Darrell's *The Idol of Paris.* Surveying the response of the *Irish Times,* the *Independent,* and even *Sinn Féin,* the *Leader* condemned its competition for offering "Cead mile failte to imported British smut."[37] Its proposal to curtail the influx of foreign filth was for other publications to join them in an extralegal ban on advertising and to use theatre reviews to urge public boycott. Perhaps the most striking feature of the *Leader's* agenda was not its eagerness to prescribe and proscribe what might be seen, but its efforts to historicize its campaign against stage smut. "Nearly ten years ago when we suddenly came upon the scene, we attacked a performance at the now defunct music hall, the Lyric, as indecent," begins the two-thousand-word essay. *The Idol of Paris* is linked with other imported plays, such as *Spring Chicken, Zaza,* and *Sappho,* which are "putrid, smutty, and dangerous to public morals." The *Leader's* crusade was no less against its journalistic competitors than against the theatre proprietors or the plays themselves. The extralegal brand of censorship envisioned, a collusion of publishers and reviewers who would decide what was suitable for Dublin audiences, makes the Lord Chamberlain's licensing of plays look like the transparent rule of law.

Despite pressures from the *Leader* and the *Catholic Bulletin,* Irish producers and managers grew bolder in offering cosmopolitan choices to Dublin audiences over the next several years when a series of minor skirmishes, most confined to isolated articles in the daily press, exposed the varying and contradictory standards for theatre. The Theatre of Ireland's 1911 production of Alexander Ostrovsky's *The Storm* (1860) was challenged not because of the Lord Chamberlain's banning (the play was not licensed until 1929), but because its venue, Molesworth Hall, did not have a license. The production lucidly demonstrates that an Irish production of an unlicensed play was far less controversial. The threat to this production concerned not the play's decency but the potential challenge it posed to the patent theatres. Lodged on behalf of the Dublin Theatres, the complaint targeted the company's employment of professional actors and claimed to be protecting the patent theatres' investments.

In December 1911, two years after *Blanco Posnet,* Flora MacDonnell and members of the Players Club appeared at the Gaiety in another play that the Lord Chamberlain had banned, Maeterlinck's *Monna Vanna.* Over the previous year, Maeterlinck had proved very popular, both at the Abbey and elsewhere. Advertised in Dublin as "the first public production on the British stage," *Monna Vanna* was banned for its indecency because the title character, according to stage directions, presents herself to the enemy officer, a former suitor, who now holds her town captive, "nue sous son manteau" (nude under her cloak). Monna Vanna is prepared to offer herself to him to save her community, but no sexual impropriety ensues. (Its plot anticipates that of *Roly Poly,* which was to be pulled from production during the Emergency.) In the *Irish Independent* Jacques savaged the production, asserting that what was performed was not only a sanitized version of Maeterlinck's original, but that the production itself was very weak. Borrowing a line from the play, Jacques called it "a bad dream." But like *Blanco Posnet, Monna Vanna* drew a large audience attracted to what Jacques described as the "morbid sensation" of an unlicensed play—what he called "the boom of the ban."[38] The ban, in fact, brought with it the boom. From the first decade of the century to its last, the publicity campaigns for Irish productions of plays banned in England or elsewhere were extremely effective in attracting audiences. In 1999, a Dublin revival of J. P. Donleavy's *The Ginger Man* used the headlines from its withdrawal in 1959 as the basis for its publicity campaign. In 1912 Jacques and other Dublin critics voiced what Robert Hogan refers to as "obsessively puritanical" objections to the language and subject of St. John Ervine's *The Magnanimous Lover,* in which an unwed mother rejects the marriage proposal of her child's father. Not only was Maggie Cather's independence shocking, so was Ervine's use of the word "whore." Ervine wrote to accuse the Dublin theatre critics of their own de facto censorship. His play, like those of Maeterlinck and Shaw, went on. Tenuous as it seemed, the freedom of the theatre survived the decade, *The Playboy* and all.

5

The Riot in Westport; or, George A. Birmingham at Home

Words, then, have only mobile and transitory significations which change from age to age and people to people; and when we desire to exert an influence by their means on the crowd what it is requisite to know is the meaning given them by the crowd at a given moment, and not the meaning which they formerly had or may yet have for individuals of a different mental constitution.

—Gustave Le Bon, *The Crowd* (1895)

On Wednesday, 4 February 1914, the performance of George A. Birmingham's *General John Regan,* punctuated by catcalls throughout the first act, was stopped during the second act when angry protesters stormed the stage. Members of the audience who were not part of the preplanned action, which was cued by the cry "Now boys!" fled the theatre. Although alerted to the likelihood of trouble by posters calling for the protest, the police were unable to restore order in the theatre so that the performance might continue. Chairs were hurled, stage properties and scenery destroyed, the theatre itself badly damaged. The actor playing the Catholic parish priest was the focus of the attack. Rioters ripped off his Roman collar and burned it in the Octagon (Westport's town center) where the crowd, by police accounts, had swelled to seven hundred. The windows of the box office, theatre, and hotel accommodating the actors were broken. In the course of what the police called a riot, a constable was badly injured and five "baton charges" were made against the crowd. The riot was quelled only after the intervention of the parish priest, Father Canavan, who pleaded for order. Twenty people, young men described as students, were arrested.

This now-obscure incident in Irish stage history was anomalous in that it occurred not in Dublin but in Westport, yet in other respects it was entirely characteristic of the disorders associated with stage protests in Ireland before and after 1914. It was not a spontaneous but an orchestrated demonstration. It presumed the audience's right to express its displeasure by interrupting a performance. The protest responded to publicity that the play had received in the press and triggered its own sustained press coverage, although not on a scale to rival that of *The Playboy* or *The Plough*. As so often, the Westport riot directed its violence against the actors in a confrontation that pitted Catholic demonstrators against a Protestant playwright. The riot over Birmingham's *General John Regan* was the most violent Irish theatrical confrontation of the century and raised familiar questions about an audience's prerogatives and the play's realism, sources, and politics.

In 1914, George A. Birmingham, the pen name of Canon James Owen Hannay, was at the peak of his popularity. Forty-nine years old at the time, Hannay served as rector for the Church of Ireland in Westport between 1892 and 1913. As George A. Birmingham, he wrote over fifty comic novels, most of them set in Ireland. A native of Belfast and second-generation Church of Ireland clergyman, Hannay was a strong advocate of Home Rule and numbered among his friends Horace Plunkett, Arthur Griffith, Standish O'Grady, and Douglas Hyde, with whom he shared the growing cultural nationalism of the times. Once a member of the Gaelic League, he also authored a pamphlet entitled "Is the Gaelic League Political?" Hannay enjoyed a favorable public opinion and the further he got from Westport, the more favorable that opinion grew. Newspaper accounts of his lectures typically describe him as "genial" and "delightful," an author known for "his warmth and wit." Hannay's affable public image contributed to the popularity of his many novels and of himself as a lecturer, especially outside of Ireland. Hannay was wont to speak of Birmingham in the third person, as in "I have a great deal of respect for George A. Birmingham because I think he is a serious sort of chap trying to make an honest penny and maintaining an attitude of fair consideration and regard for his neighbor."[1] Birmingham's career as a playwright dates from 1911 when he wrote *Eleanor's Enterprise,* which the Abbey and then the Haymarket Theatre under the management of Herbert Trench, a member of London's Irish Literary Society whom Hannay knew at school, declined to produce.[2] However, Constance Markiewicz and the Independent Company performed *Eleanor's Enterprise* at the Gaiety in Dublin on December 12, 13, and 16, 1911, with considerable success.

Playwrighting was an unlikely avocation for clerics, especially in Ireland in the early decades of the twentieth century. As Hannay himself recalled, "the theatre in Belfast was frowned on when I was a boy, and to see a play there was regarded as a sin."[3] While Hannay tried to distance himself from Birmingham through the use of a pen name and coy third-person references, his Westport neighbors had long been suspicious of his satires. In *Irishman All* (1913), his collaboration with Jack B. Yeats, Birmingham offered a dozen sketches of common Irish types: the politician, the squireen, the publican, and so on. In his study of "The Parish Priest," he recalls that "one particular priest, a man of great gentility but humble origin, took it into his head that he was the prototype of one of [Birmingham's fictional] characters."[4] Although Birmingham couches his account of the misunderstanding entirely in the third person (as his other self— Hannay—sometimes did in speaking of Birmingham), he drew on his own experience. In his 1934 autobiography, *Pleasant Places,* Birmingham describes the response of the Catholic priest in Westport, "a man with whom I had hitherto been on friendly terms, [who] conceived the idea that I had caricatured him in *The Seething Pot.* This charge," writes Birmingham, "might have been brought against me quite justly by George Moore or by Standish O'Grady; for that first novel of mine was a *roman a clef.*" Although Birmingham insists that he created his clerical character a year before this priest arrived in Westport, the priest "in his fury, stirred up the people of Westport against me. He used to write weekly articles in the local papers with such headings as 'The Author of *The Seething Pot* Unveiled.'" Hannay was burnt in effigy. Other priests "made things as unpleasant for me as they could on all occasions."[5] Such ad hominem attacks on authors were not uncommon, as could be seen four years after the Westport riot when the villagers of Delvin, County Westmeath, recognized themselves in the pages of *The Valley of the Squinting Windows* and savaged Brinsley Macnamara and his family.

Despite the publication of Brian Taylor's critical biography *The Life and Writings of James Owen Hannay* in 1995, Birmingham today is largely forgotten for the anodyne, conventional works that he produced in such great numbers. He was expelled from the Gaelic League, and after his derisive comic account of the Easter Rising, *Up the Rebels!* (1919), moderate nationalists joined their more radical colleagues in denouncing him. Although two of his most popular novels, *Spanish Gold* (1906) and *Northern Iron* (1907), were translated into Irish in the 1930s (by Padhraic Og O Conaire and Muiris O Cathain respectively), his reputation has been in decline probably since leaving Westport the year before the riot over *General John Regan.* The assessment that Stephen Gwynn offered in 1936 still pertains: Birmingham's work "lacks the concentration of serious art; but it is, especially in its beginnings, a significant product of the general movement which sought to quicken Ireland out of the stagnation left by Parnell's death."[6]

In 1913, however, Birmingham was the toast of London and New York because of the success of *General John Regan.* He dined with Shaw and Prime Minister H. H. Asquith. His travels, engagements, and lectures were widely reported in the British press. *General John Regan,* which Birmingham said that he wrote in an intense three-day period, premiered to very strong reviews at the Apollo Theatre in London on 8 January 1913 with a cast that included W. G. Fay. Typical of the London reviews was the *Observer's* judgment that Birmingham "has achieved the difficult feat of clothing a satirical plot with the loving kindness of pure comedy."[7] Like other works that provoked celebrated Irish theatrical disorders, Birmingham's play earned praise from several reviewers for its realistic qualities. After a successful London run, the play opened at the Hudson Theatre in New York on 12 November 1913. Although the American tour of *General John Regan* came only two years after the controversial Abbey tour that included Synge's *The Playboy* and provoked the anger of Irish American audiences, the American reviews, like those in London, were superlative, largely because of the play's accessibility, humor, and predictability. Acton Davies wrote in the *New York Sun,* "*General John Regan* is easily the cleverest as well as the wittiest play which has come across the water in many a long year." The London *Daily Telegraph* reported: "It is ten years since a New York first night audience has been so responsive as it was at the Hudson Theatre last night." The *New York Times* devoted all of page 2 to an interview and profile of the playwright who was quoted in the *Evening World* headline on 25 October 1913: "There are no stage Irishmen in Ireland, says the Irish Mark Twain, now in NY."[8] What proved inoffensive to sensitive Irish American theatregoers, whose hackles had been raised by *The Playboy,* prompted riots in Westport. That Birmingham had revamped and revivified the stage Irishman was precisely the charged leveled against him in the *Irish Independent* and elsewhere after the Westport riot. The very success the play enjoyed was provocative to the Westport audience who thought they were being caricatured for the delectations of foreign, especially London, audiences.

So great was the anticipated Irish demand for this play in early 1914 that two separate productions of *General John Regan* toured Ireland. Leonard Boyne's company played major Irish cities—Belfast, Cork, and Dublin—before touring England; the W. Payne Seddon company began its tour in Kilkenny on 26 January and moved on to Clonmel, setting attendance records in both. In Galway, despite some hissing and jeering, the play was so popular that its run was extended an additional night.[9] After the Westport melee, the tour continued in Sligo, Mullingar, Athlone, Ennis, and Armagh without incident.

Birmingham credits AE with telling him a story that became the basis of the plot of *General John Regan.* The same narrative as related by AE to Lady Gregory inspired *The Image,* which opened at the Abbey on 11 November 1910 to tepid reviews. In her hands, AE's tale evolved into a dramatic work that more closely resembles her one-acter "Spreading the News" (1905) than Birmingham's highly commercial play. Whereas *The Image* dwells on regional rivalries and squabbles that sidetrack the energies of her characters, the singular focus of Birmingham's play develops a comic momentum characteristic of commercially successful stage farce.

Birmingham embellished AE's story by drawing on the Irish ancestry of Bernardo O'Higgins, the "Supreme Dictator" of Chile between 1817 and 1823, whose father, Ambrosio O'Higgins, viceroy of Peru, was born in Ballinary, County Sligo. *General John Regan* also alluded to an incident that occurred in France early in the century, one of the earliest of media hoaxes. There a journalist named Birault solicited endorsements from prominent politicians and elected officials to erect a statue to one Hégésippe Simon, doer of great deeds. Ready to lend their names to a worthwhile civic venture, many notables obliged with their support. Birault was, however, having them on: Hégésippe Simon existed only in Birault's imagination.[10] Such is the outline of *General John Regan*: an American named Horace P. Billings arrives in the quiet town of Ballymoy in the West of Ireland in a flashy motor car to inquire about the great Irish "patriot statesman, the deliverer of Bolivia" (23), Ballymoy's native son, General John Regan. Billings's offer of a five-hundred-dollar contribution toward a memorial rouses the leading citizens to concoct a scheme to erect a statue to Regan in the town square.

Dr. Lucius O'Grady, Birmingham's recurrent schemer and master of mirth, sees Billings's inquiries as an opportunity to take the American's five hundred dollars and not only erect a statue but also exact a commitment from the Lord Lieutenant for some gesture of public largess. Townsfolk are recruited for a gala celebration at which the Lord Lieutenant will unveil the statue. If the Lord Lieutenant is to visit, however, the town band will have to play a patriotic British melody in his honor and none of the nationalistic members would dream of doing so. O'Grady, however, plays on the fact that none of them has ever heard "Rule Britannia" and teaches it to them as "The War March of King Malachi the Brave." Disastrous hilarity ensues: two townswomen bitterly contest how to outfit Mary Ellen, the servant girl impersonating the General's niece, in an appropriately Irish costume. The green frocks for the schoolchildren playing the fairies attending Mary Ellen fail to arrive by the big day. The Lord Lieutenant doesn't arrive at all. "The Wearing o' the Green" is fobbed off as the Bolivian national anthem. The third act of *General John Regan* mocked what Birmingham described as "the ornamental part [of the Lord Lieutenant's position], the ceremonial opening of all sorts of things, the laying of foundation stones, and the reception of debutantes fell to the lot of the Lord Lieutenant, who also had a say in the distribution of that lavish government charity which was supposed to pacify the hearts of the rebellious Irish and make them contented with their lot."[11] Whereas nationalists would bristle over phrases like "lavish government charity," the Lord Chamberlain had sought to purge any mockery of the king's representative in Ireland. Birmingham's play was licensed only after the excision of several of the derogatory comments about the Lord Lieutenant. The remark that "The way Ireland has been governed for the past twenty years, nothing that a Lord-Lieutenant did would surprise me in the least" (30) and references to the Lord Lieutenant's behavior as "shabby" (80) and his position as "purely ornamental " (78) were all blue-penciled. The officious ineptitude of British officials that offended the Lord Chamberlain would have been welcomed by many in Ireland; conversely, what might offend the Westport audience was of no concern to the Lord Chamberlain.

Birmingham's Home Rule politics are evident throughout the play, although coming from Thaddeus Golligher, the proprietor and editor of the *Connaught Eagle,* they take on a comic dimension. Golligher attributes what the American sees as the "backward" state of Ireland to "the tyranny of the landlords and the system of grazing ranches" (16). Golligher's refrain foresees a happier day: "But, glory be to God, when we get Home Rule, it won't be that way with us" (38). The pageant, in which Mary Ellen, impersonating General Regan's niece, is attended by a troupe of fairies, parodied the tableaux vivants that were regular features of the Gaelic League's feisanna and nationalistic theatre groups. Golligher's oft-repeated clichés, combined with the gullibility of the band and the mock pageant, do indeed satirize Irish nationalism. Militant nationalists, however, saw this as gross caricature served up for the amusement of foreigners. The *Leader* described Birmingham and "Pensioner Yeats" as greedy "playboys" who "within the last decade [have] ultilise[d] the Irish Ireland movement as a jumping-off board for English pence and fame. . . . They exploit Ireland in England and America for gain and they do it fairly successfully."[12]

Although accounts vary, the real flashpoint for the rioters was the portrayal of the Catholic parish priest. The company manager Payne Seddon anticipated that one exchange, although approved by the Lord Chamberlain, might be particularly offensive to Irish audiences. On the day of the big unveiling, Doyle encounters an overwrought Father McCormack:

> DOYLE: It's worried to death you are, Father, and half a glass of it—what with Dr. O'Grady not being here and the children's frocks going wrong on you and that fellow Golligher—it's in my room I have it, behind the bar, and there's never anybody goes there only myself. It isn't as if I was asking you to taste it in public, for that's what I well know you wouldn't do.
> *Fr. McCormack goes slowly into the hotel.*[13]

That scene was, in fact, cut from the Seddon production before the play reached Westport and cut from the text as published in 1933. Writing to the editor of the *Dublin Evening Herald* after the Westport riot, Seddon defended his attention to Irish sensibilities:

> In justification of the author I may state that the part [the Catholic priest] is treated with the utmost respect; the only situation which might possibly be misconstrued being where the village hotelkeeper invites the reverend gentleman to enter his house with the object of taking a drink which he refuses. This, however, was omitted when the present tour started, at my request.[14]

Even with the suggestion of the priest's surreptitious tippling cut, audience members were enraged by the thought that one of their neighbors had been caricatured on stage. That the neighbor in question in *General John Regan* was the local Catholic parish priest compounded the audience's anger and indignation. That Birmingham's play, like Synge's *The Playboy,* was a comedy only exacerbated the protest—comedy, especially farce, having far greater inflammatory potential than tragedy.

Several provincial newspapers focused their reservations on what the *Mayo News* called the "grossly insulting" portrayal of Mary Ellen, who is transformed from "a sluttish maid of about fifteen years" (10) to the quintessential Irish colleen-goddess. Whereas London and American reviews applauded the realism of *General John*

Regan, many Irish commentators denounced hyperbolic characterizations, especially of Mary Ellen and Father McCormack. And whereas Americans praised Birmingham's contribution to the demise of the stage Irishman, an article by Liam Ó Domnaill in the *Irish Independent* entitled "Stage Irishman: A Re-Incarnation" offered this understanding:

> The revival of the Irish language has had a salutary effect even on Anglo-Irish literature; and the nation began to realise that, after all, the passionate desire for self-expression was no longer to be starved. But then the stage Irishman died; but, apparently, his disembodied spirit wandered in regions none too remote. A deliberate modern miracle of reincarnation has been performed, and Canon Hannay officiated at the ceremony.

To Ó Domnaill the stage Irishman celebrated the tyrannical oppression of the British; it was "national degradation made manifest." Birmingham's play confirmed Ó Domnaill's belief that "Ireland can never find expression in the writings of those who by education and temperament are foreigners."[15] The assault on Birmingham continued in the *Leader,* where Albert C. White saw Birmingham as pandering to the English appetite by "represent[ing] the Irishman as a drunkard, a murderer, a buffoon."[16] At the end of March, J. J. Rossiter leveled the same charge against Birmingham and some of the Abbey playwrights at a meeting of the National Literary Society.[17] To nationalists, Birmingham's play was all the more insidious not only because his stage Irishman was clothed in familiarity but also because he provoked humiliating laughter.

Many of the accounts of the Westport riot compared it, not with disturbances and riots that attended the trades union protests and general lockout of the previous year, but with other theatrical disturbances, most often with those in 1899 attending *The Countess Cathleen* and those in 1907 in response to *The Playboy.* The British press summoned up the spectre of more distant Irish stage protests, *Brighton Society* recalling that "a similar riot occurred when the late Sir Henry Irving took 'Much Ado About Nothing' [to Dublin]."[18] As days and then weeks passed, the perspective became more historical in positioning the Westport riot in a tradition of Irish theatrical disorder.

For several of the British papers, the Westport riot was demonstrable proof that the Irish would not stand "being made fun of," that they could not take a joke. In fact, just as events in Westport were unfolding, Hannay was lecturing in Manchester on his favorite subject, the Irish. There was, he told his audience, "a tremendous seriousness coming into Irish life, the purposeful seriousness of men bent on making the most of their chances [and that] this seriousness ran a risk of being overdone. [The Irish] were losing their capacity for making a joke and for seeing them."[19] Hannay later defended his play by relating that he "had received from the Principal of a Seminary in the United States a request to allow the students of the college to stage it under the supervision of the spiritual instructors on Saint Patrick's Day in the aid of the building of a Roman Catholic church."[20]

With the riot in Westport as a well-publicized introduction, the other touring production of *General John Regan* found receptive, sold-out Gaiety theatre audiences and almost uniformly positive reviews in Dublin. The *Irish Times,* ebullient about the play and its production and dismissive of the grievances expressed in Westport, commented on "the brilliant and harmless humour of the piece." In the *Irish Independent,* Jacques, who had vigorously objected to the coarse language and distorted characterizations in Synge's *The Playboy* seven years earlier, was not without reservations, but called the play "extra good as farce [and] innocent fooling." *Irish Life* offered a largely positive retrospect review on the conclusion of the Dublin run, noting that the reviewer "could not, however, accept Mary Ellen, the servant girl." A very similar response came from the *Cork Examiner.*[21] Although the priest's going into Doyle's Hotel, quite possibly for the drink he earlier declined, occasioned some hissing on opening night, the *Belfast Newsletter* reported that episode was only included in the first performance of the highly successful week-long Dublin run.

The results of the riot in Westport over *General John Regan* were both immediate and far-reaching. The Westport riot provided a notoriety that guaranteed box office success throughout Ireland and thus reaffirmed the showbiz maxim that all publicity is good publicity. Not surprisingly, the *Leader* offered the most sustained and condemnatory response to *General John Regan*. Birmingham was anathema to D. P. Moran's vision of Irish—in other words, Gaelic and Catholic—Ireland; in fact, Birmingham incarnated Moran's idea of the West Briton. Recognizing that protests like the Westport riot provide free publicity for the very work they condemned, the *Leader* even suggested that Birmingham might have deliberately incited the riot:

> The row about the "Playboy" was a great asset when Lady Gregory and British Pensioner Yeats hawked that unsavoury commodity in England and America and raked in the coin, and perhaps it was not altogether an accident that a row broke out in Westport for the wily commercial Mr. Hannay may have calculated that he would provoke a row and a free advertisement by sending his farce to the town where so many years he was glad enough to enjoy a fat and easy "living."[22]

Like many attacks against plays and playwrights in Ireland, the specific objections to Birmingham's characters were broadened to a blanket charge of immorality. By attacking *General John Regan* as immoral, Moran and others linked it with imported "dirty plays" and "smutty" music-hall revues. Perhaps more importantly, such attacks explicitly called for a dedicated Irish censorship of theatre.

The *Leader* followed up its criticism of Birmingham by praising William J. Larkin, who was arrested in Dublin for disrupting the performance of the French farce *Who's the Lady?* less than a month after the Westport riot. In response to a particularly titillating moment of stage business in which a woman's dress falls off (although only to reveal a fully clothed woman), Larkin rose in the gallery of the Gaiety Theatre on 2 March 1914 to denounce "this foreign filth. . . . It is an insult to Ireland."[23] Representing himself in court, Larkin defended his outburst by presenting clippings from the British press to confirm his belief that the play was immoral. The presiding magistrate at the Southern Police Court, Mr. Drury, upheld the principle that an audience member has as much right to express disapproval as to applaud a play. Magistrate Drury not only dismissed the charges but also praised Larkin for his "public service."[24]

The *Leader* hoped to stamp out the "dirty plays" blighting the Dublin stage, first, by calling for daily papers to refuse to advertise certain imported plays, and second, by requesting that those same papers publish a list of the alleged "respectable people, female and male," who went to see them.[25] Over the next turbulent years, the nationalistic press continued to denounce *General John Regan* as immoral and Birmingham as dangerous; three years later in 1917, *Young Ireland* was still condemning Birmingham, dubbing him "the bigot of Westport." The nationalistic press grew even more vehement in their call for theatre censorship, which was now frequently tied to the demand for an expressly Irish censorship of film. Throughout the summer after the Easter Rising, the *Freeman's Journal* joined the *Leader* in attacking the imported stage smut of the music-hall revues, what the latter called "the most demoralising and devitalising influence that our large towns and cities have to face at the present day."[26]

As the weeks and then months passed, press coverage, both in Ireland and England, linked the Westport incident with a tradition of theatre disturbances in Ireland. The Westport riot, the most violent and isolated outbreak of theatrical disorder in the twentieth century in Ireland, consolidated a pattern of theatre disorder that, while it did not begin with the protests over Yeats's *The Countess Cathleen,* had firmly established itself in recent memory. As at *The Playboy's* premiere, theatre demonstrations provided media exposure for the protesters' cause but, perhaps more important, supplied enormous publicity for, and heightened the popularity of, the very play they condemned.

The Westport riot and the Larkin incident both advanced the notion that the audience had a right to express its displeasure, the former suggesting that even preplanned theatrical disorder was acceptable. When the young men were arrested for public disorder they were "vigorously cheered by the immense crowd" in Westport's Octagon.[27] In July 1914, even with a change of venue to Castlebar and despite direct police testimony, their defense centered on their right to express offense taken at the play. The jury accepted that prerogative and deliberated for only twenty minutes before exonerating the protesters. In subsequent theatrical disruptions, especially in the case of *The Plough and the Stars,* demonstrators asserted that right to use the theatre as an arena to express cultural dissatisfaction by disruptive and sometimes violent behavior. Then, as in Westport in 1914, the actors bore the physical brunt of the audience's outrage.

That the actors were attacked sheds some light on why many were so cautious of potentially inflammatory language and stage business.

During World War I, a comprehensive British censorship was imposed in Ireland. On 12 August 1914, the Defense of the Realm Act (DORA) was passed and implemented in Ireland before the year's end. Although action was threatened against the premiere of P. J. Bourke's *For the Land She Loved* in November 1915, St. John Ervine placated authorities that such seditious nationalism would not be permitted on the Abbey stage again. That same month, Shaw's *O'Flaherty V. C.* drew the scorn of military authorities. Shaw hoped the Abbey would produce the play and score another *Blanco Posnet*–like triumph, but that was not to be. After the severe British censorship of publications that prevailed during World War I was lifted and Ireland moved toward independence, periodic calls for censorship and protest continued. In 1919, for instance, *Young Ireland* denounced the dramatic fare at the Hippodrome (Theatre Royal) as cheap, lewd, and out of control: "The obvious conclusion is that certain forces have operated to degrade public taste in the last few years."[28] The effort to cleanse the Irish stage would gather new inspiration and momentum after 1922.

Even before his success with *General John Regan,* Birmingham's situation in Westport was in decline. On the one hand, his own congregation was deeply suspicious of his Home Rule and Gaelic League associations. On the other, as the riot over his play amply demonstrated, the Catholics of Westport were openly hostile to him. He resigned his position as rector of Westport before leaving on his American tour. "The place, although I loved it very much, had become difficult for me to live in," he wrote. "Many of my parishioners felt very strongly about the views I held about Irish affairs. The Roman Catholics and Nationalist people did not like me any better."[29]

Factors well beyond either text or performance shaped the Westport audience's response to Birmingham in 1914. Patterson writes that, as Ben Jonson suggests in *Timber,* a "central principle of the hermeneutics of censorship [is] that interpretations could be radically different depending on what one selected as the context of the utterance."[30] As in *The Playboy* riots seven years earlier, the Westport riot again chose the theatre as a cultural site to contest the simmering animosity between rival conceptions of what was Irish and what constituted ridicule of the Irish. For some, like F. S. L. Lyons, the Irish yoked culture and anarchy in often violent and unexpected ways. For others, like Moran, the Irish were right, if not obliged, to protest the commodified slanders of playboys and gombeen men like Birmingham.

6

The Freedom of the Theatre in the Irish Free State, 1922–1929

How and why theatre eluded institutional censorship in the Irish Free State is rightly seen in the larger contexts of, first, the campaign for, and resistance to, censorship and, second, Irish stage history between 1922 and 1929. From a legal perspective, the reason the Irish stage retained its celebrated freedom was that the regulation of printed materials was discrete from the licensing of stage plays for production. The Free State legislation to censor printed material that became law in 1929 repealed and replaced a British act that dealt specifically with publications, not with stage performances. Although stage plays were often published, the British laws regulating print were independent of those governing theatre. But beyond this legalistic understanding lies a more revelatory tale of how and why Irish theatre escaped institutional censorship.

During the earliest years of the Irish Free State pressure steadily mounted to legislate censorship. As Robert Welch notes, "an increasingly pious set of public opinions on morality, sex, and belief . . . had formed very quickly after the foundation of the Free State, as if in reaction to the anarchy of revolution and its aftermath."[1] Film censorship was quickly enacted "under cover of night"[2] in 1923 and its scope widened to include film advertisements in 1925. Legislation affecting printed material and theatre, however, was fiercely contested in a series of articles by Richard S. Devane, S.J., in 1925; the government's Committee of Enquiry's report in 1926, Devane's *Evil Literature* in 1927; and the legislative debates that led to the eventual passage of legislation in 1929. Many argued for a specifically Irish censorship, but opposition came from government ministers, writers, and commentators. One of the most vocal opponents of censorship legislation was Minister of Justice Kevin O'Higgins, who argued that the existing law adequately addressed the problem. Frank O'Connor argues that O'Higgins's opposition to censorship was so forceful that "it was not until after his assassination in 1927 that a censorship bill could be introduced."[3] Two years after O'Higgins's death, on 16 July 1929, the Censorship Act repealed the Obscene Publications of 1857 and instituted an administrative censorship of printed materials.

Among the goals of both the legislation and the committee's 1926 proposal was the protection of the young, the poorly educated, and the vulnerable. Young, poorly educated, and vulnerable, however, were hardly descriptive of Abbey audiences. Although theatregoing in Ireland in the first half of the twentieth century was preponderantly an urban phenomenon in a predominantly rural society, calls for regulation of the stage emanated from diverse sources: urban and rural; secular as well as religious; fevered as well as closely reasoned.[4] The Irish Vigilance Association and the Catholic Truth Society, for instance, were extremely active in their censorship crusades at the same time that the latter organization was conducting a vigorous literacy campaign. As a vigilance organization, the Catholic Truth Society encouraged members to identify if not seek out obscene or objectionable material for censorship, but as a literacy advocate it also organized lectures and published hundreds of inexpensive booklets. Throughout the 1920s and 1930s it not only encouraged literacy by promoting its own publications but also annually reported its record of success in having works banned or withdrawn.[5] Theatre censorship was well within its purview. For organizations like the Catholic Truth Society, a distinctly Irish censorship, consonant with its conception of Ireland as a Catholic country, was a prerogative, if not an obligation, of the Irish Free State.

A more ambiguous attitude toward censorship could be found in *Honesty*, a muckraking Dublin weekly, whose readers included Sean O'Casey. In 1925 and 1926 *Honesty* covered a wide spectrum of issues ranging from tax reform and medical quackery to animal cruelty and public health. Although many of its concerns now appear risible or alarmist, *Honesty* was surprisingly progressive in candidly address-ing controversial issues such as divorce, married women working outside the home, nonmarital children, and prostitution. Its interest in public morality focused on dance halls, cinema, and music halls, all of which were considered far more dangerous than the "legiti-mate" stage.

A blueprint for censorship appeared in the February 1925 issue of the eminently more respectable *Irish Ecclesiastical Review*. In "Inde-cent Literature" Devane called for legislation to censor a wide range of works, including newspapers, books, pictures, and photographs as well as stage plays. For the next twenty-six years, until his death in 1951, Devane tirelessly campaigned for censorship of foreign publica-tions. Responding to the range of opinions evident in the Catholic Truth Society, *Honesty*, and Devane's essays, William Cosgrave's gov-ernment appointed a five-member Committee of Enquiry on Evil Literature that conducted public hearings in 1926 and subsequently moved into private sessions.

The committee's 1926 report was less extreme and disappointed censorship zealots.[6] Its emphasis on the medium, cost, and availabil-ity of works to be censored again drew attention away from the stage. Low-cost paperbacks were targeted, as were English Sunday papers that carried detailed reportage of divorce cases. The report made specific mention of only two works of fiction: *Ulysses* (banned in Canada at the time) and an edition of Rabelais, which drew the committee's notice because it was not only unexpurgated but also cheap. Like the legislation enacted in 1929, the committee's nominal target was neither the serious literature nor the Irish press but sleazy foreign newspapers, inexpensive paperback editions of raunchy books, and anything that dealt with abortion or birth control.

The Committee of Enquiry on Evil Literature had neither acted with the haste nor produced the results censorship proponents had hoped for. "To help maintain public interest" in censorship, Devane's *The Committee on Evil Literature: Some Notes of Evidence* offered his account of the committee's public hearings and his own refutation of witnesses and recommendations.[7] Like the committee's report, Devane constructed his argument through a comparative analysis of censorship in other English-speaking countries, a common feature of both arguments for and against censorship. Devane refers, for instance, to the Canadian model for blacklisting works such as Joyce's *Ulysses* and books by Margaret Sanger and Marie Stopes advocating birth control. The censorship of works on birth control, frequently euphemized as "race suicide" in and outside Ireland, persisted into the 1990s. Devane's own version of the evidence dismissed three "stock objections" to censorship: first, that the need for censorship was grossly exaggerated; second, that, as O'Higgins believed, existing laws were adequate to deal with obscenity; and third, that such censorship would interfere with the freedom of the press. He also drew on evidence given in the 1923 hearings of the Select Committee on the Matrimonial Causes Bill in Britain, which examined the impact of salacious newspaper coverage of domestic disputes and divorce proceedings.

Devane's was neither an overtly anti–intellectual nor an antiliterary approach. He disclaimed, for instance, the notion that his proposals would compromise the freedom of the press and, in fact, paid tribute to Irish journalism:

> We are not dealing with the liberty of the Irish press, but with the license of the extern press. Hence, I suggest that the proposed legislation be not directed against the home press, but to the outside press. To my mind Irish journalism and the Irish press are as near perfect in this matter as any press can be. (16)

Devane's nationalism compounded his indignation over foreign publications. Assuming that Ireland was morally superior to England, Devane called for "a new legal definition of 'indecent' or 'obscenity' in harmony" with the standards of sexual morality obtaining in Saorstat Eireann" (52). Censorship, he argued, would protect the fledging Free State press and publishing industry. Couched in praise of, and solidarity with, ordinary Irish people, Devane anticipated objections to his draconian proposals from "cranks . . . erotic bohemians, [and] 'unconventional' highbrows" (46). And draconian his proposals were: state licensing and taxation of wholesale and retail news vendors with provisions for fines and imprisonment; a national vigilance association "not alone as regards printed matter, but also in relation to the stage, the music halls, the commercialized dance halls" (40); and an admittedly "prohibitive" (23) tax of 50 percent on most foreign periodicals. In a flourish of rhetorical legerdemain, he argued for "a protective tax as a further and final test of the Government's unqualified sincerity in its attempt to Gaelicize the nation's youth" (22) and to nurture native Irish journalism. Devane took particular care to refute Minister O'Higgins's assertion that existing laws were adequate to deal with indecent and immoral printed materials. What was needed, Devane said, was *drastic legislation of a prohibitive character*" (38, his italics).

The committee's recommendations were not, however, comprehensively accepted in the 1929 legislation. For instance, its call for a "large censor board, numbering at least 30" was rejected.[8] Although the Committee of Enquiry as well as Devane's *Evil Literature* urged banning *Ulysses*,[9] it was not then nor at any time since banned in Ireland. Just as the committee's recommendations moderated Devane's more comprehensive proposals, the 1929 legislation moderated the committee's proposals. In the process, theatre censorship was either overlooked or sidestepped, quite possibly as a consequence of the controversies surrounding the decade's most famous playwright, Sean O'Casey.

At the beginning of the decade, the atmosphere in Dublin was hostile if not inimical to theatre. The curfew in Dublin was moved back from midnight to ten, then to nine, and finally to eight. By March 1921 all but the Theatre Royal had closed and would remain closed, even after the truce of 11 July until August of that year. Lennox Robinson recalled "a dreadful day in the spring of 1921"[10] when he had to dismiss the Abbey Company. After the curfews of 1920 and 1921 were lifted, venturing out for an evening performance could still be dangerous and theatre attendance fell off sharply. Amidst the violence and disorder of the Civil War, the nation could not agree on what the nation should be, let alone on an agenda for its national theatre. Moreover, as Robert Hogan and Richard Burnham note, "by 1922 many more people were getting their drama in the cinemas than in the theaters."[11] During 1923, in response to threats of violence against theatres that did not close on days when IRA prisoners were scheduled to be executed, armed guards were posted at the Abbey so that the theatre remained open in relative safety.

After the Civil War, the atmosphere was hardly conducive to theatregoing. Several explanations for the continued lack of audience interest were suggested. The Abbey was faulted for relying too heavily on a limited repertory of plays. In February 1924 Lennox Robinson complained to the Oxford University Irish Society that "the patrons of the theatre consisted almost entirely of visitors to the city; . . . members of neither university seemed to take any interest."[12] The Irish audiences that did make their way to the theatre were often chastised in the press for unruly, disruptive, and impolite behavior, especially inappropriate laughter. Worse, Abbey actors were criticized as unprofessional and occasionally reprimanded for mugging, scene stealing, "gagging," and interpolating extraneous dialogue. After the uncertainties and disruption of the Anglo-Irish and Civil Wars, Robinson lamented that "the stariest of the [Abbey] players sought their living elsewhere."[13]

The Abbey's ability to attract Dublin audiences reached a celebrated turning point in April 1924 with the appearance of O'Casey's *The Shadow of a Gunman*. With the subsequent premieres of *Cathleen Listens In, Nannie's Night Out* (both 1924), and *Juno and the Paycock* (1925), O'Casey quickly established himself as what the Abbey had lacked since Synge's death: a native playwright who would not only win international acclaim but also attract Irish patrons. The two-week rule, restricting the number of consecutive performances of any given play, was soon waived for the sensationally popular *Juno*.[14]

In the mid-1920s, vigilance societies continued to target specific stage productions for protest. Vigilance societies were not unique to Ireland. Britain's National Vigilance Association (1885), its National Council on Public Morals (1910), the London Morality Council, and the London Council for the Promotion of Public Morality all engaged in analogous activities, as did their counterparts in the United States. In 1925 the Gaiety Theatre produced Leon Gordon's *White Cargo,* which premiered in New York on 5 November 1923 and proved a commercial success in several American cities as well as London. It dealt explicitly with a sexual relationship between an unmarried West African woman and one of four white men living on a rubber plantation. Although its Dublin run was uneventful, *White Cargo* caught Devane's attention and was singled out in *Evil Literature* as demonstrable proof of the inadequacy of existing controls and the need for stage censorship.

By 1925 the state subsidy of the Abbey vastly complicated the question of theatrical censorship. In November 1923, the Free State established a precedent for theatrical subsidy through an annual grant of £600 for An Comhar Drámaíochta, the consolidated Irish-language company. In the face of growing Abbey debts, Yeats and Lady Gregory wrote President Cosgrave on 27 June 1924 to "offer the Abbey Theatre, its entire contents, scenery and wardrobe and the property it owns to the Irish Nation."[15] Fourteen months later, the Abbey received a subsidy of £850 from the Free State. The subsidy mandated government representation on the Abbey board, bringing the number of directors to four: Yeats, Gregory, Robinson, and now the economist George O'Brien, the first director who was not a playwright. Although repeated stipulations specified that no measure of control or censorship would be afforded the government representative, O'Brien was conscious of the vigilance societies and nationalistic organizations that were prepared and eager to stage their protests against the Abbey.

Only a month after the subsidy was announced, in September 1925, O'Brien expressed reservations over the language and the suggestion of incest in Lennox Robinson's *The White Blackbird.* To Joseph Holloway, O'Brien voiced his fear that the "Catholic Truth Society might picket or demonstrate."[16] But like *White Cargo,* Robinson's play did not arouse the public animus that was to greet O'Casey's next play. O'Brien's concern over *The White Blackbird* was, however, only prelude to much graver anxieties over *The Plough and the Stars.* On 5 September 1925, O'Brien wrote Yeats to argue that Rosie Redmond's "professional side is unduly emphasised."[17]

His most vigorous objections to O'Casey's play, specifically to the song sung by Rosie and to the use of the word "bitch," were addressed in cuts before rehearsals began. The other directors—Yeats, Gregory, and Robinson—assured O'Brien that more cuts would occur during rehearsals. O'Brien's concern, at least as expressed to Yeats and Robinson, was that he act not as censor but "as the watchdog of the subsidy," to guard against attacks on the theatre and, concomitantly, its state subsidy.[18]

The ensuing and now legendary battle over O'Casey's play was central in assuring that stage censorship was never enacted in Ireland and, as Julia Carlson asserts, was never seriously considered.[19] Offensive language was the primary concern both for O'Brien, who focused on "objectionable expressions" and "vituperative vocabulary,"[20] and for Michael J. Dolan, O'Casey's detractor and the play's original producer, who found the language "beyond the beyonds."[21] Ria Mooney, who played Rosie Redmond, recalls that "some of the company tried to frighten me out of playing the part. I need hardly say that it was some of the women who tried to put me off, because they felt that they would be besmirched by the fact of one among them playing such a role."[22] During rehearsals, Eileen Crowe objected to her character, Mrs. Gogan, saying that none of her children had entered this world within the boundaries of the Ten Commandments. With the playwright's consent, additional cuts were made but on 10 January 1926, O'Casey wrote to Robinson to protest what he described as "a Vigilance Committee of the Actors. . . . [T]o avoid further trouble, I prefer to withdraw the play altogether."[23] Even before the play opened on 8 February 1926, it had already endured potential censorship from many sources: O'Brien and others successfully argued for cuts and alterations; the rejection of certain lines by actors necessitated recasting; at least three clerics, consulted by O'Brien, Crowe, and May Craig (who eventually played Mrs. Gogan), vetted the play; Robinson replaced Michael J. Dolan as producer; O'Casey himself threatened to withdraw the play.

No opening night in Dublin was more anticipated in the decade, probably none since 1907. The first week was sold out. The opening night audience included prominent politicians, public officials, and artistic figures. The well-documented Dublin reviews were very positive, some ecstatic. Box office for the second week was very strong. Despite all the preproduction challenges *The Plough* faced, the premiere itself was a huge and conspicuous success.

So conspicuous was its success that *The Plough* became an obvious target. Once again the Abbey theatre became the very public staging area for a wrenching, albeit profitable, cultural confrontation over the freedom of the theatre. The exact nature of what transpired in the theatre has been the subject of widely disparate, even contradictory, accounts. Several of the cast members recalled the violence visited upon them. Others reported disturbances or protests.[24] Yeats famously proclaimed the disorder as O'Casey's apotheosis. Writing in the *New Statesman* only a month after the premiere, R. M. Fox played down the disorder and noted only that "the play nearly provoked a riot when it was produced at the Abbey Theatre, and it was held up one evening while a protest was made."[25] For others, however, especially for American critics of the past quarter century, what happened was a riot: Robert Lowery in *A Whirlwind in Dublin* referred repeatedly to "riots" and David Krause, the editor of O'Casey's letters, described the audience as a "rioting Irish mob."[26]

The disruptions of the play's fourth performance exposed just how numerous and diverse were the objections to the play, its author, the Abbey, its subsidy, and the Cosgrave government. Most of the preproduction challenges focused on language, often on individual words, but subsequent challenges shifted the focus to the political realm. Although Mrs. Gogan's line about the Ten Commandments remained and no one else appears to have found the line disturbing, the coarse language was still a source of complaint. Others objected to bringing the Irish flag into a public house. Joseph Holloway took umbrage at the character of Rosie Redmond; Mooney, who played Rosie, wrote that "the fuss was not, apparently, over the flag, or the Volunteers about to drink port [*sic*] on the stage— but about the prostitute."[27] Still others complained that O'Casey's Citizen Army was portrayed as cowardly. In *Unmanageable Revolutionaries,* Margaret Ward asserts that the "relatives of some of the men of 1916—Mrs. Barrett, sister of Sean Connolly, . . . Fiona Plunkett, Sheila Humphreys, Hanna Sheehy-Skeffington, Maud

Gonne—together with members of Cumann na mBan and the IRA all turned up to protest that 'their men didn't drink.'"[28] Among the widows and sisters of the 1916 martyrs, the most outspoken and articulate, Hanna Sheehy-Skeffington, attacked the Abbey subsidy by speculating: "Could one imagine [Shakespeare's *Henry VI, Part 1*] being received with enthusiasm in the French theatre of the time, subsidised by the State?"[29] She and others vigorously objected to the use of police to quell the demonstrations. Astutely and perhaps consciously rebuffing an institutional censorship, she asserted that there was no basis for a moral objection to *The Plough;* her protest was on national grounds alone. Under the aegis of "national grounds," however, would have fallen resentment over, first, the government subsidy of the Abbey; second, the play's treatment of the 1916 rebels; and third, the fact that the Cosgrave government not only subsidized the theatre but turned out in force for this premiere. Three of the protestors, Dorothy Macardle, Hanna Sheehy-Skeffington, and Kathleen Pearse, would all serve in the Fianna Fáil Executive formed in opposition to the government later in 1926.

The precedents for the disruption of *The Plough*, especially the turmoil surrounding the 1907 Abbey production of *The Playboy* and the more recent 1914 Westport riot over *General John Regan*, assured demonstrators what they most coveted: extensive, sustained press coverage. Lady Gregory, who traveled from Coole to Dublin after learning of the Thursday night demonstration, contemptuously dismissed the protesters as habitual publicity hounds: "These disturbers were almost all women who have made demonstrations on Poppy Day and at elections and meetings; have made a habit of it, of the excitement."[30]

The ensuing debate over *The Plough* recapitulated many of the arguments over censorship in general and over the landmarks of stage controversy in Ireland. Peter Kavanagh, for instance, argues that "the situation was reminiscent of Edward Martyn's objection to *The Countess Cathleen*, for it was said O'Brien had also submitted *The Plough and the Stars* to a theologian."[31] Yeats's inaudible denunciation of the disruption from the Abbey stage initiated the linkage of *The Plough* and *The Playboy*. Hanna Sheehy-Skeffington extended that linkage to support her position by citing Arthur Griffith's argument that in suppressing protests of *The Playboy,* Yeats had compromised the freedom of the theatre:

> Mr. Yeats has struck a disastrous blow at the Freedom of the Theatre in Ireland. It was, perhaps, the last freedom left to us. Hitherto, as in Paris or Berlin to-day or Athens two thousand years ago, the audience in Ireland was free to express its opinion on the play. Mr. Yeats has caused that freedom to be taken away. It is the Freedom of the Theatre for the playwright to produce what he pleases and for the audience to accept or reject as it pleases.[32]

This assertion of "freedom of the theatre" cut two ways: both the advocates and detractors of *The Plough* used the identical argument, that they were exercising a cherished and by now distinctly Irish freedom—to hear or to disrupt a play—that their enemies would deny them. In the protracted and well-documented exchange of letters and articles in the press as well as in the public debate between Sheehy-Skeffington and O'Casey, the question of the audience's freedom to express offense by disrupting the performance (by booing and hissing and, in this case, throwing shoes and storming the stage) was hotly contested. So diverse were complaints about language; slurs on Irish womanhood; the perceived cowardice and drinking habits of the Citizen Army; the precedent for bringing the tricolor into a public house; the mission of a national theatre; the propriety of a government subsidy; and the nature of the freedom of the theatre that the threat of stage censorship was diffused rather than intensified.

The most immediate effect of the disruption and subsequent debate was seen at the box office. Yeats was once again correct in recognizing how good for business controversy was. Perhaps that is why before he strode on stage to deliver his now-famous "You have disgraced yourself again" speech, Yeats had not only prepared his remarks but also arranged for their distribution to the morning newspapers. So politicized were the disruptions of, and debate over, *The Plough* that the threat of stage censorship diminished. Many of the attacks on *The Plough* implicitly embraced the ideal of a morally superior Catholic Ireland, but Hanna Sheehy-Skeffington perceptively defused the censorship threat by denying any challenge to the play's morality. Politics were quite another matter—one that remained open to dispute. Although O'Casey openly provoked moral outrage, over the neglect and death of Mollser for instance, the attacks on *The Plough* did not rise to his challenge. In the year of the tenth anniversary of the Easter Rising, *The Plough* exposed how little political consensus there was in the Free State and how impossible stage censorship would have been to legislate.

The models for stage censorship, especially those that might have been drawn from Britain, were unworkable, if not unthinkable, in Ireland. Living or recently deceased public figures were proscribed in London but commonplace in Ireland—as seen in several plays from the 1920s, including *The Plough and the Stars*. Dramatizations of Irish history, such as Frank D'Alton's *Wolfe Tone* (1924) or Dorothy Macardle's *The Old Man* (1925), not only brought historical figures on stage but would have been seen as treasonous by the Lord Chamberlain. In 1927, moreover, the *Irish Statesman* attributed the rise of the Theatre of Commerce to the Lord Chamberlain's censorship.[33]

In the 1920s, despite, if not because of, the disruption of *The Plough,* Irish theatre again claimed a privileged and anomalous place. The Irish stage gloried in flaunting its freedom from the Lord Chamberlain. In much of the thinking and writing about censorship in Ireland in the 1920s and beyond, considerable attention was paid to the likely prospective audience or readership, and theatre, especially the Abbey Theatre, was not susceptible on this count. Two years later the Catholic Truth Society protested the Limerick production of *Biddy,* "in which the priesthood was caricatured,"[34] and forced the cancellation of plans to honor its playwright, Laurence Cowen, in Dublin. But its energies now focused on printed material, not theatre. The Irish stage eluded the censorship Devane envisioned and remained sui generis, not only in comparison to the harsh censorship of printed matter that emerged in Ireland in the 1930s and 1940s in comparison but also to Britain and other English-speaking countries. Like their counterparts in 1899 and 1907, the most conspicuous theatrical protesters in 1926 were neither hostile toward theatre nor enthusiastic about censorship. In November 1928 Hanna Sheehy-Skeffington denounced the pending censorship legislation as a "ridiculous and impossible" instance of Free State paternalism "fostered or suggested by the monastic, celibate type."[35]

Three decades later, in 1956, Seán O'Faoláin would speak of seven censorships (potential censorship by producers, by directors, by government representatives, by actors, by playwright, by public disruption, by mob action) affecting printed material in Ireland.[36] At least that number figured in the 1926 Abbey production of *The Plough*. The fledging Irish Free State was not even four years old when O'Casey's play illustrated that its citizens were hardly monolithic in their values or their sense of Irish history, let alone their understanding of the freedom of the theatre. Moreover, the consciously self-referential actions and statements of the principals significantly advanced the construction of a tradition of Irish stage protest counterbalanced by its inevitable twin: a tradition of Irish freedom of the theatre.

7

Irish Stage Censorship from *Salome* through *Roly Poly*

All censorship is political censorship.
—William Seagle, *Cato*

Proponents took pains to characterize the 1929 Censorship Act as other than a literary censorship, but in practice, it quickly became exactly that. Within three years, the Censorship Board banned serious literary works and expanded its remit to enact literary censorship predicated not on "the general tendency of the work" but on isolated passages. Yeats and Shaw, in the second sentence of their announcement of the Irish Academy of Letters, lamented: "There is in Ireland an official censorship possessing, and actively exercising, powers of suppression which may at any moment confine an Irish author to the British and American market, and thereby make it impossible for him to live by distinctly Irish literature."[1] Critics like Terence Brown and Paul Scott Stanfield emblematize the cultural stagnation, repression, and isolationism of the 1930s and 1940s in its censorship: "[T]he Irish writer was so hampered by the official censorship of the state and the unofficial censorship of various religious and political watchdog associations . . . [that] Irish spirituality seemed confined to Jansenistical piety and commercialised pilgrimages."[2] Irish theatre, as well as creative works critical of censorship and periodicals like the *Irish Statesman* (1923–30), *Ireland To-Day* (1936–37), and the *Bell* (1940–54), resisted and challenged the literary censorship. With Lynn Doyle's resignation and the exposure of the actual procedures of the Censorship Board in 1937 and the banning of literary works by a who's who of Irish writers, censorship remained a hotly contested subject.[3]

Concurrent with the drafting of the 1929 censorship legislation, Hilton Edwards and Micheál Mac Liammóir founded the Gate Theatre "for the production of modern and progressive plays."[4] With few resources and no subsidy, the Gate management was, of necessity, culturally sensitive and usually very astute in its management decisions. Mac Liammóir, a man who reinvented himself from Alfie Wilmore of Wilsenden Green, was acutely aware of the power of image. The conundrums of identity were never more convoluted than in the life of a gay man from North London who became a matinee idol and passed himself off as a native Irish speaker. What Oscar Wilde had done for London society when he first came down from Oxford, Mac Liammóir did for himself in the Dublin theatre world—both were outsiders who transformed themselves into the apotheosis of their adopted worlds. With *Diarmuid agus Grainne,* Mac Liammóir first established himself as an Irish-language playwright at an Taibhdhearc in Galway. He fooled everyone.

The Gate came into existence the same year the Dublin Drama League ceased operation. Lennox Robinson argues that "the League had prepared a path for them [the Gate] . . . and the League, not being a money-making concern, gladly stepped aside to make room for the Edwards-Mac Liammóir Company."[5] Unlike the Dublin Drama League, the Gate strategically included Irish as well as international plays in its repertory. Since 1923 the Abbey had been producing many more international plays—Henrik Ibsen, Anton Chekhov, Eugene O'Neill, and even Shakespeare—but as Peter Kavanagh notes, "foreign classics were abandoned [by the Abbey] in 1928, when the Gate Theatre Company was founded in Dublin with the specific object of producing them."[6]

In selecting the plays for the inaugural season of the Dublin Gate Theatre at the Peacock, Edwards and Mac Liammóir first chose *Peer Gynt,* for which the ratio of audience members in a full house to

scripted characters would be two to one—an undertaking as aston-
ishing as it was financially risky. Press releases in September 1928 announced a double bill of two short plays by Nicholas Evreinov, but
those plans were changed to make room for what the Gate pointedly
identified as "an Irish play" by Oscar Wilde.[7] *Salome* offered two
obvious footholds for publicity: first, it was written by an Irishman
whose Irishness was rarely celebrated. In its first twenty-five years
of operation, the Abbey had produced only one play by Wilde, *The
Importance of Being Earnest* in 1926. The very antithesis of Abbey
Theatre's sense of what an Irish play was, *Salome* was a stylized parable
of decadence. The Gate would in later years become Dublin's home
to Wilde, not least in Mac Liammóir's signature *The Importance of
Being Oscar*.[8] Second, *Salome* followed *Blanco Posnet* and *Monna
Vanna* in bringing to the Irish public what the London public could
not see. The formula was by now well established: audiences were reminded of the potentially sensational elements in the work (although
only the most naïve or gullible of punters would be drawn in on that
basis alone); the British as well as the Irish papers would cover the premiere; and the Irish could again rejoice in its freedom from institutional stage censorship. Only a year before, the Lord Chamberlain's
office again refused to license *Salome*.[9] Aubrey Beardsley's scandal-
ously explicit illustrations of Wilde's text and the play's role in the
1892 parliamentary hearings on stage censorship only enhanced its
notoriety. Moreover, the Dublin Gate Theatre's British counterpart
and predecessor, the London Gate Theatre, had established "a reputation for staging banned plays,"[10] including *Salome*.

The Lord Chamberlain banned *Salome* for the same reason he
proscribed *Blanco Posnet*: blasphemy, specifically the portrayal of religious personages—Herod and John the Baptist—in Wilde's play.
This remained an especially sensitive nerve in British thought, both
in regard to the censorship of film and drama. Indeed, the 1928 Gate
production of *Salome* was widely publicized as "the first production
in the British Isles" or in "these Isles" to reinforce the liberality of the
Irish stage as opposed to the repressiveness that prevailed in London.
Mac Liammóir fondly recalls that "naked and in a few elaborately
painted head-dresses and loin-cloths, it was played on a series of
black curving steps and green cube-like thrones, and ours was the

first public performance in these islands, a fact in which we took a modest pride that was only a little damped by the fact that two of the minor parts, chosen for their physique, spoke in rich and incurable Dublinese."[11] Although Edwards and Mac Liammóir successfully finessed a work that climaxes with the erotic dance of the seven veils, the production was not a great success. The *Irish Times* described the acting as "unequal and uneven," an opinion seconded by the *Irish Independent,* which wrote that although "delightfully staged," Coralie Carmichael's performance in the title role was only a "limited success."[12] Undeterred, the Gate included *Salome* in its touring program at an Taibhdhearc in Galway the next year. No less important than the relative merits of this production was its influence on the impending Free State censorship legislation. Once again, the Irish public was reminded of the ridiculous and inflexible British stage censorship. Mac Liammóir's credentials as a native Irish speaker and Irish-language playwright were invaluable in facilitating the production of *Salome* and in allowing the Gate to stake out an international agenda in Dublin.

The Censorship of Publications Act spared the stage, but many Irish Catholics thought the act deputized them to seek out objectionable works. In 1930 the Catholic Truth Society (CTS) reported its massive examination of printed material:

> [S]ome hundred of these [the Society's friends] were invited to assist in the examination of imported newspapers and magazines, and of books. A sufficient number responded to enable each of the 160 publications to be systematically examined and reported on, not only from the point of view of the Censorship of Publications Act, but also in respect of their attitude to Catholic Truth in its varied aspects.[13]

Describing the Censorship Act as "deficient," the CTS envisioned a wider purview, "Catholic Truth in its varied aspects," that ranged from anticlericalism and communism to sexuality outside marriage and homosexuality.

The ascent of Eamon de Valera in 1932, the same year of Augusta Gregory's death, brought important changes to the Abbey and its subsidy. The depression and de Valera's economic policies compelled financial sacrifices in Ireland; one of the first was the Abbey subsidy.

The Abbey had received governmental subsidy since 1926, but in April 1933, after de Valera's Fianna Fáil had achieved an absolute majority in the Dail, the grant was cut by 25 percent to £750 (Irish). Another skirmish ensued over the government's representation on the Abbey board. Although a Catholic, Dr. Walter Starkie could no longer serve as the government's appointee on the executive board because, as a Fellow at Trinity College, he was unacceptable to de Valera's government. "Yeats, ever resentful of political intrusion in the theatre's affairs," in the words of Hugh Hunt, "retaliated by appointing Starkie as an ordinary shareholding member of the Board."[14] This inched de Valera and Yeats closer to a very public confrontation that might pit their mutually exclusive notions of Irishness against one another. After Dr. Richard Hayes, the film censor, declined the government's appointment to the Abbey board, Yeats threatened to close the theatre if an unacceptable replacement was imposed. To avert a crisis, Hayes relented and accepted the appointment.

Another potential crisis was the repertory for the Abbey's American tours. Previous Abbey tours of America in the 1930s had included Synge's *The Playboy of the Western World* as well as O'Casey's *The Plough and the Stars,* both of which not only were largely responsible for Ireland's worldwide reputation for theatrical riots[15] but also travestied de Valera's conception of Ireland. Irish Americans pressured de Valera to bring the Abbey to heel. On 13 April 1934 the *Manchester Guardian Weekly* ran an article headlined: "De Valera as Play Censor." The Abbey board, it reported, had been made aware that the government would not sanction the Synge and O'Casey plays in the 1934–35 tour of America under the same conditions as previous tours. When de Valera, erroneously described as having "never set foot in the Abbey Theatre,"[16] finally met with Yeats the result proved anticlimactic. In compromise, the Abbey would omit the description of the tour as presented "with the permission of the Irish Free State government." Yeats later described de Valera in surprisingly congenial terms: "I was impressed by his simplicity and honesty though we differed throughout. It was a curious experience, each recognising the other's point of view so completely. I had gone there full of suspicion, but my suspicion vanished at once."[17]

Asserting its artistic independence, the new, expanded Abbey board staged Sean O'Casey's *The Silver Tassie* in August 1935. The outrage that greeted this production, like so many earlier theatrical protests, combined nationalist and moralistic pieties. The protests of Catholic groups, led by a Dominican priest, Father M. H. Gaffney, joined by those of the Gaelic League called for the end of the Abbey Theatre. And they were not an isolated fringe minority. Brinsley Macnamara, then a member of the Abbey board, denounced O'Casey's play in the daily press and demanded (and got) certain cuts. In turn, Yeats demanded and got Macnamara's resignation from the Abbey board of directors.

Mere cuts could not secure Yeats's next play a premiere in Dublin. Although Yeats wrote Ethel Mannin to say he had withdrawn the play, in 1937 the Abbey rejected *The Herne's Egg* on grounds of obscenity. Certainly, Yeats knew how unpalatable its subject was. As Susan Cannon Harris aptly remarks, "*The Herne's Egg* makes Synge's *Playboy* look like *Brigadoon*. Realistically, the only way the play could possibly *not* have caused a riot would be if it proved, in the words of Ernest Blythe, to be 'so obscure that no one would notice it was obscene.'"[18] Despite their nearly antithetical views of what was Irish and what was culture, Yeats and de Valera probably both realized the value of a negotiated resolution of these tangled issues and, in that regard, anticipated the less confrontational strategies of recent decades.

The Abbey Theatre Festival of 1938 produced Yeats's last play, *Purgatory,* and with it came his last public confrontation. After several unimpressive seasons, the Abbey celebrated its thirty-fifth anniversary with a festival. Like the An Tóstal festivals in the 1950s, the Abbey Festival of 1938 intended to attract an international audience—tourists as well as theatre critics and reviewers. Held the week after the Dublin Horse Show, the festival featured morning lectures by F. R. Higgins, Lennox Robinson, and others and a repertory of plays in the evenings.[19] On 10 August 1938 *Purgatory,* the only new play presented, received a single performance, quite possibly to exclude all but the most enthusiastic patrons. Yeats was very much an *eminence gris,* with only months left to live. From all reports, including Yeats's own, *Purgatory* was very well received by both an appreciative audience and enthusiastic reviewers. Under the headline "Great Poet Has Warm Reception," the *Irish Independent* was effusive: "I cannot remember any piece of production in the Abbey that so impressed me as the skillful manner in which the presence of the ghosts stole into my consciousness."[20] Although generally positive, in the *Irish Times* Andrew E. Malone wondered about "the meaning which Mr. Yeats intends to be taken from the play. . . . 'Purgatory' [is] a frail container for such a large message; rather like pouring a vat of philosophy into a half-pint bottle of time."[21] Malone was, and is, not alone in his perception of *Purgatory* as a problematic work. Indeed, it is difficult to imagine any reading of the work that was less than an affront to Irish, let alone Irish Catholic, sensibilities in 1938. On the day after the only performance of *Purgatory,* the *Irish Times* reminded readers of their Abbey heritage: "Just as James Joyce has changed the entire current of novel-writing on the Continent of Europe, the Abbey Theatre has been responsible for the reformation of the European stage."[22] On the same day, the *Irish Times* also reported that, at a lecture by F. R. Higgins, Father Terence L. Connolly, S. J., drama critic for the Jesuit publication *America* and professor at Boston College, asked Higgins: "What does 'Purgatory' mean?"[23] At an earlier lecture, Connolly, raising questions that recalled Arthur Griffith's and D. P. Moran's response to *The Playboy,* had challenged Frank O'Connor about Synge's plays. Connolly claimed to have read *Purgatory* and followed its performance at the Abbey carefully, "but he had to admit frankly that he was still in ignorance as to what it symbolised." Connolly was baiting Higgins, but Higgins demurred. He offered only a vague, unresponsive answer, and, when Higgins asked the audience for its opinion, the audience demurred as well. On 13 August 1938, Yeats responded in an article that appeared in both the *Irish Times* and the *Irish Independent,* saying, "My play is my meaning. I think the dead suffer remorse and recreate their old lives just as I have described." He continued:

> In my play a spirit suffers because of its share, when alive, in the destruction of an honoured house. That destruction is taking place all over Ireland to-day. Sometimes it is the result of poverty, but more often because a new individualistic generation has lost interest in the ancient sanctities. I know of old houses, old pictures, old furniture that have been sold without apparent regret. In some few cases a house has been destroyed by a mesalliance.

I have founded my play on this exceptional cause, partly because of my interest in certain problems of eugenics, partly because it enables me to depict more vividly than would otherwise be possible the tragedy of the house.

In Germany there is special legislation to enable old families to go on living where their fathers lived. The problem is not Irish, but European, though it is perhaps more acute here than elsewhere.[24]

Connolly's question, Higgins's tactful unresponsiveness, and Yeats's response set in train a lengthy correspondence in the press that recalls the controversy surrounding *The Countess Cathleen* thirty-nine years earlier. On 16 August, the same day it ran an article on Lynn Doyle's plea for government funding to build a new theatre for the Abbey, the *Irish Times* also published a letter by Frank O'Connor that described Connolly's "attempt to bully Mr. Higgins" and himself into "a religious free-for-all."[25] Indeed, one of the substantive links between the response to *The Countess Cathleen* and that to *Purgatory* was a clerical intrusion—the letter from Cardinal Logue and the question from Father Connolly—that challenged Yeats's theological assumptions. The other substantive link was, of course, the implication that Yeats's dramatic offenses to Catholics should not be tolerated, especially in Ireland's national theatre. Like later theatre festivals, this was not the celebratory retrospective envisioned for the Abbey Theatre Festival.

Yeats remained a powerful opponent to censorship. His late plays and poetry, especially the Crazy Jane poems, have been profitably read in the context of a censorship that in practice brutally overreached its purview. Throughout the 1930s the Censorship Board banned more and more works, Irish ones in particular, as censorship itself became the subject of numerous works. In 1931, for instance, in response to the ouster of a Protestant librarian, a satirical playlet called *Sensorship* by C. Page appeared in a short-lived periodical, the *Muse*.[26] Liam O'Flaherty anatomized the pathology of censorship in his 1932 novel *The Puritan,* one of his five novels banned in the 1930s.[27] Mary Manning, the editor of *Motley,* the house publication of the Gate Theatre, authored hilarious satires on film censorship.[28] Seán O'Faoláin's play *She Had to Do Something* portrayed the angry reception of a ballet in a provincial Irish town; his preface to the published text recalls the play's angry reception at the Abbey in 1937: "Those Puritans objected to the play as the Puritans in the play objected to the ballet."[29] A one-act farce by D. J. Giltinan, *This Book Is Banned,* appeared at the Gaiety in July 1943.[30] Patrick Kavanagh's "The Wake of the Books: A Mummery" appeared in the *Bell* in 1953. Three of O'Casey's late plays, comprising a second Irish trilogy (*The Bishop's Bonfire* [1955], *The Drums of Father Ned* [1958], and *Behind the Green Curtains* [1961]), foreground censorship and repression. Just as *Blanco Posnet* carried a subtext on vigilance committees, numerous Irish authors, those most directly affected by the practices of the Censorship Board, took censorship as their text.

In 1937 Paul Vincent Carroll's *Shadow and Substance* dramatized the passion devoted to tracking down smutty works. In Ardmahone, two young curates whip Father Skerritt's parishioners into a frenzy over a book that is critical of rural education, clientalism, and parochial attitudes, written by the local schoolmaster, O'Flingsley. A cultivated man who appreciates Renaissance painters, Father Skerritt fires O'Flingsley but forbids the younger priests to stage a public book burning. Already incensed, the townsfolk attempt to run O'Flingsley out of town. Skerritt's aloof restraint collapses when he learns that his congregation has turned into a vicious mob: "All men in the mass are barbarians. Every year scores of decent Christians in America sprinkle Negroes with petrol and burn them because they love God and his justice. Yet, you will indulge in this—free Presbyterianism, this Lutheran zeal that the Church has never had any nonsense with in history."[31] As in O'Flaherty's *The Puritan,* the human cost is steep: in both works, the zealots of censorship inadvertently cause the death of an innocent young woman. Like O'Flaherty's novel, *Shadow and Substance* concerns what the CTS enthusiastically reported: that the hunt for censurable materials had become a common activity for sodalities, confraternities, and vigilance societies. Carroll links the smut hunts with sporting activities promoting the health—literal, spiritual, or metaphoric—of the parish. From the pulpit and on the ground, some clergy endorsed and encouraged these censorship quests as spiritual exercises. By the mid-1930s the Censorship Board had indeed become a literary or, more accurately, an antiliterary one. Through the 1950s when a complaint triggered the arrest of the producer of *The Rose Tattoo,* individuals targeted works as immoral, indecent, and illegal as part of their religious regime. Worse, the Censorship Act was not only responsive but receptive to these practices. And worse still, the "general tendency of the work," the criterion stipulated in the act, was less important than a single underlined sentence. For both O'Flaherty and Carroll, the effects of these censorship crusades were lethal.

Carroll's play premiered at the Abbey in January 1937. In late 1938 the Birr Little Theatre, a small amateur company in its fifth season, undertook a production of the play in hopes of clearing the company's mounting deficit. An account of an "unauthorised, and extralegal form of censorship" by Michael Farrell appeared in the second issue of the *Bell:*

> "Never did we attack a play with so much determination and belief." Three nights a week for eleven weeks they rehearsed it; one member (a Church of Ireland clergyman) coming 17 miles and going 17 miles every night in Irish December weather. . . . They slaved and slaved, and then . . . on the night of the dress-rehearsal, the players, dressed and tuned tautly on the stage, were told that the producer had just received a decided and formal objection to the performance of the play.[32]

Intimidated by a whispering campaign that alleged communist and anticlerical tendencies, the company canceled the production. Although it performed other plays, the company's crippling debt combined with suspicions about its intentions undermined its reputation. Undone by its choice of *Shadow and Substance,* the company was victimized by the very forces at which Carroll's play took aim. Life recapitulated and verified art.

Farrell's article in the *Bell* was part of his yearlong survey of Irish theatre outside Dublin. More importantly, it initiated a long campaign that eventually forced Irish readers to question the actual implementation of the 1929 legislation. The *Bell* published not only articles on censorship but also the works of authors who were or would be banned. In early 1941 the *Bell* serialized excerpts from some of the most celebrated banned books of the decade, including Eric Cross's *The Tailor and the Ansty* and Frank O'Connor's translation of Brian

Merriman's *The Midnight Court.* It ran "documentaries" on taboo subjects: out-of-wedlock children, homelessness, and sanitarium conditions. The *Bell* attacked censorship for the same reason that the censorship had banned many works: as not only foreign, but as un-Irish, the vestige of an alien, planted, and now outmoded Victorian sensibility. Even more damning than its articles on the insidious impact of censorship were the *Bell*'s articles on the disparity between the legislation and its implementation. Lynn Doyle, a contributor to the *Bell* who had resigned in protest after only weeks on the Censorship Board, reported that the board had so many works to evaluate that it had no time to assess, let alone to read, the entire work. Instead, the board often examined not "the general tendency of the work" but only the marked passages identified by zealous groups, like the CTS, from all over the country. On that basis, Kate O'Brien's *The Land of Spices* was banned for a single sentence. Moreover, the *Bell* pointed to a fundamental hypocrisy at work. Everyone knew that with a modicum of discretion, Irish citizens could travel to Belfast, buy any book, and, as long as they did not resell or distribute it in the Irish Free State, read it in peace.

In the early 1940s the campaign to reform censorship devoted immense energy to explaining exactly how it worked.[33] In November 1942, the Seanad debated a motion to constitute the Censorship Board, during which Sir John Keane read into the record passages from *The Tailor and the Ansty* and *Land of Spices* that were subsequently deleted lest the proceedings themselves become an obscene publication. Keane's motion failed on a decisive 34–2 vote and inflamed critics who argued for a more expansive censorship.[34] A nongovernmental Council of Action, formed in November 1942, sought "to secure the administration of the Censorship of Publications Act in accordance with the provisions of the Act."[35] Three years later, in October 1945, legislation was introduced, although not implemented until 1949, to provide an appeals procedure to the board's decisions on printed materials.[36]

With the passage of the Emergency Power Order at the outbreak of World War II to assure its claim to neutrality, Ireland undertook a far more radical censorship than had ever been envisioned in the 1929 legislation. During what Ireland knows as the Emergency and other nations as World War II, virtually every form of communication—letters, telephone calls, telegrams, radio broadcasts, and, as before, books, newspapers, and films—was censored. Again, theatre found itself an anomaly, because no preproduction approval was implemented. Instead, "a warning was issued by the Department of Justice to the managers of theatres and music halls, pointing out that all objectionable references to heads of foreign states or any matter which might cause conflict with Ireland's position of neutrality were to be rigidly excluded from performances."[37] Such a delegation of censorship responsibilities was the model found in the letters patent. Although no specific powers over theatre appeared in the legislation, the state directly intervened in two instances when plays raised political rather than moral complaints.

The wording of the Emergency Power Order of 1939 spells out three criteria by which the Emergency censorship would judge films: those "prejudicial to the maintenance of law and order or to the preservation of the State or would be likely to lead to a breach of the peace or to cause offense to the people of a friendly foreign nation."[38] The film censor's announcement directly echoed these goals: "In order to avoid demonstrations prejudicial to the maintenance of law and order, or the creation of scenes likely to lead to a breach of the peace, films showing pictures of rulers, statesmen, warriors and flags of the belligerents must not be shown."[39]

The clearest instance of theatrical censorship during the Emergency was the coerced withdrawal of the Gate Theatre production of *Roly Poly,* Lennox Robinson's adaptation of Guy de Maupassant's short story "Boule de Suif" (inelegantly translated as "Ball of Fat").[40] Robinson updated the setting from the Franco-Prussian war to what his script describes as "a few years ago"[41] but most reviewers saw as a contemporaneous setting. The residents who escape Rouen would, under any other circumstance, have nothing to do with one another. The group is a microcosm of class and status consciousness: the petty bourgeois shopkeepers; two nuns; a pair of pompous aristocrats, who remind everyone that they are escaping with the "king's necklace"; the "notorious" Peter Cornudet, now a communist (rather than de Maupassant's anarchist), best known for "spouting his wicked, un-Christian ideas to innocent people coming out of Mass" (12). But Elizabeth Rousset, known as Roly Poly, causes a real sensation. The Count and Countess Loiseau initially refuse to travel with this "gay" woman. When their dilapidated bus breaks down, first from a flat tire and then with a broken axle, Roly Poly selflessly offers to share her food and wine. Loiseau suggests that she couldn't have done otherwise: "in a situation like this, we are all in the same ship. We are brothers and sisters" (23). Roly Poly establishes herself as a French patriot by reviling the Germans as "those fat swine" and inviting the group to toast France. When the group arrives at a hotel in Tours that evening they are relieved to find an excellent dinner. It comes, however, at a price. The German lieutenant asks for Roly Poly's presence in his room. She repels his crude advances and denounces him to the group as a cad and a swine. By the next morning it becomes clear that they will not be allowed to continue their journey until the German officer is satisfied. Breakfast is only the simplest of fare. During four days on very meager rations, the group discovers many reasons for Roly Poly to give into the officer's demand. Even the nuns reveal their venality when Sister Beatrice asks, "Did [Abraham] hesitate to sacrifice his son, his only son, when he was called on to do so by the Lord?" (68). Mrs. Carré-Lamadon mocks Roly Poly's airs: "A thing like her to turn up her nose at any man" (70). Roly Poly eventually succumbs; the group is rewarded with champagne. Once she returns, she is isolated—she "sits in a far corner, alone" (73). She has sacrificed herself for them only to be even more cruelly ostracized and despised.

The initial reviews in Dublin ranged from mixed to very enthusiastic. Although the *Irish Times* found "it hard to see what [Robinson] gained by" updating the play from the Franco-Prussian War to 1940, the *Evening Herald* thought it gave "the play immense topical value."[42] The most favorable notice, in the *Evening Herald,* described *Roly Poly* as "a brilliant play, one of the finest Robinson has written," and the *Evening Mail* called the production and the performances "courageous," especially since the dramatization of tedium, hunger, and boredom is usually inimical to exciting theatre. Many of the reviews reported an enthusiastic reception from the audience.

The *Irish Independent,* like the *Irish Press,* noted the introduction of a sympathetic note in Robinson's adaptation: "Whereas the great French genius wrote with an acid, unforgiving contempt for his fellows, calculated to inspire the reader with a loathing of humanity, the Irish adapter has softened somewhat the cruelty of the outlines of the characterisations." It is not only an excellent short story, but also a well-crafted and clever play; a fact not lost on the reviewers. In the *Irish Independent*, D.S. praised it as Robinson's finest work: "As a piece of dramatic construction, 'Roly Poly' will rank with the best work we have had from this master craftsman."[43] Moreover, Robinson, anticipating problems, pulled his punches in making the German officer less than the beast he is in earlier versions. Indeed, after the completion of the script in August 1940, Robinson wrote an additional scene specifically to offer a human dimension to the German, who, according to the *Irish Times,* was now "scarcely the Prussian Officer that de Maupassant saw in 1870." Several of the reviews commented on the penultimate scene in which the German speaks of his loneliness and lost love.

After the play's first night, Tuesday, 19 November 1940, Joseph Holloway described the updating as "an indiscreet thing to do, to say the least, and I wouldn't wonder if the play wasn't stopped by military direction."[44] After complaints by both the German and French (Vichy) representatives, the Department of Justice told the Gate that the play violated the Emergency legislation. That eighteen years had passed since Independence did not deter the Censorship Board from pointing out "the equivocal position of the Gate under the 1745 Act relating to the licensing of theatres."[45] The menacing implication echoes "the threat of further and better powers" that was used to bring the private screenings of the Irish Film Society into "voluntary" compliance with the Emergency censorship. Mac Liammóir recognized the danger not just to Robinson's play but also to the very existence of the Gate.

Christopher Fitz-Simon reports that "Lennox Robinson was quite determined that that night's performance should take place."[46] On Thursday, 21 November, with the audience already seated, Edwards and Micheál Mac Liammóir came on stage to offer a refund because the play could not be performed, whereupon Robinson announced that he had bought the house, would donate the admissions to a relief fund for victims of a fire in Athlone, and invited the non-paying audience to stay as his guests for a private performance. Evoking the extralegality of private performances for charity benefit, Robinson had his third performance on 21 November 1940, but then *Roly Poly* was withdrawn. Several papers reported that a member of the Vichy legation stormed out of the theatre and denounced the play's depiction of their compatriots. On Thursday, 22 November 1940, Holloway reported: "Mrs. James Montgomery . . . told me of last night . . . at the Gate when the play *Roly Poly,* was stopped by order of the authorities on the grounds of a breach of neutrality. . . . Mrs. Montgomery added that an emissary from the French [Vichy] legation called on Robinson this morning and stated that the French minister wished to fight a duel with him."[47]

The government was eager that its action be seen as moral rather than political censorship. Ó Drisceoil writes that "an 'unofficial' Government Information Bureau statement to the press suggested that the authorities had requested the withdrawal of the play on 'moral grounds.'" Several papers including the *Cork Examiner* and the *Irish Press* reported exactly that, but Bertie Smyllie, editor of the *Irish Times,* correctly said that this was "baloney" and refused to print the statement; his report instead referred to the real reason for the withdrawal: "offence to other nationalities."[48] This item was stopped by the censor, as were similar pieces, in line with a general instruction to the press censors to prohibit all references to *Roly Poly.* What did appear in Dublin papers was a bitter exchange of letters from Norman Reddin and Lord Longford who, having split with Edwards and Mac Liammóir in 1936, disclaimed any responsibility for the production. The *Irish Independent* reported only that a representative of the Gate "had been given permission by the Department of Justice to make the following statement: "The play 'Roly Poly' has been withdrawn at the request of the Department of Justice" and that booking for the three-week run, specifically the November 22 performance, had been "very heavy." [49] The cancellation of a well-reviewed new play by Robinson that showed every sign of a profitable run was a serious financial blow to a company that had lost its patronage only four years earlier. The coerced withdrawal of *Roly Poly,* however, received coverage outside Ireland. The *Belfast*

Newsletter did not consider the action a withdrawal and headlined its story "Play Banned in Dublin." Sidney B. Whipple reported in the *New York World-Telegram:* "[T]he play was removed from the stage on direction of the Ministry of Justice, on the flimsy and groundless pretext of 'immorality.'" J. J. Hayes, writing in the *Christian Science Monitor* in February 1941, reported the withdrawal and extolled the dramatic merits of the play. The British press was less concerned with Robinson's artistry than with the Irish capitulation to Vichy and German demands. Typical was the *Yorkshire Evening Post* article "Dublin Remains in Blinkers," which commented: "Eire's neutrality is neutrality in a strait-jacket. Mr. de Valera's censorship has seen to that."[50] The next month the *Irish Times* covered the debate in the Seanad over the coerced withdrawal of *Roly Poly* as an abuse of the Emergency censorship's power. On 4 December 1940, Sir John Keane moved "that, in the opinion of this House, the manner in which the powers of Press Censorship in domestic matters are exercised is unreasonable." Keane raised the questions not only of the banning of the play, but also of the Emergency censorship's attempt to advance the notion that Robinson's play was morally objectionable.[51] After Emergency censorship expired at the war's end, Thomas J. Coyne recognized that the omission of theatre censorship was a dangerous oversight. In a September 1945 recommendation for future emergencies, Coyne proposed a comprehensive stage censorship:

> In the time of war or emergency the power to control the production of stage plays and, indeed, of theatrical presentations of all kinds is clearly needed and such power should be provided in any future emergency. What is needed is power (1) to stop the production or the production of any stage show which is prejudicial to morale or public order or which consists of or includes propaganda for or against any foreign nation; and (2) to require the submission for censorship of intended productions including stage plays of any particular class or classes.[52]

If another emergency arose, he recommended not only expanded powers, but pre-production approval.

In late 1942 Robinson's *Roly Poly* was denied a license for public performance in Britain partially on the basis that, altering the setting from the Franco-Prussian War to World War II, in the words of senior examiner of plays, H. C. Game, "makes the satire intentionally topical."[53] The Lord Chamberlain's comptroller wrote Robinson's agent, Joan Ling: "But the satire of the play, in which the scene has been changed to France of 1940, becomes definitely topical, and consequently renders the play very unsuitable for public production at the present time. It will be realised that, in these circumstances, no alterations can be suggested that would make it suitable for a licence."[54] Withdrawn in Dublin as anti-German, *Roly Poly* was banned in London as anti-French (Free French). When Robinson revised *Roly Poly*, employing de Maupassant's 1870 setting, and applied for a license early the next year, the Lord Chamberlain consulted the foreign office, which advised: "I have no doubt at all that its presentation upon the stage during the times we are living in would cause the gravest offence to the Fighting French in this country, and not to them alone, . . . while there are Frenchmen here who, whatever their faults—and I admit they are many—have given up everything to fight at our side."[55] In turn, the Lord Chamberlain's secretary, Henry Titman, informed Joan Ling that there would be no "[l]icence for its public performance, during the period of the War."[56] In late 1943 Ling asked to speak directly with the Lord Chamberlain, but her request was rebuffed. Ling persisted, but on 19 October 1944, Titman's response was again categorical: "the LC will not consider the possibility of licensing it for public production so long as the war lasts."[57] At the end of the war, Ling again applied for a license and the Lord Chamberlain again sought the advice of the Foreign Office. On 28 June 1945 Sir Alexander Cadogan wrote the Lord Chamberlain, then the Earl of Clarendon:

> I still think it would be inadvisable to let this play be performed on the English stage in present circumstances. Anglo-French relations have been a good deal strained lately by our inability to do more to help the French in the economic field and by events in Syria. De Gaulle is in a particularly intransigeant [*sic*] mood and there seems to be a widespread feeling among the French that we are bent on relegating them to a secondary rôle in world affairs. . . . The production of "Roly Poly" in the near future might be regarded by many Frenchmen as a calculated attempt to discredit their country and thus cause some political embarrassment.[58]

Two years later, a French film adapted de Maupassant's short story for the screen and the Lord Chamberlain's office was advised that there was little if anything to prevent the licensing of *Roly Poly*. But neither Ling nor Robinson was notified of that recommendation. No license for the play was ever issued.

A similar fate awaited a new play by a young Jewish Lithuanian refugee, Emil Slotover. A Special Branch intelligence report described the title character, Eric, in Slotover's "The Refugee," as "a man who is running away from himself," through amnesia. In Dublin an author, Peter, tries to reconstruct Eric's life. Peter's account proves accurate but cannot prevent Eric's eventual death. An anonymous letter alerted Edward Hempel, the German diplomatic representative in Ireland, to the play's content; Hempel protested the play's "unconcealed [anti-German] propaganda" to the government because the play suggested that Nazi atrocities contributed to Eric's amnesia and guilt. On 29 March 1943, an intelligence report from Detective Inspector Martin O'Neill in the Garda Siochana summarized the play and an interview with Emil Slotover, from whom O'Neill obtained the script. "Certain matters," O'Neill reported "were cut out by the producer, Evelyn Bowen, . . . and Frank O'Connor, her husband." A meeting between Slotover and the controller of the Censorship Board, Thomas J. Coyne, on that same date "indicate[d] to him [Slotover] the changes which should be made."[59] Sanitized of any references the German ambassador found objectionable, the production premiered at the Peacock Theatre on 6 April 1943 to very brief notices and passed without public controversy. The Emergency censorship insisted on cuts because even stage dialogue about German atrocities would undermine Irish neutrality.

Not coincidentally Mac Liammóir, Robinson, and O'Connor were three of the many contributors to the *Bell* in the early 1940s and were immediately affected by the censorship. After the threat to its always-precarious existence, the Gate was even more cautious about the Emergency censorship after 1940. It declined to risk the board's wrath and reneged on its announced plans to present Frank O'Connor's *The Statue's Daughter*,[60] which, despite having the out-of-wedlock child of a national hero as its central character, was later produced without incident. Mac Liammóir feared that another challenge from the "hoodlums" who had closed *Roly Poly* might "hasten a general censorship of theatre in Ireland."[61]

The coerced withdrawal of *Roly Poly* and the threats against the Gate unquestionably tainted Micheál Mac Liammóir's attitude toward Ireland. In *All for Hecuba,* written during the War and published in 1945, his most despairing and vitriolic attacks against Ireland foreground his comments on the fate of *Roly Poly:* "[Ireland] has decided . . . that there is no pain and no disease; she has also decided that there is no pleasure and no health; nor is there any desire; there is no war, there is no song, there are no women, and there is very little wine. We live in a waiting-room for passengers to Heaven; . . . airless, claustrophobic and self-centered we sit, refusing all news, all significant plays, all perilous things from the outer world."[62] Describing the censorship action as "a mingling of neutrality and puritanism," Mac Liammóir hit upon the common denominator to virtually every effort at stage censorship in Ireland—the deadly combination of politics and religion that has threatened stage freedom in Ireland throughout the century.

8

The Fifties

Nobody has explained why there is not an official stage censorship here [in Ireland] too. Literature of all kinds is censored and so are films. I cannot isolate the principle which decrees that anything can pass so long as it is animately presented on the stage. If I had my way there would be a very severe censorship based on aesthetic as well as moral standards, so playwrights and actors would be curbed a bit in their tireless search for way to inflicting [sic] pain on us.

—Myles na Gopaleen (Flann O'Brien), "Cruiskeen Lawn: Tóstal War,"
Irish Independent, 19 February 1958

Cultural activity in present day Dublin is largely agricultural.

—Brendan Behan, 1949

At the end of the 1940s, individuals and groups as well as the government in Ireland recognized the need for, and benefits of, arts enterprises. The Inter-Party coalition that came to power in early 1948 under John Costello saw the importance of tourism as an industry and the potential of theatre to attract foreign visitors to Ireland. In 1949, the Cultural Relations Committee of Ireland, operating under the auspices of the minister for external affairs, undertook production of a series of pamphlets designed "to give a broad, vivid, and informed survey of Irish life and culture."[1] The next year Seán MacBride founded the Irish News Service. In 1951 the Republic of Ireland established the Arts Council; the first National Fleadh for traditional music was held in Mullingar; Liam Miller founded the Dolmen Press; and Comhaltas Ceoltoiri Eireann was established. Even after the 1951 election returned de Valera and Fianna Fáil to power, the organizational infrastructures to support the arts continued to appear: the Irish tourist board, Bord Fáilte, and Gael-Linn both debuted in 1952. Cork held its first International Choral and Folk Dance Festival and its first International

Film Festival in 1953. Some of these developments may have anticipated the imminent inauguration of regular air passenger service to North America, but all responded to cultural opportunities precluded during the Emergency. These agencies and events all sought to project a positive, progressive image of Ireland. Most importantly, they mark a departure from the isolationism that prevailed in Ireland before and during the Emergency and that characterized de Valera's tenure as Taoiseach in the 1930s and 1940s.

These initiatives celebrated an Irish culture that was more democratic and, hence, more accessible, both to tourists and the Irish, than the Celtic Twilight or the Irish-language fare on offer at the Abbey Theatre in the 1940s and 1950s. Dance, film, and theatre festivals, for instance, announced themselves as "international" in the hope of achieving visibility not simply with tourists, but within larger European and English-speaking artistic communities. Because several of these enterprises were sponsored, supported, or subsidized by the government, they, like the Abbey Theatre when it first received its subsidy in the 1920s, were subject to very public scrutiny and criticism. As earlier in the century, Irish Ireland—isolationist, with a goal of purity in moral affairs—came into conflict with a more permissive, progressive, internationally oriented conception of the nation.

The very first publication of the Cultural Relations Committee was Micheál Mac Liammóir's *Theatre in Ireland*. Still smarting from the coerced withdrawal of Lennox Robinson's *Roly Poly* and the more invidious threat to shut down the Gate, Mac Liammóir penned his short study in "Rome—Marakech—Venice," anywhere, it seems, but Ireland. He offered a less than sanguine view of cultural opportunities in Dublin: "With her innate resentment of the specialist, her dread of perfection, her conscience-stricken sense of inherent artistic inferiority which leads her at times to assume an attitude that is cynical without knowledge, blasé without experience, and full of the deep suspicion of uncertainty, Dublin of course is not ready for the reception of great drama."[2] Although hardly guilty of boosterism, Mac Liammóir duly celebrated the history of the Irish theatre while acknowledging the formidable obstacles in its path.

Mac Liammóir's perception of Ireland's "inherent artistic inferiority" and its hostility toward the arts was shared by many, especially in regard to theatre.[3] Eric Bentley wrote that the visitor to the Abbey Theatre in 1952 "feels himself the victim of a hoax, a gigantic hoax that has been written into the history books and engraved on the general mind."[4] That same year the playwright Paul Vincent Carroll lamented: "Since the death of Yeats in 1939, and of his superb body-guard of artists, the Abbey Theatre has been in retreat, and Ireland has at the moment no artist fearless enough to rally this broken and disrupted creative force."[5] Three years later Gabriel Fallon offered an even more scathing assessment: "[A] people gets the theatre it de-serves, and . . . [t]he Irish Theatre lacks vision because we, its audi-ences, lack vision."[6] A series of theatre controversies in the 1950s more than justified a chorus of assertions that Dublin wasn't pre-pared to welcome great drama. No one, not even the most pessimis-tic of Irish directors, actors, and playwrights, however, could antici-pate the scale of the serial censorship battles that beset Irish theatre in the last thirty-two months of the 1950s. As earlier in the twentieth century, the Irish people, inflamed by Catholic prelates and the press, would take to the streets; the police would be called and ar-rests made. Again Dublin's theatres served as the staging area for the paroxysms of change that marked what Mary Kenny sees as the be-ginning of the end of Catholic Ireland.[7]

Even after the Abbey Theatre burned down in 1951 and despite the candid consensus that mediocrity (or worse) ruled, Irish theatre could still attract visitors and their spending power. As Alan Simp-son wrote, "apart from horses, the word 'theatre' would probably be the first thing to spring to the mind of an educated foreigner, if asked what he knew of our country."[8] Coupled with Irish theatrical fame was the fact that, as at the beginning of the century, a number of journalists, politicians, and government officials had influential connections with theatre.[9] What evolved from this context in the late 1950s was a succession of attempts to impose a de facto theatre censorship beginning with O'Casey's *The Bishop's Bonfire* in 1955, ex-tending through the arrest and trial of Alan Simpson for the Pike Theatre's production of Tennessee Williams's *The Rose Tattoo* in 1957, the debacle that was the International Theatre Festival in 1958, the withdrawal of *The Ginger Man* in 1959, and culminating with the postponement and eventual revision of Sam Thompson's *Over the*

Bridge that same year. This series of controversies pitted a conservative, isolationist puritanism against a liberal, progressive permissiveness that transcended the interests of nationalism. At play was the complex interaction of theatre managers, actors, directors and producers, living playwrights, audiences, reviewers, politicians, lawyers, newly minted American Ph.D.s, and the Gardai.

As the 1950s began, the *Irish Times* ran a lengthy debate in its letters to the editor on the subject of censorship that was later published as a booklet, *The Liberal Ethic.* As Michael Adams points out, even the Catholic publications, which devoted less attention to censorship than the *Irish Times,* "reveal a whole range of opinions on the question [of censorship, and] . . . no uniform attitude emerges."[10] As in the 1940s, censorship remained central to the Irish culture wars of the 1950s. From the extremes, two voices indicate the breadth of opinion in the early fifties. In 1950 R. S. Devane, S.J., author of the polemic that informed the Censorship Act of 1929, revived his campaign against foreign publications in *The Imported Press: A National Menace.* As in earlier decades, Devane emphasized three features of these publications: first, they were cheap and easily accessible; second, they targeted an uneducated, often young, and hence vulnerable audience; finally, they were not Irish and if allowed in the country would corrupt the nation.[11] Devane's death in 1951 was hardly the end of an era. New vigilance societies, including the League of Decency (which took as its special agenda the revocation of "the right of appeal" clause in the 1945 legislation on censorship) appeared in the 1950s.[12] Two newly established, extremely conservative Catholic periodicals, *Fiat* and the *Maria Duce Bulletin,* fueled such reactionary conservatism. The second issue of the latter lambasted the major Catholic newspaper, the *Standard,* for its endorsement of the Irish Association of Civil Liberty in May 1952 and reached back to attack a 1 April 1949 editorial in the *Standard* supporting that organization.[13] Despite their intensely isolationistic stand, *Fiat* and the *Maria Duce Bulletin* imported several of their causes from America: rigid opposition to communism, to the fluoridation of water, and to Irish membership in the United Nations and the Common Market. Indeed, many of the articles in *Fiat,* including one of the two obituaries it ran for Senator Joseph McCarthy, were reprinted from the *Brooklyn Tablet.* Fiercely anticommunist and anti-Semitic, *Fiat* unsuccessfully attempted to prevent Danny Kaye's appearances at the Theatre Royal in June 1952 because of "his established connection with several Communist organisations."[14] Although the blacklisting attack on Kaye failed, it was part of an overt xenophobia that feared and resented the growing internationalism of the arts.

In the early 1950s an anticensorship voice no less extreme than Devane appeared in the person of Paul Blanshard. An American socialist and career anti-Catholic, Blanshard came to Ireland looking for his worst nightmare and found exactly that. In *Irish and Catholic Power,* published in 1953, Blanshard described Ireland as ruled by an "ecclesiastical dictatorship,"[15] the ne plus ultra of "the horrors of Catholicism."[16] As Michael Adams effectively demonstrates, Blanshard's diatribe is riddled with factual errors and exaggerations as well as the author's own prejudice.[17] Even Hubert Butler joined that fray by noting that Irish Protestants were not the "depressed or resentful community" that Blanshard imagined them to be.[18]

No less important than the extremes represented by Devane and Blanshard was the increasing willingness to examine the censorship dispassionately. *The Liberal Ethic* pamphlet was a forum for conflicting opinions, not a polemic. The Irish Association for Civil Liberties, founded in 1948, pursued anticensorship strategies similar to those of the *Bell:* education, public debate, and transparency.[19] Especially important were voices from within the ranks of the clergy, particularly that of Peter Connolly, S.J., that undertook a methodical critique of censorship. In *Christus Rex* beginning in 1954, Connolly's well-reasoned, even philosophical, analysis of the church's and the state's censorship gradually yet dramatically altered the framing of the censorship question.[20]

Censorship as Text: O'Casey's *The Bishop's Bonfire*

The period after World War II was one of tumultuous change in European and American as well as Irish theatre. Both in and outside Ireland, plays written in the 1950s dealt with psychological and sexual subjects with far greater candor and directness than ever before. Plays reflecting more permissive attitudes were hardly unknown in Ireland. In Denis Johnston's *A Strange Occurrence in Ireland's Eye*

(Abbey Theatre, 1956), for instance, the former mistress of an accused murderer is rumored to have had an abortion. *Waiting for Godot* enjoyed a very successful run at the Pike Theatre in Dublin before touring Ireland in 1955. As Ulick O'Connor wrote in the *Listener,* in Dublin "strangely enough there were no cuts in the play. We have no censor here as in London."[21] Like Behan's *The Quare Fellow* (1954), *Godot* was licensed for performance in Britain only after changes and cuts; both, however, were performed without the Lord Chamberlain's cuts and with great success in Ireland.[22] Between the premiere of Brendan Behan's play and the Irish debut of Beckett's, in a rapidly changing theatrical landscape, came O'Casey's *The Bishop's Bonfire,* a play that, like Carroll's *Shadow and Substance,* portrays a powerful, censorious clergy.

The Gaiety Theatre production of *The Bishop's Bonfire,* directed by Cyril Cusack, opened on 28 February 1955 and was the precursor to the stage censorship controversies at the end of the decade. This was the first premiere of an O'Casey play in Dublin since *Red Roses for Me* in 1943. The publication of *Cock-a-Doodle Dandy* in 1949 "led to bitter reaction in Ireland, where, until 1975, it was almost totally taboo."[23] Lead articles on the front pages of the 18 and 25 February 1955 editions of the *Standard* alleged that the anticlericalism and blasphemy of O'Casey's plays insulted the church, the nation, and the Irish people. Both articles were openly provocative: "Mr. O'Casey's name is now in the public eye—his bishop's bonfire is shortly to be ignited. Is it inflammable material?" and "Where is the nation's self-respect?"[24] Hundreds heeded the call to protest.

Tyrone Guthrie offers an embittered, vivid recollection of the scene outside the theatre:

> By lunchtime on the day of the performance you could not get into the street where the theatre stands. At three in the afternoon the mounted police were called to clear the crowds. When the doors opened the police had to be called again, because about a thousand people were storming into a gallery which holds less than three hundred. There was another storm when Catholic students from the National University started to boo in the street, because they regarded O'Casey as a renegade Irishman. They were answered by Protestant students from Trinity College who made a counter-demonstration in O'Casey's favour.[25]

The *New York Times* reported a quite different and certainly more subdued scene: "For an hour before the play began the groups of young men, reported to be anti-Catholic, lined the approaches to the theatre and demonstrated. They were still there in force near midnight when the crowds were emerging at the close."[26] Writing under the name Donat O'Donnell in the *New Statesman and Nation*, Conor Cruise O'Brien wrote that "the audience itself was . . . ready to shout down the interruptions that were expected from militant pietists, maddened by the muezzins of a local weekly paper."[27] In a news article, independent of Harold Hobson's theatre review, the *Times* reported that "the play was listened to without interruption until nearly the end, . . . the applause and booing contending with each other on fairly equal terms."[28] The protests both for and against the play had created enormous tension in and outside the theatre that at least in Ireland recalled the protests over Synge's *The Playboy* in 1907 and O'Casey's *The Plough* in 1926. In 1955, a year before the emergence of John Osborne and Pinter, a new O'Casey play could still lure London critics to Dublin in force. W. A. Darlington, the critic for the *Daily Telegraph,* writing in the *New York Times,* downplayed the hubbub: "And it is accepted here that twenty years ago, or even less, there could have been no prospects of staging 'The Bishop's Bonfire' in Dublin without causing a major rumpus. . . . Today feelings do not seem to run so high. . . . On opening night an organized group of young men in the balcony booed and hissed the performance. But most of the audience greeted the comedy of the piece with laughter and applause."[29]

The reviews of the play were mixed. Harold Hobson, writing in the *Christian Science Monitor,* described it as "ramshackle, ill-conceived, and clumsy. . . . Even Mr. O'Casey's biggest admirers . . . are puzzled to know what his latest play means."[30] Irish reviewers were almost universally disappointed, but unlike their British counterparts, several were openly malicious. Thersites in the *Irish Times* not only panned *The Bishop's Bonfire* but also challenged O'Casey's reputation, crediting the Abbey management and actors rather than the playwright with the success of O'Casey's great works of the 1920s.[31] Despite the Irish reviews, *The Bishop's Bonfire* was very popular during its five-week run at the Gaiety. A. J. Leventhal, reviewing for the quarterly *Dublin Magazine* rather than the daily press, speculated that by the eighth performance, "cuts and speeding of tempo may explain the enthusiasm of the audience and my own enjoyment of the production."[32] Theatregoers were not alone in endorsing the play. The diversity of opinion, even among Catholics, is seen in a motion passed, with a margin greater than two to one, by the Literary and Historical Society at University College, Dublin, in early March 1955: "This house deplores the attitude of the *Standard* newspaper towards the new O'Casey play."[33]

No playwright paid closer attention to the reviews of his plays than did O'Casey. His essays, collected in books like *The Green Crow* (1956), include meticulous scrutiny of the reception of his plays. His extensive correspondence with reviewers—notably Brooks Atkinson, George Jean Nathan, and Gabriel Fallon as well as scholars like Robert Hogan and David Krause—were letters to friends. O'Casey was outraged by the negative reviews in the Irish press and made no secret of his anger. In "Bonfire Under a Black Sun," he accused the Irish reviewers of resenting the interest shown by English and American critics and of "carrying on a cold war against O'Casey and all his works."[34] With largely negative reviews from Dublin and mixed notices from the London papers, O'Casey seized upon the most flattering phrases of the American and English reviews to create the impression that there was a "cabal" of Irish drama critics conspiring against him. The biting anticlerical satire of "Bonfire under a Black Sun" may well have precipitated the seizure of *The Green Crow* by Irish customs officials. That volume contained essays in which O'Casey mocked the puritanism of the Catholic hierarchy, endorsed Blanshard's charges as "indisputable," and described Irish drama as "hobbled . . . by fear of the clergy" (157). Prophetically, he also wrote that "a Bishop can make himself felt without showing himself" (140). Before the decade's end, Archbishop John Charles McQuaid would do just that, twice.

Fun An Tóstal

One of the many Irish cultural enterprises that had its origins in the 1950s, An Tóstal epitomized the spirit of boosterism. The first Tóstal, held for three weeks in April 1953, combined Holy Week,

Easter, and springtime celebrations and featured historio-religious spectacles with a strong patriotic flavor. Billed as "Ireland at Home," the Tóstal offered scores of competitions and concerts, but, as the *Irish Times* succinctly acknowledged in 1958, "the primary function of An Tóstal has been, and is, to attract visitors to Ireland."[35] In its second year, 1954, An Tóstal began on 17 and 18 April, Holy Saturday and Easter Sunday. As advertised in the *Dublin Evening Mail,* its centerpiece was "The Pageant of St. Patrick. . . . Cast of 1,700—Massed Choir of 400 voices—Greatest Pageant ever produced in Ireland—Four episodes extending over two days."[36] As such, An Tóstal imbricated the religious celebrations of Easter, the nationalistic commemoration of the Easter Rising, and the cultural agenda of Bord Fáilte. President O'Kelly inspected a guard of honor outside the General Post Office and, on Easter Monday, a solemn high mass at the Pro-Cathedral, an event that would soon take on huge importance, was celebrated by the apostolic nuncio. Although the Belfast Arts Theatre's production of Eugene O'Neill's *A Moon for the Misbegotten* was playing at the Gas Company Theatre, the only professional theatrical performance connected with An Tóstal was stage comedian Jimmy O'Dea in "Fun on Tóstal" (and its sequel, "Fun on Tóstal 2") at the Theatre Royal. Clearly, in its early years An Tóstal was far less an arts festival than, in A. J. Leventhal's words, "a rather inchoate jumble of national aesthetic jollifications illumined by fireworks."[37]

An Tóstal expanded to include the Dublin International Theatre Festival, which in 1957 relied heavily on Irish plays. Now held several weeks after Easter, the 1957 Tóstal was opened by the Tanaiste, Seán Lemass, on Sunday, 12 May. At an Irish theatre exhibition at Trinity College, the minister for external affairs, Frank Aitken, reported, "We are very proud of the standard of theatre in Ireland."[38] Such ministerial reassurances may have been thought necessary because, although thirty years had passed since the disorders associated with *The Plough,* Irish theatre was still seen as a staging area for cultural confrontations. In reviewing *The Bishop's Bonfire* of two years earlier, J. C. Trewin reminded his readers: "I know the reputation of these Irish playgoers when their blood is up."[39] To counter any adverse publicity over *The Bishop's Bonfire,* a wide range of local and national government officials expressed great pride in Irish theatre for the first Dublin International Theatre Festival.

While the Abbey languished under the stewardship of Ernest Blythe, several upstart theatre companies challenged its dull hegemony in the 1950s. As earlier in the century, small amateur companies operating in makeshift theatres provided Dublin with international, contemporary offerings. Among the tiniest of these theatres was the Pike Theatre with a seating capacity of only sixty-two and a stage about six feet by ten feet. Under the artistic direction of Alan Simpson and Carolyn Swift, the Pike Theatre had produced the Irish playwrights the Abbey was loathe to acknowledge, especially Samuel Beckett and Brendan Behan. Actor and director Phyllis Ryan suggests that the Pike had a certain notoriety, and not only for producing Beckett and Behan: "The Pike was certainly off-beat and had more of a reputation for so-called decadent parties than for what went on in its theatre."[40] The decision to produce a play by Tennessee Williams, whose *The Roman Spring of Mrs. Stone* (banned 20 February 1951) and *Cat on a Hot Tin Roof* (banned 16 March 1956) were already proscribed by the Censorship Board, promised further notoriety. Williams surely would be numbered among the many pernicious foreign influences whose importation, Devane argued, would offend and corrupt. Williams's plays had aroused controversy elsewhere: In Britain, the Lord Chamberlain refused to license *Cat on a Hot Tin Roof* (1955) three times, in 1955, 1963, and 1964; *Battle of Angels* (1940) caused outrage in Boston; the film version of *Streetcar Named Desire* (1951) had been drastically sanitized. Only months before the Pike production of *The Rose Tattoo*, *Cat on a Hot Tin Roof* provoked the wrath of a New York City license commissioner who demanded a cut ten days after the production had opened. As Donald Spoto notes: "The salty language, an off-color joke . . . and the psychosexual turmoil sent shock waves through the 1955 [New York City] audience."[41] Although "there had been no attempt to have it brought before the censorship body"[42] and the published text was readily available (in Duffy's "Catholic" Bookshop no less), the film version of *The Rose Tattoo* would be banned in 1956.[43]

Late in 1957, the Dublin journal *Studies* carried an article about

Williams by Desmond Reid that not only echoed but also reinforced Devane's line of thinking about censorship in general and foreign authors in particular. Although it appeared after *The Rose Tattoo,* in the winter issue of *Studies* (that is, the issue following the Fall 1957 number), the essay makes no specific mention of the Pike production and may well have been in press as the controversy unfolded. Reid's article provides a measure of conservative Catholic, but hardly anti–intellectual, opinion in Ireland at the time. While acknowledging Williams as "a playwright of high talent,"[44] Reid claimed the authority of the same tenets that inspired the censorship acts: "the objective norm of the natural law and its precepts" (438). Perhaps Reid's most expansive comment is also his most telling. In objecting to the language of *Cat on a Hot Tin Roof,* he writes: "The use of other words, of anatomical slang and of phrases involving the Holy Name are out of place and objectionable on the stage, as they are in real life. . . . If used repeatedly and immoderately, . . . [this language] can lower the moral tone of a person, a group—or a nation" (442). Although Williams was not in the same class as the trashy English papers or the imported horror comics of the day, Reid saw him as a threat to the moral fabric of Ireland, and a foreign one at that.

Carolyn Swift, Alan Simpson's wife and codirector at the Pike, reports that before the production opened, the director of Dublin International Theatre Festival, Brendan Smith, "had received a letter from a body calling itself The League of Decency [that] alleged the play 'advocated the use of birth control by unnatural means.'"[45] The charge owes to Williams's stage direction: "A small cellophane-wrapped disk falls on the floor [from Alvaro's pocket], escaping his notice, but not Serafina's." She immediately challenges his intentions by asking, "Is that a piece of poetry that dropped out of your pocket?" Once he realizes that she has seen the condom, Alvaro kicks it under the furniture. Swift recalls that in this production nothing was dropped, that the entire action was mimed, although others say a paper disk was used. A devout Catholic, Serafina berates and dismisses Alvaro: "I told you good night. Here is *no casa privata. Io, non sono puttana!*"[46] Anna Manahan, who played Serafina, offered this succinct summary of the scene: "Serafina rejects him because of this action and throws him out of her house. She could not possibly love any man except as her religion ordained her, which makes the play entirely acceptable from a Catholic point of view."[47]

The initial reviews of the play were nearly unanimous on two counts: the quality of the play and Manahan's performance as Serafina. Gabriel Fallon in the *Evening Press* described the play as "undoubtedly one of the major creations of modern drama" and her Serafina as "magnificent."[48] Even the Fianna Fáil *Irish Press* saw in the play "a deep and seemingly genuine spirituality" and in Manahan "a remarkable performance which was beautifully shaded."[49] Although the *Irish Independent* judged Manahan's acting "brilliant," it objected to the play as "oppressive in its sordidness, . . . too shocking to awaken sympathy."[50] R. M. Fox, writing in the *Dublin Evening Mail,* acclaimed the production "a minor miracle" and Manahan's performance "her greatest triumph."[51] The British papers were similarly enthusiastic. With such strong notices from both the Irish and British press, the Pike signed a lease with Lord Longford for the play's transfer to the Gate Theatre.

The facts of *The Rose Tattoo* case have a near legendary standing: shortly before eight o'clock on 21 May 1957, police investigators demanded that Simpson cancel the performance for which the audience was already seated. Simpson refused, and the curtain went up ten minutes late. On 23 May 1957 Simpson was advised that the Gardai were waiting for him at the theatre; again, with the consent of the cast, he refused to cancel and was arrested under a summary warrant that precluded bail before a court appearance. Despite the fact that the cast was threatened with arrest, the final performance went on as scheduled on the last day of the festival, 26 May 1957.

Swift writes that "I have since been told it was probably a certain member of the Knights of Saint Columbanus, acting on his own initiative," who filed the protest. She also quotes a friend as saying "'I can only tell you it comes from the very top. . . . Dev himself wants action taken against you.'"[52] Complaint led to formal charges alleging that Simpson produced "for gain—a performance which was indecent and profane."[53] The 1929 Censorship Act allowed individuals or societies to identify offensive material. And here was an instance in which a single individual may well have demanded the Gardai act as dramatic censor. After the final performance in Dublin completed

its scheduled run, the production did transfer, with a slightly different cast, to Belfast, where the *Irish Times* reported on 18 June 1957
that "three high-ranking R. U. C. officers last night watched the
opening performance at the Belfast Opera House of the Dublin Pike
Theatre's production of *The Rose Tattoo*."[54] They had no inkling
why the play was considered indecent or profane.

The question of censorship of printed material was much in the
news as Simpson's case moved through the courts over the next year.
Anticipating Reid's warning that Williams's drama might corrupt a
nation, the *Irish Press* headlined their coverage of Simpson's arrest,
"Garda Action on American Play." O'Casey's letters to the *Irish
Times* on censorship in general and the suppression of *The Green
Crow* in particular appeared with regularity.[55] Six days after the *Irish
Times* published O'Casey's letter, "Irish Writers," the prosecution of
Simpson had worked its way through the courts and its litigation
now appeared frivolous. At the hearing on 5 June 1957 to determine
whether Simpson's case should come to jury trial, his counsel, Sean
Hooper, argued that the charges against Simpson were groundless.
District Justice Cathal O'Flynn decided not to send the case to trial,
holding that because "a prima facie case had not been made, no rea-
sonable jury would convict."[56] Simpson was exonerated.

The consequences of Simpson's arrest and prosecution reverber-
ated over many months and, in fact, years. The financial effects were
among the most immediate and the hardest hitting. Unlike the box
office benefits reaped by almost every earlier attempt at Irish stage
controversy, the Pike was financially battered by Simpson's arrest.
The *Pike Newsletter* lamented: "Had we taken off the play when or-
dered to by the Garda under threat of arrest on the second Tuesday
of the Festival, we would have lost £100."[57]

The Belfast run did not show a profit. With the release of government papers, Swift and Gerard Whelan uncovered documentation
of just how the case against Simpson and the Pike developed. Perhaps the most intimidating dimension to the strategy outlined in the
Department of Justice's seven-point memorandum is labeled 5.b:

> approach the management of the Gate and tell them that if the play
> is put on with the objectionable passages and situations included,
> they will be prosecuted and that *the matter will be noted for the*

information of the Attorney General when their application for Letters Patent for the Theatre comes before him in due course (my italics).[58]

Fearing legal entanglements, Lord Longford reneged on his commitment to lease the Gate; once *The Rose Tattoo* completed its run at the Pike, there would be no foreseeable opportunity for larger audiences to see the play in Dublin. Shortly after Simpson's arrest, the Gate, already having difficulty renewing its license, announced that it was closing for repairs. Not one but two legal defense funds were established—the first in London by *Encore* magazine, supported by O'Casey, John Osborne, Peter Hall, Harold Hobson, John Gielgud, George Devine, and others; the second by Jim Fitzgerald in Ireland. Litigation dragged out for more than a year, and the costs were crippling. Although Bord Fáilte hoped the Dublin International Theatre Festival would promote Dublin to international theatregoers, the litigation of *The Rose Tattoo* case did little to enhance the reputation of Irish theatre. Reports of Simpson's case noted the prosecution's secretiveness: the offending passages in the play were not identified until long after the production had closed (so the management never had the option of emending); and Simpson and the Pike received support from neither An Tóstal officials nor Lord Longford. On 5 June 1957, Sam Wanamaker, heeding advice that he might encounter problems similar to Simpson's, cancelled the Dublin booking of Tennessee Williams's *Cat on a Hot Tin Roof*.[59] Ireland still had no institutional censorship, but the atmosphere in 1957 was even more hostile to great drama than that reported by Mac Liammóir at the end of the 1940s.

Several commentators believe that this case had a long-term positive effect. Certainly, the risks that Simpson personally took seem heroic in retrospect. In the early 1970s Brendan Smith said, "It is quite significant that from 1959 onwards we have had little or no trouble from minority nuisance groups trying in any way to impose censorship on the stage."[60] Terence Brown sees Simpson's acquittal as a turning point: "As it was the judgment meant that adventurous experiments could be embarked upon in the assurance that the police would be less inclined to proceed against a play even when they received complaints from the public or from the various self-appointed watch committees that sought to protect the Irish moral environment from theatrical pollution."[61] In writing that "at least the absurd court case ensured that no censorship of any kind would trouble Irish theatre again,"[62] Phyllis Ryan overlooked Archbishop McQuaid's hand in the 1958 Tóstal and the 1959 withdrawal of *The Ginger Man.*

That Mass

By 1957 An Tóstal was one of several enterprises that assured a boom in Irish tourism. With the inauguration of regularly scheduled air service to North America, the number of American visitors had risen more than ten-fold from four hundred in 1953 to forty-five hundred in 1957. In the apparent belief that the debacle over *The Rose Tattoo* would not, could not, be repeated, the Dublin International Theatre Festival ambitiously expanded its offerings for 1958. This time, however, neither Irish reviewers nor outraged citizenry but rather the Archbishop of Dublin, John Charles McQuaid, would elicit charges of censorship. The stakes now were higher than anyone realized: Ireland was about to be denied the works of its two greatest living playwrights.

On 18 October 1957 Brendan Smith wrote Hilton Edwards, "I have secured the rights to world premieres of a new O'Casey play and Alan [*sic*] McClelland's dramatisation of 'Ulysses.' I should like to see Micheál [Mac Liammóir] and yourself about the latter at the earliest possible moment."[63] Later that month Edwards wrote back from London to say: "I have come to an arrangement with Allan McClelland whereby I am assisting him in the production on paper of 'Ulyssees' [*sic*]." On 28 November 1957, Smith wrote separate letters to Mac Liammóir and Edwards confirming their participation in the adaptation of *Ulysses,* the former to play the reader-narrator and the latter "to devise the production [and] to direct."[64] On 13 February 1958, Allan McClelland, as yet unaware of what had happened in December and January, sent Hilton Edwards act 3 of what was now called *Bloomsday.* Still at work on the play at the end of February, McClelland may have been among the last to learn what had transpired in Dublin.

By 1957 O'Casey clearly wanted to force the issue of censorship—and for good reason. After *The Green Crow* was seized by a customs official under the Customs Consolidation Act of 1876, O'Casey endured more than a year without either a hearing or an official judgment on the de facto banning of his book. His letters to the *Irish Times* and, on one occasion, the *Irish Press,* were alternately embittered, openly provocative, hostile, and hopeful. Moreover, as Christopher Murray notes, *The Drums of Father Ned* "challenges, by its insertion into the debate on censorship, the traditional attitudes and values which had choked freedom of expression in the arts in Ireland since the foundation of the state."[65] Long before any public controversy over *The Drums of Father Ned* or over the play's selection for the 1958 Dublin International Theatre Festival, O'Casey, in his very first letter to Brendan Smith, wrote that he had already "thought of refusing to allow a performance of any of my plays in the Republic."[66] If, as this statement suggests, O'Casey was looking for a reason to ban production of his plays in Ireland, perhaps as a token measure of revenge for the negative reviews of *The Bishop's Bonfire* and possibly even for grudges of much longer standing (like the Abbey's rejection of *The Silver Tassie*), the archbishop obliged. On 28 December 1957, Archbishop McQuaid refused to permit "any religious ceremony whatever and more particularly the Holy Sacrifice of the Mass" in conjunction with the 1958 An Tóstal.[67] After this correspondence, the archbishop refused further comment, specifically on the question of the inclusion of *Bloomsday* and O'Casey's new play. Such was the power of Archbishop McQuaid that no explanation could be demanded and no criticism of his decision tolerated.[68]

On 10 January 1958, the *Irish Times* reported: "Last week the Council became aware that the Most Rev. Dr. McQuaid, archbishop of Dublin, did not approve of their inclusion in the programme. As a result of their inclusion, this year's Tóstal will not be marked by an official opening Mass."[69] The archbishop's refusal to permit the votive Mass could not have been based on *The Drums of Father Ned* or *Bloomsday,* since neither was available to him. His targets were any new play by O'Casey or any dramatization of Joyce's *Ulysses.* Like Cardinal Logue in 1899, textual analysis was beyond the archbishop's remit. But unlike Logue, McQuaid took decisive and disastrous action. McQuaid had clearly set out his principles in regard to censorship and morality two years earlier: "in this Catholic country we do not entertain two moralities, one for aesthetics and one for living."[70] With the prosecution of Alan Simpson still underway and Mc-Quaid's powers at their zenith, there was no possibility of appeal. A marginal note handwritten on the typed account prepared for the archbishop on 6 January 1958 summed up the situation: "AB has dealt with it."[71]

What may have begun as benign, if not the best of, promotional motives—asking the archbishop for permission to celebrate Mass in the first place—triggered the eventual postponement and abridgement of the Dublin International Theatre Festival. Brendan Smith tried to salvage the festival and, specifically, to provide for a Dublin production of *Father Ned* by an amateur company. Smith believed that the debacle was not simply a series of misunderstandings: "all [the archbishop] was concerned with was one author, James Joyce; it was not O'Casey. . . . I am convinced to this day that the situation developed as it did because members of the Tóstal Council representing non-theatrical interests provoked a public row quite unnecessarily. They did this deliberately as a means of sabotaging the Theatre Festival. They had an idea that *Ulysses* was dirty and that O'Casey might be anti-clerical."[72] In the aftermath, O'Casey devised a brilliant strategy in his editorial and dramatic protests against censorship in Ireland that assured that the world, especially outside of Ireland, would see these events from a perspective sympathetic to him. His letters to critics, editors, and scholars, especially those in America, advanced the view that *The Drums of Father Ned* had been banned in Dublin, a view that did, in fact, become the received understanding of events. In 1958 Robert Hogan's article on O'Casey in the *New Republic* reached a wide American audience—much wider than that of any scholarly journal—and offered an understanding of the events in Dublin surrounding *The Drums of Father Ned* from O'Casey's point of view. In "O'Casey and the Archbishop," Hogan copper-fastened what happened in 1958 with what took place when the Abbey rejected *The Silver Tassie* in 1928: "The [Abbey] directors took precisely the same stand taken thirty years later by the Tóstal Council," wrote Hogan. "The Tóstal Council has parodied the refusal of *The Silver Tassie,* by using the same specious reasoning put forth by the Directors of the Abbey Theatre in

1928."[73] On 24 January 1958 the directors of the Globe Theatre Company, Godfrey Quigley and Norman Rodway, asked O'Casey for blanket permission for the director, Jim Fitzgerald, "to make such alterations as he requires" in *The Drums of Father Ned*.[74] O'Casey wrote back on 29 January 1958 saying that he had submitted no work to them and asking for the immediate return of his script. On 8 February 1958 the Tóstal Council had, in fact, voted eight to six in favor of presenting both *The Drums of Father Ned* and *Bloomsday*, although evidence in the Dublin Diocesan Archives and elsewhere suggests that everyone assumed that O'Casey would not agree to alterations in the script.[75] Eventually O'Casey banned all professional performances of his works in Ireland and settled for a world premiere of *The Drums of Father Ned*, directed by and starring Robert Hogan, by a community theatre company in 1959 in Lafayette, Indiana, where its politics were indecipherable to a Hoosier audience. Hogan and others created the clear impression that the play had been banned by festival or Tóstal officials as a result of clerical pressure, rather than withdrawn by O'Casey.

Beckett also withdrew his plays from the festival and then banned all production of his plays in Ireland. Writing to Alan Simpson on 15 January 1958, Beckett rescinded permission for three mimes as well as a reading of *All That Fall* at the Pike Theatre. Beckett's opposition to censorship was long-standing and profound. In 1926, he and his friend Geoffrey Thompson were at the Abbey for the premiere of O'Casey's *The Plough and the Stars;* they returned for the tumultuous Thursday evening performance when Yeats delivered his famous "You have disgraced yourselves again" speech.[76] Beckett was intimately familiar with the trials Joyce endured and admired Joyce's "refusal to bow to censorship."[77] After the 1934 banning of his own work, Beckett wrote his essay "Censorship in the Saorstat," in which he proudly identified *More Pricks than Kicks* as the 465th work banned in Ireland.[78]

Just as the Tóstal Council was meeting, Beckett was having his own problems with censorship in England. In February 1958 the Lord Chamberlain refused to license *Endgame* on the grounds that it was blasphemous. Beckett had agreed to four of the five alterations demanded by the Lord Chamberlain, changing the translation of "*salaud*" from "bastard" to "swine" for instance, but refused to alter the prayer scene. Compounding the outrage was the fact that the Lord Chamberlain had licensed a production of *Fin de Partie,* the very same play in French, the previous spring. Among many dubious decisions by the Lord Chamberlain, this was the most dubious; by October 1958 even he recognized the silliness of permitting in French what he banned in English, reversed his decision, and licensed the play for production in English by George Devine at the Royal Court.[79]

Beckett had promised Simpson and the Pike the right of first refusal for other plays that he might translate into English in the future. On 21 August 1957, Simpson appealed to Beckett for rights to the "translation of *Fin de Partie* which would get the Pike Theatre out of the 'ghastly jam' caused by *The Rose Tattoo.*"[80] The Pike production of the uncensored *Godot* gave the company a brief interlude of financial stability in the mid-fifties. Not only was the run of *Godot* at the Pike extended, but the production also toured Ireland and returned to play Dublin's much-larger Gate Theatre. "Apart from *This Other Eden,*" the *Pike Newsletter* boasted, "this was the longest consecutive run in Dublin and, with the tour, constitutes a unique dramatic record for the country."[81] Once again, a wide Irish audience had seen what a London audience was, and would be, denied. On 17 February 1958, Beckett wrote Carolyn Swift: "As long as such conditions prevail in Ireland I do not wish my work to be performed there, either in festivals or outside them. If no protest is heard they will prevail forever. This is the strongest I can make. I have therefore to cancel the permission I gave you to present *All That Fall* and *Endgame.* I hope you will forgive me."[82] On 27 February 1958 Beckett withdrew all of his plays from production in the Republic of Ireland. Padraic Colum and others believed that "Beckett was misled" about the exact circumstances in Dublin,[83] but Beckett was not to be compromised. Had he had access to the archbishop's files, Beckett might have made the decision earlier, but his deep regret over the implications of his decision for individuals and small companies is glimpsed in a 7 May 1960 letter supporting Cyril Cusack's Dublin performance of *Krapp's Last Tape:* "I have decided it is now time I fell off my high Eire moke."[84]

The success of *Godot* in Ireland and the growing international acclaim for Beckett's works had not escaped the scorn of the archbishop and the ecclesiastical hierarchy. On 14 January 1958, Father O'Grady, the Jesuit provincial, "directed the Rector of Gardiner Street [Church] to refuse tha [*sic*] application of the Theatre Festival Committee of the Tóstal for permission to stage a play of Beckett's in the new St. Francis Xavier Hall."[85] Although Brendan Smith believed that Joyce was the real target of McQuaid's actions and others think it was O'Casey who provoked the archbishop, Beckett, too, must be counted among the usual suspects.

The abbreviated 1959 International Theatre Festival, postponed from May to September, was not without controversy either. The most provocative offering, Dominic Behan's *Posterity Be Damned,* presented at the Pike Theatre outside the official festival program, was described in the *Irish Press* "as a sickening stew of puerilities, cynicism, clownings and downright blasphemies."[86] Again, Irish audiences saw what London audiences could not. When *Posterity Be Damned* was submitted to the Lord Chamberlain for licensing, the excisions demanded were much more extensive than those imposed on *Godot.* For Gabriel Fallon what was paramount was that the 1959 theatre program survived at all and that it "established Dublin's right to have a Festival."[87]

Banned in France

The stage adaptation of J. P. Donleavy's *The Ginger Man* is the most blatant instance of Irish stage censorship in the fifties. Like the 1955 novel, the stage version of *The Ginger Man* was calculated to *épater* not just *la bourgeoisie* but *le monde* as well. Indeed, the novel's publication caused controversy in the United States and, as the review in the *Irish Times* reminded readers, even in France. Donleavy, who adapted his novel at the request of the play's director, Philip Wiseman, recalls registering surprise when told that the production would play in Dublin. After all, *The Ginger Man* offended many, but Catholics and Irish Catholics in particular. In the play, Dangerfield's English wife, for instance, says of the Irish: "The whole country is Catholic. I hate them. . . . They can't be trusted. Nor do they bathe."[88] Kenneth O'Keefe, Donleavy's persona, adds late in the play, "Do you know, Dangerfield, if it weren't for the British this place would be so many wild savages" (148). In addition, as the first act ends, Dangerfield, having driven his wife and infant daughter away, strikes the pose of Christ crucified and cries out, "Put in the nails" (89). The play offered abundant potential for charges of pernicious foreign influence, demeaning characterization of the Irish, indecent and obscene action, and blasphemy. The London premiere of *The Ginger Man* in September 1959 "had police protection on its first night at the Fortune Theatre because the management decided that it contained controversial matter concerning Ireland and the Irish."[89] That police presence may have been as much to generate publicity as to protect the cast and crew. The London reviews of *The Ginger Man* were far from enthusiastic—the *Times* referred to it as "an exasperatingly empty little play."[90] Recast, but with Richard Harris still in the title role, the play opened in Dublin on 26 October 1959 to similarly poor reviews.

The most positive of the Dublin reviews, by M.K. in the *Irish Times,* found "Wiseman's production is brilliant" and described the acting as uniformly excellent, but concluded that the play is "strong and often rancid meat." Although also favorably impressed by the acting, M. M. in the *Irish Press* wrote: "There is one scene near the end of the second act which is probably the most offensive ever performed on a Dublin stage and which I sincerely hope will never be repeated again. In a short five minutes a travesty is made of everything that stage entertainment is supposed to mean, morals are mocked at and indecency is flaunted. It is all very well to talk of art and freedom of expression in the theatre, but I think we have gone far enough. Up to this scene, the play had been rude, vulgar and even offensive to a degree, but I think we might still have stomached it but for this intrusion. I thoroughly agreed with the gentleman in the gallery who shouted, 'You have gone far enough.'" As troubling as was the staging of Dangerfield's copulation with Miss Frost, the play's only Irish character, his mockery of her moral scruples further incensed critics. The reviewer in the *Evening Mail* called it "the most tasteless, trivial and empty play that I have yet seen." D.B.'s three-sentence review in the *Irish Independent* was even harsher: "The current production in the Gaiety Theatre, Dublin, is one of the most nauseating plays ever to appear on a Dublin Stage and it is a matter of some concern that its presentation ever have been considered. It is an insult to religion and an outrage to normal feelings of decency. Now that it has shocked everyone with an average sense of values that has seen it, the best course open to all concerned is to withdraw it with the greatest possible speed."[91] Philip Wiseman was quick to write the *Irish Independent* threatening legal action by claiming that its incendiary review was "a deliberate attempt to incite a breach of the peace." In fact, Wiseman himself sought to provoke the public disorder that could make this production a *cause célèbre.* From the outset Wiseman hoped for the public outrage that greeted *The Bishop's Bonfire.* Such disorder would ally *The Ginger Man* with *The Playboy* and *The Plough,* in what was looking more and more like the best-known, if not most reliable, tradition in twentieth-century Irish drama. Although Wiseman's comments were an open invitation for protesters to disrupt the performance, none did; instead, another force, a *force majeure,* intervened.

In the plainest instance of stage censorship in Ireland since the Ministry of Justice coerced the withdrawal of Lennox Robinson's *Roly Poly* in the name of Irish neutrality during the Emergency, clerical pressure, brought to bear on a theatre manager, forced the closing of *The Ginger Man.* The pressure, according to Donleavy, came from Archbishop McQuaid through an emissary, a Father Nolan, most likely Reverend G. Nolan, S.J., who had advised the archbishop on the 1958 Dublin Theatre Festival. This instance provides a textbook example of why theatre managers had spoken so highly of the Lord Chamberlain's office in the 1909 hearings. Claiming that their contract with the Gaiety stipulated that the author had the right to refuse enforced revisions, Donleavy and Wiseman declined any negotiation over possible cuts. Louis Elliman, manager of the Gaiety, found himself between his playwright's ironclad contract and the envoy of the second most powerful man in Ireland. After the production's third performance, Elliman canceled the run of the play. The *Times* reported that for that third performance the house was half-full. Unlike *The Rose Tattoo,* which completed its scheduled run, *The Drums of Father Ned,* which was withdrawn by its author, and *Over the Bridge,* which was produced, *The Ginger Man* was unceremoniously pulled. As with the archbishop's refusal to permit a votive Mass for the 1958 Tóstal, no explanation would be given, no explanation would even be requested.

Donleavy's own account of the play's reception, "What They Did in Dublin with *The Ginger Man*," which includes many of the Irish reviews, appeared as the preface to the published version of *The Ginger Man* in 1961, again in 1963, and in subsequent editions Donleavy began his dedication of the published text, "To all those fuckpigs."[92] What the Lord Chamberlain did to the play in London is also worth comment. While Irish audiences saw the play unexpurgated, British audiences did not. The initial reader's report, prepared by St. Vincent Trowbridge in April 1959 for a production of *The Ginger Man* in Hull, described it as "an Irish *Look Back in Anger,* crossed with something by James Joyce"[93] and recommended forty excisions, often of entire lines rather than single words. Even after these cuts to the version performed in Britain, the Lord Chamberlain's office received a number of complaints from both private citizens and the stage plays subcommittee of the Public Morality Council that challenged the wisdom of licensing the play at all. Viewed in isolation, the abrupt termination of the Dublin run of *The Ginger Man* is an egregious example of the capricious use of clerical power. In comparison to the preproduction licensing of the Lord Chamberlain and the complaints received at Saint James Palace, the withdrawal of the play in Dublin was indicative of the times. Unlike the other plays discussed here, however, *The Ginger Man* was withdrawn; its run canceled. McQuaid's action was perhaps most menacing because it was not only so effective but also wholly outside the rule of law.

North of the Border

Given the machinations and unassailable power of Archbishop McQuaid, it is not surprising that the most public debate over theatre censorship in the 1950s occurred not in Dublin but in Belfast. The case of Sam Thompson's *Over the Bridge* is unlike the others discussed in this chapter not only because it transpired in Northern Ireland but also because it transgressed an entirely different area. Thompson's play about sectarian bigotry in the Belfast shipyards violated none of the entrenched standards of censorship in the Republic—it was not indecent, blasphemous, "foreign," anticlerical, nor profane, nor did it touch upon the subjects of birth control or abortion. The issue that provoked intense controversy was politics, and the reason given for withdrawing the play was the fear of civil disturbance and mob action.[94] Closer to the truth was that a funding agency, the Northern Ireland Council for the Encouragement of Music and the Arts (CEMA) objected to the play's graphic portrayal of anti-Catholic bigotry as an integral part of daily life in contemporary Belfast and the depiction of a vicious Protestant mob. The censorship did not involve a ban on *Over the Bridge;* in fact, it had a very successful and popular production. Instead, what took place was the withdrawal of financial support from a public arts organization.

In its early years CEMA, founded during World War II, regularly booked English theatre companies to tour Northern Ireland. This mission was fundamentally unlike that of analogous arts organizations in the Republic because it sought not the cultivation or showcasing of Northern Irish drama but the importation of culture, especially from England and Scotland, for Northern Irish audiences. In its second annual report CEMA lamented that "owing to difficulties of engaging companies from England, the Council during the year 1944/45 was obliged to depend entirely on local resources."[95] This approach is antithetical to that of the Abbey and numerous arts organizations in the Republic, including those that proliferated in the 1950s. Only as the fifties began did CEMA extend its efforts toward developing native talent by soliciting new plays from some forty writers, "chiefly Ulstermen."[96]

Despite the consolidation of three small companies as the Ulster Group Theatre and the emergence of the Lyric Theatre, the situation for Northern Irish dramatists—for all Northern Irish writers, in fact—was bleak in the early fifties. At the Poets, Essayists, Novelists (PEN) Conference held in Belfast in 1953, an open letter signed by Mary O'Malley, the cofounder of the Lyric Theatre, and three other members of the Belfast Corporation and an MP, candidly addressed the dilemma of writers in Northern Ireland:

> Why is it that an area which is so rich in tensions, political, social and religious, has failed to throw up work of importance? The explanation is in part the fact that many writers try to ignore their

roots. The local market also creates difficulties. A quiet, but none-theless powerful censorship prevents the writer for radio or the theatre from dealing with the very tensions that are the most prominent features of life in the area. The political and economic domination by the Unionist Party is taboo as a subject as is the victimisation of political opponents. The nearest approach that can be made is on the level of broad farce. Treatment of historical questions, even of several centuries ago, is banned unless it is on an officially approved basis.[97]

In the late 1950s the Ulster Group Theatre would accept for production two plays that challenged this prevailing censorship by examining sectarian prejudice. Gerard McLarnon's *The Bonefire* and Sam Thompson's *Over the Bridge* not only shared common themes but also provoked censorship by the powerful politicians who took offense at these plays.

The Bonefire centers on a love triangle among Vanessa, "her Popish sailor boy" John Hanna, and Willy McNulty, who, as the play begins, has just been released from a prison term for the blinding of Hanna during the previous year's bonfires on the eve of the July Twelfth celebrations. The play is replete with melodramatic turns (Hanna was, in fact, not blinded, which is why McNulty has been released from prison), sensationalistic effects (including "two orange pillars of fire"), and some coarse language ("How long did you and Vanessa go rutting together in the ditches of the road?" asks McNulty).[98] As in Thompson's play, the action climaxes when a rampaging Protestant mob commits murder; the denouement shows the grief of the victim's relatives. Several scenes incorporate rhythmic chanting, physical threats, and gruesome violence. For a Canadian readership, Tyrone Guthrie described the bonfires and rituals associated with the July Twelfth commemorations as "extremely primitive, extremely interesting as anthropology, and scarcely credible in a great and otherwise modern and progressive metropolis."[99] *The Bonefire* projected unflattering images of Protestant sectarianism as atavistic and dangerously violent and directly linked those images with militant Unionism, the July Twelfth rituals, and mob action.

The 1958 production of *The Bonefire* was presented by the Ulster Group Theatre and directed by Guthrie at the Grand Opera House in Belfast. Since the production was scheduled to go to the Edinburgh Theatre Festival, Belfast reviewers of *The Bonefire* expressed anxiety about responses to the play both at home and abroad. The *Belfast Telegraph* lamented: "It is a vomit of disgust. . . . [A] foreigner seeing this presentation by the Group Theatre company at the Edinburgh Festival next month will not react to it as would an Ulster Catholic or an Ulster Protestant. He will not regard the Orange bigots and the spineless Catholics on the stage as crude caricatures."[100] As criticism of the play raged in the press, the Lord Mayor of Belfast, W. Cecil McKee, demanded cuts in the play and, "under pressure from him and other sources the Group acceded to these changes."[101] Compounding public anger and resentment over Thompson's play was the fact that the Group Theatre received public funds. The previous year, as a condition of accepting a subsidy, the board of the Group Theatre had been reconstituted to include representatives from CEMA and the Belfast Corporation. As the Abbey Theatre discovered in 1926, the year it accepted its government subsidy and produced O'Casey's *The Plough and the Stars,* state funding intensified public scrutiny. Fearing that acceptance of the subsidy would entail the loss of artistic freedom, both J. G. Devlin, the actor who would play the role of Rabbie White in the 1960 production of *Over the Bridge,* and the actress Margaret D'Arcy resigned from the Group Theatre company in 1958.[102]

Early in 1959, Sam Thompson approached the same Ulster Group Theatre with his first stage play, *Over the Bridge.* The central conflict in Thompson's play is between trade unionism, with its ideal of "unity, tolerance and loyalty,"[103] and sectarianism. The conflicts that drive part 1 all exist within the Protestant community: between the fanatically devout Billie Morgan and the worldly trade union, between an older generation that remembers the depression and a younger one that does not, between Archie and Rabbie, and between the obnoxious George and Nellie Mitchell and their former neighbors. In part 2, the larger sectarian conflict between Protestants and Catholics overshadows local tensions and overwhelms even the conflict between the workers and management. After an explosion, presumed to be the work of the IRA, the Protestant workers "ferret out" (94) any Catholics who have reported for work. One Catholic,

O'Boyle, refuses to be intimidated out of his job. As a gesture of union solidarity, Davey, a dedicated trade unionist, joins him to face an angry mob that injures O'Boyle and kills Davey.

Although the mob attack on Davey and O'Boyle is the starkest example of physical violence, Thompson's play is suffused with menace expressed in threatening, provocative language. The quarrels between Archie Kerr and O'Boyle, the slanders of which they accuse each other, employ language that is uncharacteristically strong for a play for the 1950s; as performed in Belfast, it would not have been licensed by the Lord Chamberlain.[104] The most incendiary language is that of casual bigotry: Archie Kerr refers to O'Boyle, the only Catholic character to appear on stage, as "that Fenian get," while other Catholics are "the advancing scum of Popery" (44); Catholics are almost invariably called "popeheads" or "taigs." The unapologetic Kerr is quick to label any Protestant who doesn't support these characterizations as "mealy mouthed" (35) or "half-baked" (45). Although Rabbie White claims there is as much sectarianism among Catholics as Protestants, all but one of the characters, like most of the workers in Belfast's shipyards of the time, are Protestants who express ferociously anti-Catholic sentiments.[105]

Despite its daring subject and shocking language, *Over the Bridge* was accepted by the Group Theatre for production in the spring of 1959. On 5 May 1959, Thompson's documentary, "The Long Back Street," was broadcast on BBC television. The next day, with *Over the Bridge* already cast and in rehearsal and with less than two weeks before the opening, the theatre directors withdrew the play. Thompson describes it as "a very strange and sudden decision. I wonder if Siobhanitis has anything to do with it. They were particularly concerned about a mob scene."[106] John Ritchie McKee, the chairman of the directors of the Ulster Group Theatre and brother of Belfast's Lord Mayor W. Cecil McKee, explained the 6–2 vote to stop rehearsals and cancel the production as an expression of the public will: "The Ulster public is fed up with religious and political controversies. This play is full of grossly vicious phrases and situations which would undoubtedly offend and affront every sector of the public. . . . It is the policy of the directors of the Ulster Group Theatre to keep political and religious controversies off our stage."[107] *Over the Bridge* incurred the wrath of McKee and the board because of its candid, realistic depiction of sectarianism, the characters' use of "gross and vicious phrases" (which were less numerous, less gross, and less vicious than those in *The Bonefire*), and the "vicious" sectarianism of the mob scene. As Devlin and D'Arcy feared in 1958, CEMA funding of the Ulster Group Theatre had brought with it not only representation on, and a new chairman of, the board of directors but censorship as well. In response to the withdrawal, James Ellis (who subsequently produced the play) and two other directors resigned from the board of the Ulster Group Theatre. The *Belfast Telegraph* editorialized: "But two points must be firmly made. One is that 'The Bonefire' proved that an adult society can now be trusted to look at itself in a way that would not have been possible, even a few years ago. The other is that Northern Ireland must go on widening this self-examination, and so its understanding."[108] Less optimistically, Lord Mayor McKee stated, "I think that most people of any intelligence, whatever their creed, are sick, sore and tired of anything which seeks to stir up sectarian strife."[109]

Commentators, ranging from Stewart Parker and Sam Hanna Bell to D. E. S. Maxwell, assert that *Over the Bridge* broke new ground in its depiction of sectarianism and religious discrimination and opened new possibilities for dealing with contemporary issues on the stage in Northern Ireland. Roy McFadden, poet and lawyer, also indicated the limits that inevitably come with government subsidy: "The official purse is open only to those who will rehash the mixture without changing the ingredients."[110] In the summer of 1959, essays by McFadden, Janet McNeill, and Mary O'Malley about the *Over the Bridge* controversy appeared in *Threshold*. All three writers acknowledged that state funding of the arts, especially of theatre and especially in a highly polarized political system such as Northern Ireland's, necessarily entailed some measure of control if not outright censorship. McFadden pessimistically concluded that "the objection to the play is, I suspect, rooted in the notion that art is not a serious business: it may divert, and in a general way instruct, but it must never impinge directly on our social living."[111]

The theatre controversies of the late 1950s are today seen as turning points in the theatre histories of Ireland and Northern Ireland, cathartic moments in the emergence into the international arena. Despite attempts to impose an ad hoc censorship, several of these theatrical events were extraordinarily popular. So successful was Danny Kaye's appearance in 1952 that the Theatre Royal employed additional staff "to deal with the flood of postal bookings which reached the theatre when the week of two shows daily was announced."[112] Both Alan Simpson and Sam Thompson eventually triumphed not only in their legal proceedings but also in very popular productions of *The Rose Tattoo* and *Over the Bridge*. Indeed, rather than being intimidated by the assertion that these were dangerous, inflammatory, or immoral works, audiences were attracted to all of these plays, save *The Ginger Man*. With the case against Simpson finally resolved, Phyllis Ryan undertook a revival of the Pike's *The Rose Tattoo* in Dublin's Eblana Theatre. Again, the reviews were enthusiastic, especially about Anna Manahan's performance; its run of over three months indicated a wide base of popularity. *Over the Bridge* was even more commercially successful during its Belfast run that began in January 1960. Although it closed after only four performances at the Princes Theatre in London, *Over the Bridge* also did extremely well in its transfers to Dublin and Glasgow. Thompson's influence is seen in works as diverse as Frank McGuinness's *Factory Girls* and Martin Lynch's *Dockers* that consider sectarianism in the workplace. The enduring legacy of *Over the Bridge*, however, is that Northern Irish drama after 1960, especially after 1969, would often and openly address sectarian questions. That these two instances occurred within four years of each other suggests not mere coincidence but a sea change in the attitude toward drama. That significant percentages of the populations of Dublin and Belfast went so far as to purchase tickets is indicative of rapidly changing attitudes about not only theatre and the arts in general but also the freedoms to which ordinary people thought themselves entitled. Two plainer examples of how the efforts to censor theatre can backfire might be difficult to find.

One of the very few, perhaps the only, common element in these controversies is that the target of censorship was eager to see the case aired in the Irish and international press. Especially in Ireland, the tradition was by now a venerable one that recalled *The Countess Cathleen, The Playboy,* and *Blanco Posnet.* Just as William Boyle's decision to withdraw his plays from the Abbey was newsworthy in 1907, so were the bans imposed by O'Casey and Beckett. O'Casey was hardly an opportunist in exploiting stage censorship, but he astutely recognized the importance of airing his case in the press. Rather than backing away from the threat of clerical intervention, O'Casey insisted that it be exposed and did much to ensure that the wider world saw events from his perspective. Simpson, too, certainly recognized the importance of press coverage, especially since after his arrest he was by law severely restricted from commenting on his case. The day of his arrest, Simpson personally delivered a manifesto to the newspapers and arranged for an ideal photo opportunity of his being taken into custody: "My instinct of the last couple of days [prior to his arrest] that the whole affair would be of fantastic interest to the Press, was correct. . . . I had tried to avoid publicity as long as possible, but now that the die was cast, I was determined that the publicity should be exploited to our advantage."[113] He was not only correct in his judgment, but also successful in his strategy: the photographs of his arrest ran on the front pages of Dublin papers as well as London's *Daily Telegraph.* More venally, Wiseman hoped to provoke protest and to generate media hype over *The Ginger Man.* Ironically, when *The Ginger Man* was revived in Dublin in 1999, the publicity campaign for the production centered on its 1959 withdrawal. In his comment about "Siobhanitis," Thompson showed that he knew he was caught up in a sectarian struggle over media control.

If Bord Fáilte had hoped to attract foreign tourists to Ireland for theatre, they had seen more negative than positive publicity, especially in the American press, but the campaign was successful nonetheless. The dull and dire situation of Irish theatre described by Mac Liammóir, Bentley, Carroll, and Fallon at the beginning of the fifties was certainly livelier by the decade's end. In 1957 the arrest and prosecution of Alan Simpson eventually precipitated the demise of the Pike Theatre and Simpson's departure from Ireland. The next year Irish theatre had lost all access to its two greatest living dramatists, one of whom was unquestionably the most popular of the Abbey dramatists. Although none of the episodes of attempted censorship discussed herein directly involved the Abbey, it bore an enormous loss of potential revenues as a result of O'Casey's (and Beckett's) decision. The coerced withdrawal of *The Ginger Man* may have been one verse in McQuaid's long swan song. After Vatican II his powers would decline steeply, but even in his heyday, McQuaid could not dim the enthusiasm of Dublin audiences for O'Casey. The instance of *Over the Bridge* anticipates the often-heated debates over artistic freedom and state funding that have proved typical of theatrical controversies in the last four decades in Ireland and elsewhere. Moreover, each was, in its own way, cathartic, putting to rest another manifestation of a reactionary extreme.

9

New Theatrical Economies

In the early 1960s the Abbey was hardly the welcoming home to new Irish playwrights one expects to find in a national theatre. The Abbey turned down Behan's *The Quare Fellow* (1956), Hugh Leonard's *Walk on the Water* (1960) and *Madigan's Luck* (1963), John B. Keane's *Sive* (1959) and *The Highest House on the Mountain* (1960), and Tom Murphy's *Whistle in the Dark* (1960). So while Behan and Murphy were all the rage in Stratford East or in New York and Beckett was remaking the contemporary stage, an established calm prevailed at the Abbey. Beyond neglecting these Irish playwrights as too critical of Ireland, too violent, or too experimental, Ernest Blythe likewise declined to produce non-Irish contemporary dramatists, arguing that their works were beyond the terms of the theatre's remit. Whereas the commercial theatre was once denounced as a hegemonic threat to native Irish playwrighting and, in the first three decades of the century begot the Abbey and the Gate, the Abbey itself had become as rigid, narrow, and hidebound as the commercial stage. Wedded to a selection of plays that was the cultural legacy of the isolationism and conservatism of the 1930s and

1940s, Blythe's Abbey precluded nonrealistic plays as tainted by an alien avant-garde dramaturgy as well as works that cast too cold an eye on contemporary Irish life.

Two distinct attitudes toward censorship are in evidence by the end of the 1950s, both of which apply to theatrical performances as well as publications. The first judged that provoking the forces of conservatism and censorship was the duty if not the inevitable consequence of the creative artist's work. John Ryan recalls "that in time it became a badge of artistic distinction and intellectual courage to have had at least one book banned."[1] Similarly, Benedict Kiely remarked "by the time I got around to the distinction, you'd be damned nearly ashamed if you weren't banned. You were annoyed in one way, but you also felt you had joined the elect."[2] When asked his personal reaction to the banning of *The Dark,* John McGahern replied: "I didn't really care for myself because it was something of the time. If you were a writer, you half expected it; there actually would be no shock or surprise."[3] A much bleaker reality prevailed in the expressions of the demoralization, harassment, and misery created by a repressive and, in the case of theatre, capricious censorship. That atmosphere contributed to Alan Simpson's decision to leave Ireland in the 1960s, a decision that hastened the demise of the Pike. The Globe, as Christopher Murray points out, endured fatal losses first from the withdrawal of *The Ginger Man* and then the cancellation of *The Drums of Father Ned.*[4] At the end of the 1950s, the sluggish condition of Dublin's stages occasioned articles by Thomas Kilroy and Gabriel Fallon in *Studies;* both, however, suggested the potential for another renaissance in Irish theatre. By decade's end, despite, or perhaps because of, the conservative policies at the Abbey, at least four theatre companies, with a number of even smaller groups following in their wake, brought new Irish as well as international dramatists to Dublin. In the early 1960s, while the Abbey languished in its self-induced torpor, rejecting the works that found international acclaim, one by one these companies dropped from sight as their personnel pursued distinguished careers in London, Hollywood, and New York. As for earlier generations, emigration and exile continued to exact a heavy toll.

By 1960 the standards of the Censorship Board had become more liberal, in part because of Peter Connolly's commentaries on the negative effects of an overzealous censorship. Delicate questions of the stage presentation of homosexuality, nudity, violence, and coarse language were all successfully, although not painlessly, negotiated, both in the Republic and Northern Ireland. The introduction of homosexual characters on stage (*Walk on the Water, The Death and Resurrection of Mr. Roche* [1968]), a greater sexual candor, and the dramatizations of Irish history (Murphy's *Famine* [1968]) characterize Irish theatre in the 1960s. In 1968, after 231 years, Britain eliminated the licensing of plays by the Lord Chamberlain. In the parliamentary hearings on stage censorship, John Osborne was specifically asked about the production of his plays, including *Look Back in Anger* (1956), in Ireland and said that there had been no problem.[5] Although the abolition of the Lord Chamberlain's licensing had no direct impact on the Irish stage, it produced a greater openness on the British stage that did influence Irish theatre. The development of Irish television service, the increasing accessibility of British television broadcasts, and fundamental changes in the film industry all expanded the entertainment opportunities and exposure to previously taboo subjects. Since the 1960s, Irish theatre reflects a receptivity to controversial material and nonrealistic dramaturgies as new theatrical economies emerged.

Evincing a latter day "boom of the ban," revivals of controversial plays such as *Over the Bridge* and *The Rose Tattoo* were among the most popular productions of the 1960s. One of the most celebrated banned books, Eric Cross's *The Tailor and the Ansty,* was adapted for the stage and performed at the Peacock on 3 October 1968. Archbishop McQuaid did indeed prevent the Dublin International Theatre Festival from presenting *Bloomsday,* but dramatic adaptations of Joyce soon flourished. Mary Manning's *The Voices of Shem,* an adaptation of *Finnegan's Wake* written in 1955, played at the Eblana in October 1961. A year later, Hugh Leonard's *Stephen D* appeared at the Gate Theatre. Siobhan McKenna's one-woman show, *Here Are the Ladies* (1970), incorporated excerpts from Molly Bloom's soliloquy in *Ulysses.* The audience's horizon of expectations was drastically remade by playwrights like Beckett, companies such as Charabanc, and the cultivation of nontraditional spaces in which plays could be performed. The nature of theatregoing continued to evolve, with the pace of change quickening, as the democratization of theatregoing continued. The practice of dressing for the theatre faded. Not only was admission often fixed at a single price and seats unassigned, but new, nontraditional theatre audiences were targeted, sought, and developed.

In the last thirty years, institutional censorship of drama yielded to a more diffused and vastly more complex system of control over plays, both in Ireland and elsewhere. At work is the intricate interaction of theatre boards, state arts agencies, actors and their unions, playwrights, corporate sponsors, directors and technical personnel, community constituents, religious organizations, the press, and the public at large. In Northern Ireland, the complexity of these interactions was further complicated by the renewal of sectarian violence in 1969. There are, of course, still laws that govern what may be performed on stage in Ireland. Criminal as well as civil laws against libel, sedition, blasphemy, common-law offenses (including obscenity), breach of the peace, and incitement to riot, however, regulate stage plays in both the United Kingdom and Ireland. Moreover, both Northern Ireland and the Republic have statutes against hate speech that are applicable to the theatre.

A potent brand of de facto control emanates from the use of public funds. Most plays are performed by theatre companies that receive grants from the Arts Council or other state agencies, including employment or training schemes. Municipal governments provide support, as did the Belfast City Council in the early days of Charabanc. The continuity and, in fact, the survival of these companies typically depend on annual funding renewals, if not increases in the level of financial support. Retributive cuts or simple inaction may mean the end to a theatre company. Like all arts organizations, theatre companies now exist in a symbiotic relationship with public arts councils and with the public at large. A company's relationship with a corporate sponsor is comparable, although theatre companies typically are not bound by contractual obligations to corporate sponsors beyond advertising that sponsorship.

In the mid-1960s the theatre scene in Dublin underwent remarkable changes. Ernest Blythe relinquished his hold on the Abbey in 1966, the same year Jim Fitzgerald and Colm Ó Briain launched the Project Arts Centre (PAC). Intended as a multimedia forum for theatre, the visual arts, music, poetry readings, and lectures, the PAC hoped to accommodate a burgeoning arts scene in Dublin. In its early years, the PAC was housed in several venues. In the mid-1970s it had settled in the block that includes the Olympia Theatre where it operated on relatively short-term leases. By now the PAC drew support from a wide range of agencies and organizations, including the Goethe Institute, the Arts Council, Bord Fáilte, and the Dublin Theatre Festival. The venue was not without its problems. Dissatisfied with safety precautions, Dublin's chief fire officer required substantial improvements. "Given to understand that they would get a £6,000 grant if they did the work," the PAC undertook the mandated changes.[6] The corporation, however, "never publicly stated that it gave any undertaking."[7] The requisite improvements were made, but the Dublin City Council denied funding for the PAC. At risk were the ambitious plans for a season of new plays by Irish playwrights, now-substantial debts, and the very survival of the PAC. Many on the Council argued that the short-term lease made the stability of the PAC uncertain; others argued that the Council was imposing its own theatre censorship because council members objected to the use of public funds to support, among many things, two productions by the Gay Sweatshop.

The PAC controversy might serve as a model for the direction that stage censorship has taken since 1960. As in earlier decades, the exact point of controversy was diffused and itself a source of contention. Was *The Countess Cathleen* provocative only because of its theological implications or was not the sight of an Irish peasant hurling a dead wolf on his starving family's table a profoundly disturbing image? The flashpoints in *The Plough* were many. The charges against *Roly Poly* in the press quickly expanded from offending the Germans to being immoral. In the case of the PAC, the safety of the venue and the duration of the lease were offered as the ostensible, less controversial, reasons for withdrawing funding.

Community and regional theatre companies, in particular, stand in a very unusual relationship to commercial theatre. In the 1960s desperation over the fading fortunes of the Gate, drove Micheál Mac Liammóir to create the most successful production of the decade, *The Importance of Being Oscar*.[8] His partner, Hilton Edwards, in cooperation with Oscar Lewenstein, produced an international success for Brian Friel's *Philadelphia, Here I Come!* The 1970s and 1980s saw the proliferation of small companies, such as Rough Magic and Passion Machine (both founded in 1984) in venues like the PAC. In the 1990s, productions seen in New York City came from small regional companies like Druid or Dubbeljoint. At the end of the twentieth century two instances of controversy in Ireland and Northern Ireland illustrate the intricacies of the relationship between producing companies and the public. Both are marked by a distinctive, hypocritical brand of political correctness in public discourse that masquerades as an entirely apolitical correctness.

Quite unlike the Lord Chamberlain, state arts agencies present themselves not as the watchdogs of morality, but as advocates for the arts. The state creates arts agencies to foster, nourish, and support the arts, even if wags averred that CEMA, the forerunner to the Arts Council of Northern Ireland, stood for the "Council to Encourage Migration in the Arts." Given their shared concerns, funding agencies and arts organizations gravitated toward negotiated arrangements rather than confrontations. Typical of such accommodations was the playing of the British national anthem in Northern Ireland at the Lyric Players Theatre. The question of the national anthem was a vexing one, closely related to analogous issues concerning flags and emblems in Northern Ireland. When the Lyric became a charitable trust in 1960, the issue of the anthem surfaced at the first meeting of the trustees, who unanimously agreed "that the Lyric Players Theatre should continue its policy of having no National Anthem at productions, etc., on the premises but that it may be played at the discretion of the Trustees, at any outside function inside Northern Ireland and elsewhere."[9] The practice of playing the anthem had generally been fading in movie houses and theatres throughout Britain, but it still had enormous symbolic importance in Northern Ireland. As seen in the film *An Everlasting Piece* (2000), audience members who disliked the anthem, usually Catholics, might duck out of the cinema before the anthem began. Some theatre impresarios played the anthem twenty minutes before the play started.[10] When Dame Debra Parker resigned as president of CEMA in the early 1960s, she left a memo stating that the anthem had to be played at events promoted or supported by CEMA. The organization's secretary, Jack Loudon, "found ways to circumvent the directive. He would arrange to 'forget' to turn up the volume on the record player or it would not be played until the audience had all left."[11] Mary O'Malley, the Lyric's founder, had quietly been avoiding the anthem at the theatre she founded for years. On an Abbey visit to Belfast, the anthem was played after the curtain was lowered, so actors from the Republic were not confronted with the prospect of standing respectfully during it. As the decade progressed, so did Arts Council funding. With the help of a £20,000 grant from the Arts Council of Northern Ireland, and the stipulation that the anthem be played nightly, the Lyric built a new auditorium. On 29 October 1968, three days before the theatre's opening, both Pearse and Mary O'Malley resigned in protest: "The new policy concerning the playing of the Anthem at performances in the Theatre will affect, in our view, artistic independence and vision."[12] When the board asked the O'Malleys to reconsider their decision, Pearse O'Malley withdrew his resignation and returned to the board. The problem festered over the next fifteen months. At the end of 1969, W. Brian Boyd described the "sad and hopeless" state of affairs at the Lyric: "The Trustees seem to have become embroiled in an unfortunate disagreement relative to the National Anthem, and for this and other reasons have lost the support of the Fund Raising Committee."[13]

The Lyric remained a lightning rod for theatrical controversy in Belfast in the seventies. Since its founding in 1951, the Lyric Players expanded upon its original commitment to poetic drama, especially Yeats's, to become more inclusive, not least by staging popular musicals. Its 1974 production of *Jesus Christ Superstar* aroused protests in the press as well as the streets. Many of the letters to the Lyric reflected the now-eclipsed standards of the Lord Chamberlain against the representation of Christ and the treatment of Scripture. Reverend Alan Cairns of Ballymoney described a "diabolically inspired and iniquitously blasphemous production."[14] Picketers took to the streets outside the theatre. As so often, such protests had precisely the opposite effect of what they intended. True to the model, the expanded publicity brought in over fifteen thousand patrons.

But the success of *Jesus Christ Superstar* defied an undeniable trend: Theatre attendance, particularly in the North, was in decline. Just as the cultural revival at the end of the nineteenth century capitalized on increased literacy, expanded leisure, and growing urbanization, so in the 1960s and 1970s, comparable cultural forces reconfigured the place of theatre in Ireland, but to the detriment of playgoing. The most important among these forces was television, but numerous other factors loomed large: the renewal of sectarian violence in the North, the unionization of actors and technical personnel, and chronic economic problems. Many of the commentaries on the Northern Irish companies founded in the last quarter of the century, such as Field Day, Charabanc, and Dubbeljoint, mention how surprising it was to see large, enthusiastic audiences especially in remote venues.

Public funding often carries with it the charge of reaching or at least appealing to a "community." Especially in the United Kingdom, the emphasis on "bums on seats," an admittedly quantitative measure, became a criterion of success in the 1980s. In the last decades of the century, the definition of "community" was aggressively contested and greatly complicated by identity politics. Just whose bums were on those seats became an important question. Often reaching a community was synonymous with expanding the audience base to include nontraditional theatregoers (working and lower classes, the unemployed) from specific constituencies (women, Irish-speakers in Northern Ireland) and playing in unconventional, "nonbourgeois" venues. Charabanc, the Belfast women's company founded under an Action for Community Employment project in the Department of Economic Development in 1983, regularly performed in nondedicated venues: "leisure centres, hotels, community centres and bars."[15]

Many of these productions were new works that sought new audiences. Some came from writers-in-residence. Others were "texts" developed through a collaborative process involving multiple authors: researchers, a core acting company, interviewers/interviewees, and directors. The decentralization of the author and text was ideally suited to the antielitism of these companies. Seeking out hitherto unheard or silenced voices, many of these companies drew upon the workshop strategies derived from Joan Littlewood, especially via companies like 7:84 or Joint Stock, to develop or transform oral and noncanonical histories, contemporary events, or "concepts" into theatrical productions. Invariably, the subjects developed by community and regional theatres have an immediate connection in either time or space to the nontraditional audiences they hope to reach. Often these companies sought funding for the development of a new or embryonic script as well as its performance.

No less important is the well-defined, unconventional agenda if not *raison d'être* of the new companies. The stated intention and policy of companies as diverse as Charabanc, Field Day, and Druid, was not to shock, affront, or offend their audience but to build an audience. Their appeal was not only to an established, well-educated, middle- and upper-class audience, but also to people who usually did not go to the theatre. The choice of the projects workshopped and plays performed as well as interviews, manifestos, and mission statements reflect audience development as an objective. Field Day's "founding purpose [was] to take new plays to audiences unused to going to the theatre."[16] Charabanc deliberately sought to "play community centers, . . . where our real audiences are." Dublin's Passion Machine was formed in 1984, "to present theatre that depicted contemporary everyday life and to attract a large audience . . . to new original Irish play[s]."[17] Dubbeljoint "has the dual aims of creating plays with an appeal throughout the island of Ireland, and making that work as widely available as possible."[18] The impulse to startle a jaded metropolitan audience, to celebrate an elitist "high culture" tradition, or to present an idealized image of Ireland yielded to a stronger desire to appeal to ordinary people, especially nontraditional theatregoers, who would find something of themselves on stage. This meant soliciting or developing new scripts that had immediate relevance to that prospective audience and called for a repertory quite unlike that of a commercial or university theatre or even a governmentally subsidized theatre such as the Gate or the Abbey.

From the outset, Field Day, Charabanc, and other companies played outside purpose-built theatres. As at the beginning of the century, smaller companies attracted a nontraditional audience by playing in unconventional venues. Field Day held the advantage of having internationally known playwrights, Brian Friel in particular, premiering new work in Derry. And as earlier in the century, the parish halls, community centers, and reclaimed spaces were the ones unburdened by high overheads. Moreover, many of these companies were committed to touring. Charabanc provides the most celebrated example: between May 1983 and October 1984 *Lay Up Your Ends* played to over thirteen thousand people in ninety-six performances in fifty-nine different venues.[19] A 1993 report on the arts in Northern Ireland credited Charabanc with bellwether change: "The play made an enormous impact on the way theatre was seen in the city [Belfast]. Suddenly there was a new audience for theatre, and Charabanc nurtured that audience for several years. They also attracted a substantial section of the existing theatre audience who were looking for new and challenging work after the lean years of the 1970s."[20] During the same period, between 1976 and 1994, the drama budget for the Arts Council in the Republic of Ireland increased seven-fold, from £680,308 to £4,654,420.[21] The change was even more dramatic in Northern Ireland: in 1982 and 1983 funding for "Smaller-scale Drama and Cultural Traditions" was nearly nil; by 1990 it was about £50,000; in 2001–2002 it was ten times that amount.[22]

Forced Upon Us emerged from a workshop experience under the direction of Pam Brighton, a theatre professional trained as a barrister, who came to Northern Ireland in 1984 to direct *Lay Up Your Ends* and work with Charabanc. In her native England, she directed new performances at the Royal Court Upstairs and served as artistic director of the Hull Truck Theatre Company and the Half Moon Theatre. The workshop format, pioneered by Joan Littlewood, was further developed in her work with Charabanc. In 1991, along with Mark Lambert and Marie Jones, Brighton founded Dubbeljoint, its name combining the first syllables of Dublin and Belfast to suggest a cross-border cooperation, to produce *Hang all the Harpers*. Like Charabanc, Dubbeljoint produced new plays, several written by Marie Jones, as well as others developed by amateurs. Despite the slight level of funding, subversive if not offensive plays, and nontraditional audience, many were extremely popular in and outside Northern

Ireland. Brighton directed several award-winning productions, including Charabanc's *Lay Up Your Ends* and Dubbeljoint's *Women on the Verge of HRT* and *A Night in November;* both of the latter had successful commercial runs in London's West End and in New York.

In the mid-1990s Dubbeljoint entered into a partnership with a community organization, JustUs, and a drama training scheme, which was linked with the Training for Women's Network and Féile an Phobáil (the West Belfast Festival) with assistance from the Open College Network. The collaborations between Dubbeljoint and JustUs resembled the theatrical methods of Charabanc: largely feminist in orientation, based on interviews and research, developed in workshop rehearsals, and moving toward, rather than working from, a fixed, "authorized" text. In the first production, *Just a Prisoner's Wife* (1996), Dubbeljoint and JustUs won a Belfast City Council Award for arts partnership.

In 1997 *Binlids,* also directed by Brighton and presented at Féile an Phobáil, dramatized the Springhill and Ballymurphy massacres, which took place in the 1970s. When funding from the Belfast City Council for the August production was delayed in May 1997, Catriona Ruane, Féile an Phobáil director, denounced the withholding as "censorship, and a denial of our civil, political and cultural rights."[23] *Binlids* received its funding and proved as successful as it was controversial. In November 1998 *Binlids* sold out its run at the Angel Orsanz Foundation in New York City. It attracted huge audiences in Northern Ireland, but was denounced as republican propaganda. Most disturbing was the fact that some Northern Irish audiences cheered a scene in which the IRA killed a captured British soldier. That audience response, a localized interpretation of a dramatized episode, prompted the questioning of Dubbeljoint's use of public funds. On the one hand, the festival director had accused the Arts Council of Northern Ireland (ACNI) of censorship; on the other, some Conservative MPs called for withdrawal of ACNI funding of Dubbeljoint.[24]

In February 1999 the ACNI announced an £18,000 grant to Dubbeljoint for Brighton's work in the development of a play, unwritten at the time of funding, concerning policing in Northern Ireland. This sum represented 30 percent of the £62,500 ACNI had committed to Dubbeljoint in 1999. The script was developed by two members of the JustUs community theatre company: Brenda Murphy, who conducted much of the archival research for the project and who was interned as a member of the IRA in the 1970s,[25] and Christine Poland. Like previous Dubbeljoint/JustUs productions, *Forced Upon Us* was to premiere as part the West Belfast Festival, Féile an Phobáil, held annually since 1988 to direct energies away from violence on the anniversary of the introduction of internment in Northern Ireland. Robert Ballagh, the Dublin artist who has designed sets for Dubbeljoint, offers this account of Féile an Phobáil's genesis: "Kids were regularly getting whacked up and put away . . . in West Belfast. They decided to put their energies into the arts. This is the kind of thing I'd been talking about for years, and suddenly they were doing it—so I became an enthusiastic supporter. I designed their logo, did everything I could."[26] In the 1990s the festival underwent a comprehensive change: no longer would its feature attractions be limited to "the Pound Loney day (all pints £1), Scooty's disco or the West Belfast guider grand prix."[27] Widely promoted, Féile an Phobáil hoped to attract an audience to a cultural festival that included lectures, recitals, concerts, theatre, and exhibitions held in a republican neighborhood. The festival also emerged as a radical, "people's" alternative to the Belfast Festival at Queen's, even if "the people" in question were republicans. By 2000, the festival described itself as the largest community festival in Western Europe. Its 1999 program described *Forced Upon Us* as "a powerful, painful yet witty expression of the call for the RUC to go."[28] The production opened on July 30 at the new Amharclann na Carraige, the Theatre on the Rock, in the Belfast Institute for Further and Higher Education, just off the Falls Road. As several of the reviewers from outside Belfast noticed, the graffiti "Disband the RUC" was conspicuous on walls throughout the neighborhood. Indeed, the campaign to disband the RUC had become one Sinn Féin's highest priorities.

The play begins with the screams of a Catholic woman being raped by a Protestant man. The Catholic woman refuses to call the Royal Ulster Constabulary (RUC) to report the crime because the police have verbally abused her in the past. In response to her father's question, "How did we come to this?" the play moves back in time from a contemporary setting to examine the origins of the

RUC in the decade leading up to its inception in 1922. The violence of the contemporary rape is linked with the horrific lynching of a Catholic—doused with paraffin and set afire—by two drunken Protestants after the Titanic sinks. Using historical episodes, the play dramatizes the abuse and murder of Catholics, including a "reprisal massacre in Desermartin, Co. Derry in May 1922 when seven Catholics were shot and beaten to death in front of their Catholic neighbors and relatives, who were then expelled from the village,"[29] for which the Royal Irish Constabulary, the forerunner to the RUC, and the B Specials are complicit or responsible. The words of Edward Carson, James Craig, and other unionists, excerpted from their letters, diaries, memoirs, and public speeches of the period, counterpoint the words of the Irish nationalist and socialist, James Connolly. Craig and Connolly, played by individual actors, confront each other from platforms at either end of the theatre—their actual speeches played off against one another. The contemporary RUC and unionist politicians are depicted as no less bigoted than their counterparts from the 1920s. *Forced Upon Us* invites the audience to draw direct parallels between the anti-Catholic pogroms of the 1920s and ethnic cleansing, between RIC Detective Inspector John W. Nixon and the Shankill Butchers, between James Craig and David Trimble. The play is aggressively republican, not least in its construction of a continuous past of anti-Catholic bigotry; its perspective, as one of its authors plainly acknowledges, is not objective but subjective. The play includes a reference to then First Minister Trimble as "that ginger wee shithawk."

The play's dramaturgy combines Brechtian elements, such as an episodic structure, direct address, and an unmistakable agit-prop message, with a visceral, Grand Guignol appeal. There is little emphasis on the development of a smooth, flowing narrative; rather, *Forced Upon Us* interrogates the origins of the RUC as they contributed to contemporary reality—the Catholic woman's refusal to contact the very people whose job it is to help her. Historical records are presented rather than represented. The episodic structure "is punctuated by the appearance of Catholic women (about every ten minutes), crying that their son/brother/father has been killed by the Unionists."[30] Moreover, the stage and sound design envelop the audience and dispel any sense of predictable, naturalistic theatre: the audience is assaulted by screams, horrific violence, impassioned rhetoric, formal oratory, and pistol reports.

The ACNI deemed one version of the script, submitted on 24 June 1999, incomplete. Outside assessors evaluated a second version, submitted on 15 July, as "artistically unacceptable." External evaluations described a "final version," submitted four days before the first performance, as "well below the threshold of artistic acceptability, . . . distasteful, . . . exploitative, . . . very poorly realised, . . . a propagandistic play [that] could only serve to deepen existing prejudices."[31] The ACNI withheld the £18,000 earmarked for the project, ostensibly on two counts: first, that Dubbeljoint failed to deliver the complete script on time, and second, that external assessors evaluated the script as artistically unacceptable. ACNI made no mention of the play's politics in announcing the withholding of funding. Arguing that script approval was an arbitrary requirement, Dubbeljoint promised legal action to secure its grant. Brighton denounced the ACNI's action as politically motivated and described it as "censorship."

The consequence of the Arts Council action and the extensive publicity was what the *Irish Independent* in 1911 called "the boom of the ban." As one paper reported in early August: the result of "the farcical Arts Council snub is that every theatregoer in Ireland has heard about *Forced Upon Us.*"[32] Performances scheduled during the West Belfast Festival quickly sold out and an extra Saturday matinee was added to the run. Greeted with standing ovations by its audiences, which Eoin O'Brien described as "made up of women of the same generation as that of the women from Just Us [*sic*],"[33] *Forced Upon Us* was extensively reviewed and widely praised. Several reviews pointedly dismissed the outside assessors' judgment that the play was artistically inadequate as groundless and, as proof, pointed to the large and enthusiastic audiences. Some reviews, however, denounced the play as bigoted. "What is the point in going into a community and affirming its most venomous prejudices?" asked the *Belfast Telegraph.*[34] The *Guardian,* no one's idea of a conservative paper, described "murder after murder of good Catholics, with no reference made to contemporaneous IRA violence."[35] Even the republican *Irish News* described parts of *Forced Upon Us* as "over-emotional."[36]

ACNI was not without its defenders. The reviewer for the *Belfast Telegraph,* Malachi O'Doherty, wrote in *Fortnight* that "explicitly party political propaganda is surely always bad drama" and denounced the play's politics as "simply redneck republicanism."[37] Even *Private Eye* took notice and panned the play as "a vicious anti-Protestant rant, differing in no way from Ian Paisley's anti-Catholic polemics apart from the fact that the taxpayer isn't expected to cough up for his bigotry."[38] Whereas all commentators either stated or implied that the decision to withhold funding was political, ACNI denied that it was.

Forced Upon Us was successfully revived several times throughout the next year. In September 2000, the play was performed at the SFX Theatre in Dublin, where the *Irish Times* reviewer, David Nowlan, called it a "characterless pageant" in which "its evident anger merely seethes over the very user-unfriendly ramps and platforms in a form which has little theatrical shape or dramatic purpose."[39] Its Dublin run concluded with a panel featuring Robert McBride (from the African National Congress), Gerry Adams, and Bernadette Devlin McAliskey (whose daughter Deirdre McAliskey played in the 2001 Dubbeljoint production *The Laughter of Our Children*).

In the midst of the funding crisis, on 30 July 1999, Gerry Adams had denounced the ACNI decision and prophetically spoke of the play's audience: "This is political censorship. . . . It is not the job of the Arts Council to decide what is and what is not 'acceptable' or 'proper' drama. The people who will turn out in large numbers next week to see this drama are the only judges that matter."[40] That same day, a letter to the editor of the *Irish Times* signed by fourteen authors, including Marie Jones, Frank McGuinness, and the novelist Shane Connaughton (a member of Dubbeljoint's board), described the withdrawal of funding as "a deplorable act of political interference with the freedom of artistic expression."[41] The *Andersontown News,* the *North Belfast News, An Phoblacht,* and other republican publications provided extensive and extended coverage of the play. Philip Hammond, director of performing arts for the ACNI, wrote the *Irish Times* to defend "our record of adamantly resisting any form of censorship, political or otherwise," and cited Dubbeljoint's failure to deliver the final script on time as the reason that funding

was withheld. In addition to letters to the editor and its regular review, the *Irish Times* also ran a fifteen-hundred-word piece on the
play and ensuing controversy. A forum on political theatre in the
North was held in Belfast on September 1999. *Fortnight* ran a three-
part perspective on the controversy in its September issue.

One of the most interesting attacks on the Arts Council came
from the *Anderstown News,* which accused "the Arts Council glitterati" of elitism in "pontificat[ing] about what type of art the proles
should be allowed to sample." Conflating the works of Carl Andre,
Damien Hirst, and Andreas Serano, they argued that ACNI funded
projects no one wanted, such as "a tank filled with urine or a row of
Tyrone bricks."[42] This advanced a view on what the ACNI should
be funding that had been an undercurrent in many of *An Phoblacht*'s
articles. Brighton herself recalled that *Binlids* received no ACNI
funding and criticized the 1999 funding levels: "The agenda of the
Arts Council has an effect on the access to drama for people living in
the working class areas of Nationalist West Belfast. To give such an
excessive increase in funds to the Ulster Orchestra which most working class people will find boring demonstrates the elitist mentality of
those Unionists and Castle Catholics who are attempting to sidestep
the issues thrown up by the last thirty years."[43]

On 1 October 1999 ACNI and Dubbeljoint issued a joint statement "indicating that the matter had been resolved to their mutual
satisfaction."[44] More importantly, *Forced Upon Us* precipitated a
larger debate over ACNI funding policies that pitted an expanded,
nontraditional audience base, community involvement, and the development of new works against a "middle-class" audience, professional actors, and established playwrights from Shakespeare to Friel.
Before 2000, a report entitled *Towards the Millennium* provided the
guiding principles behind ACNI policies and funding. In 2000,
Opening Up the Arts (also known as the Everitt report) prepared by
external reviewers Annabel Jackson and Anthony Everitt, offered a
highly critical evaluation of ACNI in the previous five years and suggested drastic revisions in the funding guidelines. Within a year the
Arts Council had a new chief executive, Róisín McDonough, whose
background suggests she may be quite differently predisposed than
her predecessor. McDonough was a director in the Training Network

for Women, one of the agencies supporting JustUs during the production of *Forced upon Us,* and chief executive of the West Belfast Partnership.

The priorities set in *Opening Up the Arts* are clearly seen in the significant shifts in the ACNI funding awards for 2001–2002. Grants to community arts organizations and Irish-language projects were generally increased. Among those receiving increases of at least 200 percent were Aisling Ghear (the Irish-language theatre company), the Beat Initiative, Féile an Phobáil (all in Belfast), and Sole Purpose Productions (in Derry). Organizations such as the Opera Theatre Company, the Ulster Orchestra Society, and the Belfast Grand Opera House saw their funding decline. The funding level for Dubbeljoint remained at £62,500; JustUs received its first grant of £15,000. Response to the funding decisions was mixed. In *The Belfast Newsletter,* Ian Hill, who earlier criticized ACNI for withholding the Dubbeljoint grant for *Forced Upon Us,* denounced the 2001–2002 funding decisions and the new ACNI priorities:

> Professional critical success has become an anathema. To the devil with the "pursuit of excellence."[T]he council will be seen as slavishly favouring political correctness, fostering an artistic Animal Farm; middle-class professional equals Bad; distressed, ghettoised, socially deprived and amateur equals Good.
>
> For so blinkered is this obsessive drive for socially engineered access, the Council has forgotten that without exposure to outside contemporary professional excellence, generations to come—except those able to travel to England or Europe—will be left in artistic isolation, obsessed with a resurrected past, trapped in recycling victimhood, wearing thin the artistic cliches of such projects.[45]

Several individuals and organizations responded to Hill, including Will Chamberlain and playwright Martin Lynch from the Community Arts Forum, an organization whose funding had doubled from £25,000 to £50,000. Lynch and Chamberlain argued that "not only do [the people of Northern Ireland] want the arts, they want to participate in the creation of the arts." As *Opening Up the Arts* reported, ACNI had "a pitifully low audience base (17 percent of the adult population at the last count), and a very narrow pool of creative talent to draw from."[46]

At the other end of the theatrical spectrum of Irish theatre lies another contemporaneous and comparable tale. About as far removed from the overtly political, community-oriented, collaborative, feminist, republican grass roots of *Forced Upon Us* is the wunderkind celebrity genius of the West End and Broadway, Martin McDonagh. In the late 1990s McDonagh enjoyed the most auspicious theatrical successes since Oscar Wilde's triumphs a century earlier. Before he reached the age of thirty, McDonagh had his plays performed in thirty-nine countries in twenty-seven languages. In 2000, McDonagh's plays were performed in North America more often than those of any other playwright save Shakespeare.

In 1997 McDonagh announced that he had two Irish trilogies: The Leenane Plays and The Aran Plays, the latter comprised of *The Cripple of Inishmaan, The Lieutenant of Inishmore* (the first-written of the Aran plays [1994]), and *The Rifleman of Inishturk.* And then, beginning in 1998, none of these new plays appeared because McDonagh had committed himself to seeing *The Lieutenant of Inishmore* produced before allowing his Inishturk play and two subsequent non-Irish plays, *The Pillowman* and *Dead Days at Coney,* to be performed. The difficulty came in finding a first-rate company to mount the play, which calls for delicate and dangerous stage illusions, including a *coup de théâtre* involving a cat.

Druid, the Galway company that premiered *The Lonesome West* and *A Skull in Connemara* as well as the Leenane plays as a trilogy, declined. So did Britain's Royal National Theatre, which first produced *The Cripple of Inishmaan* and sponsored McDonagh as writer-in-residence. The Royal Court, which mounted the London premiere of *The Beauty Queen of Leenane* in 1994, turned it down twice, under two artistic directors, explaining to McDonagh's agent, Rod Hall, that the problem was the artistic quality of the play, not its incendiary subject matter. After languishing for four years since the last new McDonagh play appeared and seven years since it was written, *The Lieutenant of Inishmore* opened in a "protected" performance in April 2000 in the smallest of the Royal Shakespeare Company's Stratford stages, the 170-seat The Other Place. In April 2002, the production transferred to the similarly sized Royal Shakespeare Company London theatre, The Pit.

Like McDonagh's earlier plays, *The Lieutenant of Inishmore* exploits certain Irish stereotypes and comically inverts others. While many commentators focus on McDonagh's debts to Ireland's great writers, no less influential are the mass culture images of the Irish. The dramaturgy, humor, characters, and intertextuality of *The Lieutenant of Inishmore* have obvious affinities with McDonagh's previous works, but its horrific violence and politically incorrect send-up of terrorists, whose brand of terror is too extreme for "mainstream terrorists," demanded a suitable production company. Set in 1993, *The Lieutenant of Inishmore* depicts a plot by the Irish National Liberation Army (INLA) to assassinate a renegade terrorist, Mad Padraic. To lure Padraic to his native Inishmore, three INLA men kill what he loves: his black cat, Wee Thomas. Fearing that Padraic will blame and punish them for the cat's death, his father, Donny, and the seventeen-year-old Davey hatch a ludicrous scheme to cover a tabby cat with black shoe polish and fob it off as Wee Thomas. When Padraic returns home, he meets Davey's sister, Mairead, who is equally infatuated with Padraic and the INLA. Together they execute the INLA men but when she realizes Padraic killed her cat, Mairead murders him.

Five of the play's nine scenes are set in Donny's Inishmore cottage. Except for indoor plumbing and a telephone, both used conspicuously, little has changed since Synge portrayed the rural Irish cottage in *In the Shadow of the Glen* in 1903. Austerity and intimacy, if not poverty and claustrophobia, prevail. The only setting rendered realistically, the cottage provides a playing area not much larger than the original Abbey stage (twenty-one feet by fifteen feet). In the first scene, however, the audience focuses on the dead cat, "its head half missing." Despite parallels in Synge's plays, the violence against animals—two cats assassinated, cows blinded, and a dog killed when it chokes on its owner's severed nose—is unprecedented. The most successful fusion of the grotesque and comic is in the sexual attraction between Padraic and Mairead. Their eyes remained locked on each other as he executes the three blinded INLA terrorists at point blank range. Recurrent tableaux in the play depict armed standoffs that arise from the interruption of set pieces of speechifying that parody the Irish nationalist tradition of speeches from the dock: "[I]t isn't only for the school kids and the oul fellas and the babes unborn we're freeing Ireland. No. It's for the junkies, the thieves and the drug pushers too!"[47] In the final scene, the cottage floor awash in blood, Donny and Davey dismember the bodies of the INLA terrorists, creating a gruesome spectacle, appropriate to Padraic's pathological violence.

Across the political spectrum of the British press, many of the reviews for the Stratford production were superlative. Mark Lawson in the *Guardian* called it "thrillingly written and politically challenging." In the *Independent* Paul Taylor wrote that "the show never loses its exhilaration, because method and message are so adroitly united." John Peter in the *Sunday Times* found it "cunningly constructed, deeply and intensely felt, bitterly bloodcurdling and breathtakingly funny." The exception was Patrick Carnegy in the *Spectator* who described it as "complicit with the very evil it purports to dissect." McDonagh anticipated that he would be criticized for writing a comedy about a situation in Northern Ireland that he describes as "a sick joke."[48] His play articulates "pacifist rage. I mean, it's a violent play that is wholeheartedly anti-violence." McDonagh offers a revealing comment on his own political orientation: "Attacking my own side, I believe, was the most interesting aspect. I do think if art can change anything about that situation, then anyone brought up Catholic and republican should be looking at their own side, and the opposite side should be doing the same thing. As long as we keep attacking each other's communities artistically nothing's going to change."[49]

There is a common obfuscation at work in both these productions that inhibits the "official spokespersons" from agencies that dispense or receive public monies from honesty, let alone candor. To state publicly that these plays were not being funded or not being produced because of their politics would leave the agency or company vulnerable to easy attacks. Consequently, the Arts Council and the Royal Court Theatre (like the ACNI) would not comment on the plays' incendiary politics but instead only on the nebulous and indefinable questions of "artistic merit." Riddled with doublespeak, official public discourse cannot admit politics as a reason to decline to fund or to produce a play because to do so would suggest a form of censorship, which has emerged as an unequivocally "bad" thing, especially for people involved in the arts. No one from the Arts Council described *Forced Upon Us* as having the potential to incite hatred, although at least one of the outside assessors suggested as much. Moreover, the play itself, like earlier works, profited from the charge of censorship, despite the fact that there was never an attempt to suppress the play. Similarly, the Royal Court took pains to observe that it was not the politics of McDonagh's *The Lieutenant of Inishmore* that failed to measure up; it was the play's artistic quality. Unlike one another in virtually every other way, the production histories of *Forced Upon Us* and *The Lieutenant of Inishmore* reflect a contemporary political correctness that insists that it is not political at all.

In Ireland in the twentieth century actors are second only to managers (or play-selection committees) in exerting their influence to reject the playwright's words, lines, parts, or stage directions. In 1903 Dudley Digges and Maire Quinn left the NTS over Synge's *In The Shadow of the Glen,* and in 1926 *The Plough and the Stars,* already in rehearsal, had to be recast, prompting O'Casey to protest "a Vigilance Committee of the actors." In the labyrinthine conditions governing subsidized theatre companies, the thinnest of lines separates what McDonagh calls cowardice from what others call discretion. Even the accusation of censorship carries a political and historical charge that is extremely potent and, for JustUs and Dubbeljoint, extremely effective in securing funds.

Conclusion

It is but according to ancient customs that the new truth should force its
way amid riot and great anger.

— W. B. Yeats, "On Taking *The Playboy* to London"

In 1899 when Edward Martyn expressed anxiety over *The Countess Cathleen*, Yeats was willing not only to see the play vetted
by two Catholic clergy but also to change what was deemed
offensive. At the beginning of the century, the advanced nationalist
press argued for a distinctly Irish censorship, "sanitary measures," to
purge the stage of pernicious foreign influences. Progressive authors,
including George Moore, feared that censorship was inevitable. At
century's end, the opposite was true: the consensus, especially among
arts practitioners, was that censorship was not merely "evitable," but
inherently dangerous. By the century's end, the very charge of censorship carried with it a sense of injustice.

From the beginning of the twentieth century, the freedom of the
theatre from censorship was an oft-enunciated and distinctly Irish
principle. Yeats staked a revolutionary claim to put Irish theatre outside the purview of institutional control at a time when censorship
was nearly universally accepted. But what freedom of the theatre
meant—the right of playwrights to be heard as opposed to the right
of the audiences to respond—became the subject of intense debate.

Ironically, protests, especially organized protests, against plays by those who sought a play's withdrawal by management or its boycott by potential audiences almost invariably had exactly the opposite effect: throngs of often unlikely ticket buyers besieged the box office. Performances sold out. Runs were extended. As Annabel Patterson notes, "Modern censorship reveals its most ancient and insoluble predicament: that controls against freedom of expression are as likely to increase resistance as to weaken it, and to increase the value of works that if disregarded by the authorities would become insignificant to their audience also."[1] Yeats and Gregory, Mac Liammóir, and those like Phyllis Ryan who produced the controversial plays of the fifties were astute spin doctors who recognized the value of publicity, both favorable and damning. When press coverage moved from a dramatic review to news stories, theatres often welcomed the unpaid publicity that brought full houses.

The meaning of "Irish" was often contested on stage and off, especially in these controversies over theatre censorship, not least because of its importance in mapping what was characteristically Irish or at least not British. Yeats's *The Countess Cathleen,* the ILT, the Abbey, and Synge's *The Playboy* were all denounced as un-Irish. In 1909 there was considerable debate about whether Shaw was Irish. The nature and scope of an expressly Irish, institutional censorship was contested through most of the 1920s. Many wanted an expressly Catholic, pervasive censorship; in the 1930s they got one, at least of printed materials. Only after the arbitrary, absolutist Emergency censorship and the wrenching, destructive battles over stage censorship of the 1950s, was the struggle for institutional control over the Irish stage decisively lost. More recently, questions analogous to those raised in other countries—especially the appropriate use of state funding—beset theatre controversy in Ireland.

Comparable theatre protests in other English-speaking countries in earlier centuries were typically provoked by seating policies, increased ticket cost, or the appearance of foreign actors or playwrights. The cultivation of a new, specifically targeted audience, especially at the beginning and end of the twentieth century, created an unstable and sometimes explosive dynamic among the plays, those who brought them to the stage, patrons (including the state), audiences, and the general public. Although changes in the horizon of expectations and in the material conditions of theatregoing at the end of the twentieth century, as at the end of the nineteenth, destabilized the relationship between the audience and the performance, Irish theatrical disorder owed to what was performed or at least what audiences thought was being performed on stage. While these controversies attest to the vitality of the Irish stage and its national theatre, attempts to censor plays in Ireland were hardly without deleterious effects.

Like all controls over the stage, attempts at theatre censorship were most minatory to small companies that, always in the shadow of the Abbey, played a vital role in bringing international drama to the Irish public, especially in the first two thirds of the century. The damage done to the Pike Theatre, for instance, was not only in the arrest, incarceration, and protracted trial of Alan Simpson, but in the fact that after *Bloomsday* and O'Casey's *The Drums of Father Ned* were excluded from the Dublin Theatre Festival, O'Casey and Beckett withdrew their plays from the Pike company and from Ireland. The Pike did not survive. Nor did the Globe Theatre Company, which produced *The Ginger Man* and "was ruined by [its] collapse."[2] Beckett's plays remained inaccessible on the Irish stage for eighteen months; the loss of all of O'Casey's plays to professional productions in Ireland lasted six long years (from January 1958 to January 1964). More difficult to gauge is how often producers were intimidated, as Sam Wanamaker was in 1958, from mounting or touring productions of potentially controversial plays in Ireland.

In some instances the established powers, especially clerical ones, either took decisive action or fomented protest (or allowed it to be fomented). In one notable instance, under the exigencies to assure neutrality during the Emergency, the Free State acted decisively to ban Lennox Robinson's *Roly Poly*. Efforts to impose an extra-legal, ad hoc stage censorship were usually enacted not from above, but from below—by groups that were or believed themselves to be excluded from the privileges presumed by those responsible for the play. Marginalized constituencies such as Catholic university students in 1899 or republican widows in 1926 consciously staged now famous protests. The students from Dublin University who booed

The Countess Cathleen were probably no worse—certainly, neither more violent nor more disruptive—than their counterparts from Trinity recruited to support *The Playboy* who fare less conspicuously, if at all, in most Irish theatrical histories.

Perhaps most unexpected (and most difficult to document) is the censorship exerted by actors, especially in the century's early decades. As viciously as playwrights were maligned, actors typically bore the brunt of an audience's outrage: they were the ones at whom missiles and abuse were hurled in the most violent protests. The departure of Dudley Digges and Maire Quinn from the NTS over Synge's "In the Shadow of the Glen," exemplifies the actors' rejection of certain lines, roles, or, in this case, an entire play. In the century's first decade that many of the actors were unpaid seems to have fuelled their subversive power to challenge the authority of dramatist, director, and producer. In 1926, O'Casey aligned the actors' censorious impulses with contemporaneous moral crusades by referring to them as a Vigilance Committee.

Since the nineteenth century, Irish theatre sought to define itself in contradistinction to British theatre. It sought to drive a stake through the heart of the undead stage Irishman, manipulated and redefined images of the Irish. Nowhere is the incendiary power of comedy more clearly seen than in the audience uprisings against Synge, Birmingham, and O'Casey, who consciously manipulated stereotypes and stage images of the Irish. That their comic characters provoked laughter only exacerbated the anger against them. Their portrayal of female characters that failed to conform to idealized models of Irish womanhood further envenomed the protests against their plays and ad hominem attacks against them. On the one hand, the comedies of Synge, Birmingham, and O'Casey obviously contributed to the disproportionate contribution of Irish theatre to English-speaking theatre throughout the twentieth century. On the other hand, the fluid relationship between audience and performance elicited vocal although rarely violent responses.

As the century progressed, Irish theatre celebrated its freedom and recalled the attendant notoriety for theatrical disorder with increasing self-referentiality. Perhaps more in the telling than in fact, both the freedom of the theatre and the penchant for theatrical disturbances became well-established and carefully constructed features of Irish theatre. The propensity to protest or to riot so often attributed to Irish audiences became the best known tradition of twentieth century Irish drama, accreting self-referentiality as the century progressed. *The Playboy* referred to *The Countess Cathleen,* *The Plough* to *The Playboy.* By the fifties, the tradition was well-entrenched, at least in the press coverage. The eagerness to identify a tradition of Irish theatrical disorder continues unabated today. An article in the *New York Times* on 21 June 2001, "A Vigorous Tug of War for Ireland's National Theatre," concerning the possible relocation of the Abbey Theatre, began by recalling the riots associated with *The Playboy* and *The Plough,* as if readers who knew nothing else about the Irish stage would surely recall its celebrated theatrical disorders.

Notes

Introduction

1. H.P.W., *Sligo Theatre: A Statement of the Proceedings Taken by the Rev. W. C. Armstrong* (Dublin: printed for the author, 1824), 10.

2. Ibid., 21.

3. See Roy Foster, *The Irish Story: Telling Tales and Making It Up in Ireland* (New York: Penguin, 2002), especially "'When the Newspapers Have Forgotten Me': Yeats, Obituarists and Irishness," 80–94.

4. Richard Hayes, "The Genial Censor," *The Bell* 3 (November 1944): 111.

5. Gustave Le Bon, *The Crowd* (New York: Viking, 1960), 106.

6. Roland Barthes, "Baudelaire's Theatre," in *Critical Essays,* trans. Richard Howard (Evanston, Ill.: Northwestern University Press, 1972), 26.

7. See Anne Ubersfeld, *Reading Theatre,* trans. Frank Collins, ed. Paul Perron and Patrick Debbèche (Toronto: University of Toronto Press, 1999); and Patrice Pavis, *Theatre at the Crossroads of Culture,* trans. Loren Kruger (New York: Routledge, 1992).

8. See Adrian Frazier, *Behind the Scenes: Yeats, Horniman, and the Struggle for the Abbey Theatre* (Berkeley: University of California Press, 1990), 75–77, 207–27. Frazier convincingly demonstrates that Annie Horniman censored Abbey activities "either by planting self-censorship in the minds of the directors, censoring the NTS [National Theatre Society] activities herself, or seizing upon a pretext to close the Abbey" (207).

9. Alec Craig, *The Banned Books of England and Other Countries: A Study of the Conception of Literary Obscenity* (Westport, Conn.: Greenwood Press, 1977), 131.

10. Norman St. John-Stevas, *Obscenity and the Law* (London: Secker and Warburg, 1956), 178.

1. Theatrical Censorship and Disorder in Ireland

1. John Palmer, *The Censor and the Theatres* (London: T. Fisher Unwin, 1912), 25.

2. Vincent J. Liesenfeld, *The Licensing Act of 1737* (Madison: University of Wisconsin Press, 1984), 16.

3. Ibid., 9.

4. John Johnston, *The Lord Chamberlain's Blue Pencil* (London: Hodder & Stoughton, 1990), 42.

5. Quoted in Russell Jackson, ed., *Victorian Theatre: The Theatre in Its Time* (New York: New Amsterdam, 1989), 304.

6. George Colman, *Report of the Select Committee Appointed to Inquire into the Laws Affecting Dramatic Literature, 1832*, Series of British Parliamentary Papers, Stage and Theatre 1, ed. Marilyn L. Norstedt (Shannon: Irish University Press, 1968), 66.

7. See Dan H. Laurence and Nicholas Grene, eds. *Shaw, Lady Gregory, and the Abbey: A Correspondence and a Record* (Gerrards Cross: Colin Smythe, 1993), 17.

8. Richard Findlater, *Banned! A Review of Theatrical Censorship in Britain* (London: Macgibbon and Kee, 1967), 78.

9. The infamy of Wilde's *Salome* grew over the next three decades. In 1918, J. T. Grein attempted to mount a private performance to benefit war charities with the notorious Maud Allan in the title role. The production attracted the attention of Pemberton Billing, who launched a campaign against the play as not only immoral but also seditious. See William Tydeman and Steven Price, eds., *Wilde "Salome"* (Cambridge: Cambridge University Press, 1996), 78–86; and Findlater, *Banned!* 95–96.

10. In at least one instance, Arthur Wing Pinero's *The Wife Without a Smile* (1904), the Lord Chamberlain withdrew his license after viewing the play's production. See Nicholas de Jongh, *Politics, Prudery and Perversions: The Censoring of the English Stage, 1901–1968* (London: Methuen, 2000), 35–36.

11. *Report from the Select Committee on Theatres and Places of Entertainment* (London: Her Majesty's Stationery Office, 1892), 233. The 1892 joint select committee accepted Gunn's uncorroborated testimony on 11 May 1892 as authoritative.

12. "A Copy of the Clauses in the Last Patent for the Theatre Royal, Dublin," 1909, E67, P. S. O'Hegarty Collection, Kansas University, Lawrence, Ks. (hereafter cited as O'H/KU).

13. "Dublin Corporation Act 1890," *Local Acts*, 53 & 54 Victoria, c. ccxlvi, sections 54 and 55 (18 August 1890), vol. 7, 24. The final report of the joint select committee investigating the licensing of plays in 1892 concluded that any problems in Ireland were negligible:

> There are very few theatres or music-halls in Ireland. In Dublin, no theatre can be established except by Royal Letters patent. In Belfast, the only theatre in the town is licensed by the mayor under 8 & 9 Vict. c. 142 (Local); in Cork, the only theatre is licensed by the corporation; and the same practice appears to prevail in the few other towns in which such places of amusement exist. In Dublin, the Dublin Corporation Act of

1890 gave considerable powers to the corporation, and we have been informed that it is in contemplation to adopt the Public Health Acts Amendment Act. We have no reason to think that the public or the managers of theatres and places of entertainment in Ireland are dissatisfied with the present state of the general law on these subjects (*Report from the Select Committee on Theatres and Places of Entertainment,* p. iv).

14. "Dublin Corporation Act 1890," This legislation is primarily concerned with public safety, specifically fire regulations, in "places of public resort . . . kept open for public dancing[,] music[,] or other public entertainment."

15. "Last Patent for the Theatre Royal," 1909, E67, O'H/KU.

16. "An Act for Regulating the Stage in the City and County of Dublin," 26 Geo. III, c. 57 (Ireland).

17. See La Tourette Stockwell, *Dublin Theatres and Theatre Customs, 1637–1820* (Kingsport, Tenn.: Kingsport, 1938), 152–67; Christopher J. Wheatley, *Beneath Ïerne's Banners: Irish Protestant Drama of the Restoration and Eighteenth Century* (Notre Dame, Ind.: University of Notre Dame Press, 1999), 123–26; and Helen M. Burke, *Riotous Performances: The Struggle for Hegemony in the Irish Theatre, 1712–1784* (Notre Dame, Ind.: University of Notre Dame Press, 2003), 285–90.

18. 26 Geo. III, c. 57 (Ireland).

19. See Alan Browne, ed., *Masters, Midwives and Ladies-in-Waiting: The Rotunda Hospital, 1745–1995* (Dublin: A. & A. Farmar, 1995), and Ian Campbell Ross, ed., *Public Virtue, Public Love: The Early Years of the Dublin Lying-In Hospital, The Rotunda* (Dublin: O'Brien, 1986). To finance the Rotunda, Bartholomew Mosse devised a variety of fund-raising schemes, including entertainments, lotteries, and paid admissions to the gardens that generated ten times as much as private subscriptions.

20. "Last Patent for the Theatre Royal," 1909, E67, O'H/KU.

21. Stockwell, *Dublin Theatres,* 309.

22. Francis R. Wolfe, *Theatres in Ireland,* 2d ed. (Dublin: Humphrey and Armour, 1898), 26.

23. Quoted in Richard Moody, *The Astor Place Riot* (Bloomington: Indiana University Press, 1958), 16. See Stockwell, *Dublin Theatres,* 93–101.

24. Esther K. Sheldon, *Thomas Sheridan of Smock-Alley* (Princeton, N.J.: Princeton University Press, 1967), 115. Similar reforms were not instituted at Drury Lane and Covent Garden until the 1760s.

25. See "The Marquess Wellesley's Visit to the Theatre," *Freeman's Journal,* 16 December 1822, 3; "The Recent Outrage," *Freeman's Journal,* 19 December 1822, 3; "The Conspiracy," *Freeman's Journal,* 3 February 1823, 3; and "The Trial," *Freeman's Journal,* 10 February 1823, 3. On 3 February 1823 *Freeman's Journal* published a special supplement on the Bottle Riot. See

also Mary D. Condon, "The Dublin Riots of 1822 and Catholic Emancipation" (master's thesis, University of Southern California, 1950), 54–103.

26. There are several other works that deal with specific dimensions of censorship in Ireland: Louisa Burns-Bisogno, *Censoring Irish Nationalism: The British, Irish and American Suppression of Republican Images in Film and Television, 1909–1995* (Jefferson, N.C.: McFarland, 1997); Brendan Ryan, *Keeping Us in the Dark: Censorship and Freedom of Information in Ireland* (Dublin: Gill and Macmillan, 1995); Kieran Woodman, *Media Control in Ireland, 1923–1983* (Carbondale: Southern Illinois University Press, 1985); Patrick Smyth and Ellen Hazelkorn, eds., *Let in the Light: Censorship, Secrecy, and Democracy* (Dingle, Kerry: Brandon, 1993). See also Ciaran Carty, *Confessions of a Sewer Rat: A Personal History of Censorship and the Irish Cinema* (Dublin: New Island Books, 1995).

27. Many film chains in the United States will not exhibit films rated NC-17.

28. F. O'Reilly, *The Problem of Undesirable Printed Matter: Some Suggested Remedies* (Dublin: Catholic Truth Society of Ireland, 1926), 17.

29. Peter Connolly, *No Bland Facility: Selected Writings on Literature, Religion and Censorship,* ed. James H. Murphy (Gerrards Cross: Colin Smythe, 1991), 66.

30. Quoted in Donal Ó Drisceoil, *Censorship in Ireland, 1939–1945: Neutrality, Politics, and Society* (Cork: Cork University Press, 1996), 31.

31. Quoted in Ó Drisceoil, *Censorship in Ireland,* 33.

32. Quoted in Michael Adams, *Censorship: The Irish Experience.* Tuscaloosa: University of Alabama Press, 1968), 150.

33. Annabel Patterson, *Censorship and Interpretation: The Conditions of Writing and Reading in Early Modern England* (Madison: University of Wisconsin Press, 1984), 52–53.

34. Michel Foucault, *Discipline and Punish: The Birth of the Prison* (New York: Vintage, 1995). See also Francis Hackett, *The Invisible Censor* (1921; reprint, Freeport, N.Y.: Books for Libraries, 1968).

35. Several recent studies of censorship, especially of its authorial and collegial manifestations, center on English drama and literature in the late sixteenth and early seventeenth centuries. Especially valuable are Annabel Patterson, *Censorship and Interpretation;* Richard Burt, *Licensed by Authority: Ben Jonson and the Discourses of Censorship* (Ithaca, N.Y.: Cornell University Press, 1993); and Janet Clare, *"Art Made Tongue-Tied by Authority": Elizabethan and Jacobean Dramatic Censorship,* 2d ed. (Manchester: Manchester University Press, 1999).

36. Sheldon, *Thomas Sheridan,* 81.

37. F. S. L. Lyons, *Culture and Anarchy in Ireland, 1890–1939: From the Fall of Parnell to the Death of W. B. Yeats* (New York: Oxford University Press, 1979), 137.

38. Quoted in Philip B. Ryan, *The Lost Theatres of Dublin* (Westbury, Wiltshire: Badger, 1998), 13.

39. Andrew Davies, *Other Theatres: The Development of Alternative and Experimental Theatre in Britain* (Totowa, N.J.: Barnes and Noble, 1987), 47;

40. Ó Drisceoil, *Censorship in Ireland,* 53.

41. Quoted in Sean O'Casey, *The Letters of Sean O'Casey,* vol. 3: *1955–1958,* ed. David Krause (Washington, D.C.: Catholic University of America Press, 1989), 66.

2. Theatre, Art, and Censorship

1. John Palmer, *The Censor and the Theatres,* 28.

2. St. John Ervine, *The Theatre in My Time* (London: Rich and Cowan, 1933), 15–16.

3. Ervine, *The Theatre in My Time,* 18.

4. See Gary Owens, "Nationalism without Words: Symbolism and Ritual Behaviour in the Repeal 'Monster Meetings' of 1843–45," in *Irish Popular Culture, 1650–1850,* ed. James S. Donnelly Jr. and Kerby A. Miller (Dublin: Irish Academic Press, 1999), 242–69.

5. See Marc Baer, *Theatre and Disorder in Late Georgian London* (Oxford: Clarendon Press, 1992), 195. There are a surprising number of links between theatre and the Irish temperance movement. The Dublin Coffee Palace, home to several productions by the Fay brothers, was a temperance hall. The Church of Ireland Temperance Society owned Molesworth Hall. Father Theobald Mathew (1790–1856) provides an even more substantial link.

6. A similar prohibition against theatregoing applied to Catholic priests in Britain. See Ervine, *The Theatre in My Time,* 23.

7. James Cousins and Margaret Cousins, *We Two Together* (Madras: Ganesh, 1950), 64.

8. Yeats to Gregory, 11 March 1898, W. B. Yeats, *The Collected Letters of W. B. Yeats,* vol. 2: *1896–1900,* ed. Warwick Gould, John Kelly, and Deirdre Toomey (Oxford: Oxford University Press, 1997), 198.

9. Robert Hogan and James Kilroy, eds., *The Irish Literary Theatre, 1899–1901,* vol. 1 of *The Modern Irish Drama: A Documentary History* (Dublin: Dolmen Press, 1975), 132.

10. Gabriel Fallon, quoted in Philip B. Ryan, *Lost Theatres of Dublin,* 128.

11. John Denvir, *Denvir's Monthly* 24 (December 1903): iv.

12. The Tivoli Variety Theatre, with a capacity of 1,252, was also known as Conciliation Hall. The Mechanics' Institute was formerly known as the Hibernian Theatre of Varieties, 1874–1902; later, it and a former morgue provided the site of the first Abbey Theatre.

13. Mouillot, H. H. Morrell, and the other owners hired the renowned architect Frank Matcham to remodel Leinster Hall. See Philip B. Ryan, *Lost Theatres of Dublin,* 23.

14. Eugene Watters and Matthew Murtagh, *Infinite Variety: Dan Lowery's Music Hall, 1879–97* (Dublin: Gill and Macmillan, 1975), 134.

15. Quoted in *Collected Letters of W. B. Yeats,* 2:223–24.

16. 26 Geo. III, c. 57 (Ireland).

17. See chapter 1, note 19.

18. Dawson Byrne, *The Story of Ireland's National Theatre: The Abbey Theatre, Dublin* (Dublin: Talbot Press, 1929), 38, 40.

19. Wolfe, *Theatres in Ireland,* 19, 17.

20. See Maria Tymoczko, ed., "Tableaux Vivants in Ireland at the Turn of the Century," *Nineteenth-Century Theatre* 23 (1995): 90–110.

21. Augusta Gregory, *Our Irish Theatre: A Chapter of Autobiography* (Gerrards Cross: Colin Smythe, 1972), 24.

22. Roy Foster, *W. B. Yeats: A Life. I: The Apprentice Mage, 1865–1914.* (Oxford: Oxford University Press, 1997), 188.

23. E. R. Norman, *Anti-Catholicism in Victorian England* (London: George Allen and Unwin, 1968), 17–18.

24. G. C. Duggan, *The Stage Irishman: A History of the Irish Play and Stage Characters from the Earliest Times* (London: Longmans, 1937).

25. Watters and Murtagh, *Infinite Variety,* 164.

26. Richard Allen Cave, "Staging the Irishman," in *Acts of Supremacy: The British Empire and the Stage, 1790–1930,* ed. J. S. Bratton, et al. (New York: Manchester University Press, 1991), 69.

27. See Séamus de Búrca, *The Queen's Royal Theatre Dublin, 1829–1969* (Dublin: de Búrca, 1983), 3; Cheryl Herr, *For the Land They Loved: Irish Political Melodrama, 1890–1925* (Syracuse, N.Y.: Syracuse University Press, 1991), 16–19.

28. *Irish Playgoer,* 15 February 1900, 12. The phrase was the motto of the *Nation.*

29. W. J. Lawrence, "Irish Characters in English Dramatic Literature," *Gentleman's Magazine,* n.s., 45 (August 1890): 191.

30. Herr, *For the Land They Loved,* 62.

31. William Barrett, "Irish Drama." *New Ireland Review* 3 (March 1895): 38–39.

32. W. A. Henderson, "Three Centuries of the Stage Literature of Ireland," *New Ireland Review* 7 (May 1897): 168.

33. Richard Eyre, *Changing Stages: A History of Twentieth-Century British Theatre, British Broadcasting Corporation* (BBC) broadcast, 12 October 2000.

34. William Grattan Flood, "The Inventor of the Stage Irishman," *New Ireland Review* 23 (April 1905): 118.

35. "We will show that Ireland is not the home of buffoonery and of easy sentiment." Quoted in Gregory, *Our Irish Theatre*, 20, and in Hogan and Kilroy, eds., *The Irish Literary Theatre*, 25.

36. See Herr, *For the Land They Loved*, 62–64, and Stephen Watt, *Joyce, O'Casey, and the Irish Popular Theatre* (Syracuse, N.Y.: Syracuse University Press, 1991), 84–88.

37. "Bogus Irish Drama," *New Ireland Review* 8 (September 1897): 62–64.

38. Henderson, "Three Centuries of the Stage Literature," 178.

39. Barrett, "Irish Drama," 40.

40. James W. Flannery, "High Ideals and the Reality of the Marketplace: A Financial Record of the Early Abbey Theatre," *Studies* 71 (Autumn 1982): 248.

41. See Karen Vandevelde, "Outside the Abbey: The Irish National Theatres, 1897–1913" (Ph.D. diss., National University of Ireland, Galway, 2001); and Mary Trotter, *Ireland's National Theaters: Political Performance and the Origins of the Irish Dramatic Movement* (Syracuse, N.Y.: Syracuse University Press, 2001). In "High Ideals" Flannery states that "from the very beginning of the Irish dramatic movement the principle of subsidy was established" (247).

42. Maire Nic Shiubhlaigh, *The Splendid Years; Recollections of Maire Nic Shiubhlaigh* (Dublin: Duffy, 1955), 73.

43. George Moore, "Is the Theatre a Place of Amusement?" *Beltaine* 2 (February 1900): 9–10.

44. "All Ireland," *United Irishman*, 25 March 1899, 1.

45. William Patrick Ryan, *The Irish Literary Revival: Its History, Pioneers and Possibilities* (1894; reprint, New York: Lemma, 1970), 22.

46. "From the Study Chair," *New Ireland Review* 1 (1894): 393.

47. Yeats to William Sharp, 20 November 1897, *Collected Letters of W. B. Yeats*, 2: 148.

48. Elizabeth, Countess of Fingall, *Seventy Years Young: Memories of Elizabeth, Countess of Fingall* (New York: Dutton, 1939), 235.

49. W. B. Yeats, "Windlestraws," *Samhain* 1 (October 1901): 4.

50. Edward Martyn, quoted in Hogan and Kilroy, *Irish Literary Theatre*, 26.

51. "'The Slave Market at Cairo' Exhibition," *Freeman's Journal*, 10 May 1899, 2.

52. The copyright performance was typically little more than a reading, without costumes or scenery, staged to preserve the author's rights. Although the Dramatic Copyright Act of 1833 and the American Copyright Act of 1891 advanced the dramatist's rights, printing a play before its first public performance was still an invitation to theatrical piracy.

53. W. B. Yeats, "Introduction," *Countess Cathleen and Various Legends*

and Lyrics (London: T. Fisher Unwin, 1892), 7–8. Quoted in James W. Flannery, *W. B. Yeats and the Idea of a Theatre: The Early Abbey Theatre in Theory and Practice* (New Haven, Conn.: Yale University Press, 1976), 143.

54. F. Hugh O'Donnell, *Souls for Gold! A Pseudo-Celtic Drama in Dublin* (London: Nassau Press, 1899), is appended to *Collected Letters of W. B. Yeats,* 2: 674–80.

55. See Michael J. Sidnell and Wayne K. Chapman, eds., *"The Countess Cathleen" Manuscript Materials* (Ithaca, N.Y.: Cornell University Press, 1999).

56. Michael J. Sidnell, "*The Countess Cathleen* as a Study in Theatrical Genre," *South Carolina Review* 32 (Fall 1999): 44.

57. O.Z., "From a Modern Irish Portrait Gallery—W. B. Yeats," *New Ireland Review,* 2 (December 1894): 658. Yeats himself corroborated this criticism in *Dramatis Personae, 1896–1902.* See Wayne K. Chapman, "'The Countess Cathleen' Row of 1899 and the Revisions of 1901 and 1911," *Yeats Annual,* ed. Warwick Gould, No. 11 (London: Macmillan, 1995), 110.

58. Yeats to Dr. William Barry, 24 March 1899, *Collected Letters of W. B. Yeats,* 2:379.

59. In "The Day of the Rabblement," James Joyce wrote of Yeats's "treacherous instinct of adaptability." See James Joyce, *James Joyce: Occasional, Critical, and Political Writing,* ed. Kevin Barry (Oxford: Oxford University Press, 2000), 51.

60. See Herr, *For the Land They Loved,* 47–50.

61. "'The Countess Cathleen' Controversy," *Collected Letters of W. B. Yeats,* 2:672.

62. Philip B. Ryan, *Lost Theatres of Dublin,* 149.

63. Baer, *Theatre and Disorder,* 11.

64. Mary Colum, *The Life and the Dream,* rev. ed. (Garden City, N.Y.: Doubleday, 1947), 103.

65. Padraic Colum, "Early Days of the Irish Theatre," *Dublin Magazine* 25 (1950): 13.

66. Cousins and Cousins, *We Two Together,* 96.

67. Declan Kiberd, "The Fall of the Stage Irishman," in *Genres of the Irish Literary Revival,* ed. Ronald Schleifer (Dublin: Wolfhound, 1980), 44.

68. See "The Countess Cathleen Controversy," in *Collected Letters of W. B. Yeats,* 2:669–80.

69. Quoted in Hogan and Kilroy, *Irish Literary Theatre,* 38.

70. Ibid., 39.

71. "Irish Literary Theatre," *Irish Times,* 9 May 1899, 5.

72. "Notes," *An Claidheamh Soluis,* 13 May 1899, 136.

73. "Notes," *An Claidheamh Soluis,* 20 May 1899, 153.

74. Peter Bailey, "Custom, Capital and Culture in the Victorian Music

Hall," in *Nineteenth-Century England,* ed. Robert D. Storch (New York: St. Martin's Press, 1982), 193.

75. "The Irish Literary Theatre," *Freeman's Journal,* 9 May 1899, 5. The omission of the word "organised" from Hogan's and Kilroy's excerpt from this review (*Irish Literary Theatre,* 41) is significant because whether the demonstrations were preplanned or spontaneous was a pivotal question, especially during the disorders attending *The Playboy.*

76. Joseph Holloway, *Joseph Holloway's Abbey Theatre: A Selection from His Unpublished Journal "Impressions of a Dublin Playgoer,"* eds. Robert Hogan and Michael J. O'Neill (Carbondale: Southern Illinois University Press, 1967), 6.

77. "Letter from University Students," *Freeman's Journal,* 10 May 1899, 6.

78. C. P. Curran, *Under the Receding Wave* (Dublin: Gill and Macmillan, 1970), 104. Curran notes that "the letter was signed amongst others by Tom Kettle, Frank Skeffington, and George Clancy. Other signatories included a future President of University College, Cork, the first Chief Justice of the Irish Free State and one of his colleagues on the Supreme Court" (101).

79. *United Irishman,* 13 May 1899, 2.

80. WBY [W. B. Yeats], "Letter to the Editor," *Morning Leader,* 13 May 1899, 3; *Collected Letters of W. B. Yeats,* 2:410.

81. George O'Neill, "The Inauguration of the Irish Literary Theatre," *New Ireland Review* 11 (June 1899): 249.

82. "'Irish' Literary Theatre," *An Claidheamh Soluis,* 20 May 1899, 157; "All Ireland," *United Irishman,* 6 May 1899, 1; "All Ireland," *United Irishman,* 13 May 1899, 1.

83. "All Ireland," *United Irishman,* 13 May 1899, 1; F. J. F. [Frank J. Fay], "Irish Drama at the Theatre Royal," *United Irishman,* 8 July 1899, 1.

84. Holloway, *Abbey Theatre,* 7–8.

85. George Moore, "Irish Literary Theatre," *Samhain* 1 (October 1901): 12.

86. Francis Bickley, *J. M. Synge and the Irish Dramatic Movement* (London: Constable, 1912), 70.

87. Cousins and Cousins, *We Two Together,* 57.

88. T. W. Rolleston, "Letter," *Freeman's Journal,* 10 May 1899, 5.

89. James Joyce, "The Day of the Rabblement," *James Joyce,* 51.

90. Max Beerbohm, "In Dublin," *Saturday Review,* 13 May 1899, 587.

91. George O'Neill, "The Inauguration of the Irish Literary Theatre," *New Ireland Review* 11 (June 1899): 246.

92. Yeats to Gregory, 10 April 1900, *Collected Letters of W. B. Yeats,* 2:510.

93. WBY [W. B. Yeats], "To the Guarantors for a 'Celtic' Theatre," [before 16 July 1897], *Collected Letters of W. B. Yeats,* 2:124.

3. "The Evil Genius"

1. Susan Bennett, *Theatre Audiences: A Theory of Production and Reception* (New York: Routledge, 1990), 15.

2. W. B. Yeats, "The Reform of the Theatre," *Samhain* 3 (September 1903): 9.

3. Padraic Colum, *The Road Round Ireland* (New York: Macmillan, 1926), 272.

4. Kathleen M. O'Brennan, "The Drama as a Nationalising Force," *Sinn Féin,* 10 November 1906, 3. Two weeks later another article under the same title, this one by T. B. Cronin, appeared in *Sinn Féin.*

5. W. B. Yeats, "Windlestraws," *Samhain,* 1 (October 1901): 3.

6. Nic Shiubhlaigh, *The Splendid Years,* 4.

7. W. G. Fay and Catherine Carswell, *The Fays of the Abbey Theatre: An Autobiographical Record* (New York: Harcourt, Brace, 1935), 67.

8. Nic Shiubhlaigh, *The Splendid Years,* 10.

9. Seamus O'Sullivan, *The Rose and the Bottle and Other Essays* (Dublin: Talbot Press, 1946), 120.

10. AE, "The Abbey Theatre," in *The Living Torch,* ed. Monk Gibbon (London: Macmillan, 1937), 247–48.

11. Padraic Colum, "Early Days of the Irish Theatre," *Dublin Magazine,* 24 (1949): 14–15.

12. Cousins and Cousins, *We Two Together,* 64.

13. Mary Colum, *Life and the Dream,* 95.

14. Holloway, *Abbey Theatre,* 25.

15. Quoted in Robert Hogan, Richard Burnham, and Daniel P. Poteet, eds., *The Rise of the Realists 1910–1915,* vol. 4 of *The Modern Irish Drama: A Documentary History* (Dublin: Dolmen Press, 1979), 145.

16. Padraic Colum, "The Early Days of the Irish Theatre (Continued)" *Dublin Magazine,* 25 (1950): 20.

17. Temperance halls sometimes doubled as "Coffee Palaces"—places where people could socialize without the temptations of alcohol. Despite the desperate financial constraints on theatre companies, various organizations often presented plays to raise funds. As Fay and Carswell note: "When the demand for private shows slackened, the [Ormond Dramatic] society offered its services to various temperance societies to enable them to get funds to carry on their work" (*The Fays of the Abbey Theatre,* 25).

18. Marvin Carlson, *Places of Performance: The Semiotics of Theatre Architecture* (Ithaca, N.Y.: Cornell University Press, 1989), 9.

19. *A Twelfth-Century Pageant Play: Portraying Scenes of Irish History* (Dublin: Hodges, Figgis, 1907).

20. In 1915 two editions of a "Souvenir of a Public [O'Donovan Rossa's] Funeral," compiled by a committee chaired by Brian O'Higgins writing under the pen name Brian na Banba, offered readers a "complete account, fully illustrated," D262, O'H/KU.

21. "Queen's Theatre: Letters Patent," 21 September 1951, MS 33,685, National Library of Ireland (hereafter cited as NLI).

22. Dawson Byrne, *Story of Ireland's National Theatre*, 41.

23. Yeats to Gregory, 4 August 1904, *The Collected Letters of W. B. Yeats*, vol. 3: *1901–1904*, ed. John Kelly and Ronald Schuchard (Oxford: Clarendon Press, 1994), 631.

24. Peter Kavanagh, *The Story of the Abbey Theatre: From Its Origins in 1899 to the Present* (New York: Devin-Adair, 1950), 216.

25. See Patrice Pavis, *Theatre at the Crossroads of Culture*, trans. Loren Kruger (New York: Routledge, 1992), 79–82. Deterritorialized language, the connection of the individual to the political, and "a collective enunciation" characterize Pavis's minor theatres.

26. See Nic Shiubhlaigh, *The Splendid Years*, 69–73; Frazier, *Behind the Scenes*, 123–28.

27. Nic Shiubhlaigh, *The Splendid Years*, 2.

28. Nic Shiubhlaigh implies that she replaced Maire Quinn in *In the Shadow of the Glen* (42). Ann Saddlemyer asserts that Digges "refused to perform" in Synge's play. See "Finding a Theatre," in *The Collected Letters of John Millington Synge, 1871–1907*, vol. 1, ed. Ann Saddlemyer (Oxford: Clarendon, 1983), 62.

29. George Moore, "The Irish Literary Theatre: Interview with Mr. George Moore," *Freeman's Journal*, 6 November 1901, 5.

30. The play was performed at the Arts Theatre on 2 October 1930 with Ian Fleming, the creator of James Bond, in the role of Jesus.

31. Adrian Frazier, *George Moore: 1852–1933* (New Haven, Conn.: Yale University Press, 2000), 313.

32. Ibid., 305.

33. George Moore, "The Irish Literary Theatre: Interview with Mr. George Moore," *Freeman's Journal*, 6 November 1901, 5.

34. Yeats, "Windlestraws," *Samhain* 1 (October 1901): 6–7. Within a few years, many of the Catholic clergy grew suspicious and then scornful. When Father Dineen's *Creideamh agus Gorta* was performed in 1905, he "refused to take calls (on the Abbey stage) for 'Author' because he wanted no further connection with the theatre's reputation for 'irreligion.'" See Ben Levitas, *Theatre and Nation: Irish Drama and Cultural Nationalism, 1890–1916* (Oxford: Clarendon Press, 2002), 104.

35. Yeats, "The Freedom of the Theatre," *United Irishman*, special supplement, 1 November 1902.

36. Thomas Kettle, "Mr. Yeats and the Freedom of the Theatre,"

United Irishman, 15 November 1902. Kettle went further to assert that the dramatist "will manifest the essential nullity of evil—the necessary triumph of good." Kettle was, in turn, attacked the next week by Maurice C. Joy in "Mr. Yeats and the Freedom of the Theatre," *United Irishman,* 29 November 1902, 10.

37. Yeats, "The Reform of the Theatre," *Samhain,* 3 (September 1903): 11.

38. See Watt, *Joyce,* 82–88.

39. George Steiner, *The Death of Tragedy* (New York: Hill and Wang, 1961), 8.

40. J. W. Whitbread, *Wolfe Tone* in Herr, *For the Land They Loved,* 257.

41. Fay and Carswell, *The Fays of the Abbey Theater,* 200.

42. Quoted in Byrne, *Story of Ireland's National Theatre,* 67.

43. See Frazier, *Behind the Scenes,* 64–68.

44. David H. Greene and Edward M. Stephens, *J. M. Synge: 1871–1909,* rev. ed. (New York: New York University Press, 1989), 169.

45. Una Chaudhuri, *Staging Place: The Geography of Modern Drama* (Ann Arbor: University of Michigan Press, 1997), 55.

46. Quoted in Byrne, *Story of Ireland's National Theatre,* 54–55.

47. Brenna Katz Clarke, *The Emergence of the Irish Peasant Play at the Abbey Theatre* (Ann Arbor: UMI Research Press, 1982), 44.

48. Many of these one-acters were in the acknowledged tradition of medieval mystery plays. Lady Gregory's *The Gaol Gate,* for instance, takes on an allegorical dimension as the wife and mother, two Irish Marys who recall biblical counterparts, of the Christ-like Denis Cahel. Her audience may not have known of the tenth-century "Quem Quaritis?" but authors, publicists, and critics used the label "miracle or mystery play." Localized in both time and space, these miracle plays often conflated religious faith and nationalistic sentiment.

49. Colum, *Life and the Dream,* 97.

50. John Denvir, *Denvir's Monthly* 24 (October 1903): iv.

51. In "The Soul of Ireland" Joyce wrote: "The drawf-drama (if one may use that term) is a form of art which is improper and ineffectual. . . . [It] is accordingly to be judged as an entertainment" (Joyce, *James Joyce,* 75).

52. Frank D'Alton, quoted in Robert Hogan and James Kilroy, eds., *The Abbey Theatre: The Years of Synge 1905–1909,* vol. 3 of *The Modern Irish Drama: A Documentary History* (Dublin: Dolmen Press, 1978), 116.

53. Quoted in Hogan and Kilroy, *Years of Synge,* 176.

54. Burke, *Riotous Performances,* 109.

55. Frazier, *George Moore,* 329.

56. Colum, *Life and the Dream,* 107, 116.

57. Byrne, *Story of Ireland's National Theatre,* 57.

58. Marjorie Howes, *Yeats's Nations: Gender, Class, and Irishness* (Cambridge: Cambridge University Press, 1996), 71.

59. Yeats, "The Reform of the Theatre," *Samhain*, 3 (September 1903): 9.

60. Flannery, *Idea of a Theatre*, 328.

61. Holloway, *Abbey Theatre*, 81.

62. Quoted in Greene and Stephens, *J. M. Synge*, 156. The article appeared on 8 October 1903, as did John Butler Yeats's defense of the play, "Ireland Out of the Dock," in the *United Irishman*. In *Prodigal Father: The Life of John Butler Yeats (1839–1922)* (Ithaca N.Y.: Cornell University Press, 1978), William M. Murphy notes that that issue of the *United Irishman*, although dated 10 October 1903, was on the streets two days earlier (256).

63. In December 1905, Maire Nic Shiubhlaigh, Honor Lavelle, Emma Vernon, Maire Garvey, Frank Walker, Seamus O'Sullivan, Padraic Colum, and George Roberts left the Abbey, just a year after the patent for the theatre had been issued. They gathered around them the support of George Russell (AE), James Cousins, Thomas Kettle, H. F. Norman (editor of the *Irish Homestead*), Stephen Gwynn, and Thomas Keohler (Keller) to found the Theatre of Ireland in June 1906. In all more than half the members who pledged their support to Horniman on 11 May 1904 were gone.

64. Frazier, *Behind the Scenes*, 92–93.

65. Fay and Carswell, *The Fays of the Abbey Theatre*, 140. To Fay and Carswell, "the tumultuous reception of 'In the Shadow of the Glen' was because Synge had the misfortune to be not only a genius, but a Protestant and a member of the 'Ascendancy' class" (148).

66. Lionel Pilkington, *Theatre and the State in Twentieth-Century Ireland: Cultivating the People* (New York: Routledge, 2001), 44.

67. Cousins and Cousins, *We Two Together*, 93.

68. Hogan and Kilroy, *Years of Synge*, 19.

69. Quoted in Robert Hogan and James Kilroy, eds., *Laying the Foundations: 1902–1904*, vol. 2 of *The Modern Irish Drama: A Documentary History* (Dublin: Dolmen Press, 1976), 81.

70. Synge to Masefield, 17 December 1903, *Collected Letters of John Millington Synge, 1871–1907*, 1:72.

71. Synge to Max Meyerfeld, 10 March 1906, *Collected Letters of John Millington Synge*, 1:163.

72. Quoted in Laurence and Grene, *Shaw, Lady Gregory, and the Abbey*, 24.

73. Henderson, "Three Centuries of the Stage," 157.

74. Holloway, *Abbey Theatre*, 41.

75. Ibid., 52.

76. See Hogan and Kilroy, *Years of Synge*, 15–18, and Fay and Carswell, *The Fays of the Abbey Theatre*, 166–68.

77. Hogan and Kilroy, *Years of Synge,* 18–21.

78. George Sigerson, "The Irish Peasantry and the Stage," *United Irishman,* 17 February 1906, 2–3.

79. George O'Neill, "Recent Irish Drama and Its Critics," *New Ireland Review* 25 (1906): 31–32.

80. John P. Harrington, "Resentment, Relevance, and the Production History of *The Playboy of the Western World,*" in *Assessing the Achievement of J. M. Synge,* ed. Alexander G. Gonzalez (Westport, Conn.: Greenwood Press, 1996), 5. In *"The Playboy,* Critics, and the Enduring Problem of the Audience," in that same volume, 10–23, Ginger Strand argues that "[i]f the *Playboy* audiences sought to silence Synge's play, it was in part because they themselves felt silenced by it" (18). David Cairns's and Shaun Richards's brilliant analysis, "Reading a Riot: The 'Reading Formation' of Synge's Abbey Audience," *Literature and History* 13 (1987), 219–37, assesses the breadth of the spectrum of response to *The Playboy.* Christopher Morash's meticulous "All Playboys Now: The Audience and the Riot," in *Interpreting Synge: Papers from the Synge Summer School,* ed. Nicholas Grene (Dublin: Lilliput, 2000), documents the exact sequence of events during the play's run.

81. Hogan and Kilroy, *Years of Synge,* 144.

82. Colm Tóibín, *Lady Gregory's Toothbrush* (Dublin: Lilliput, 2002), 63.

83. Fay and Carswell, *The Fays of the Abbey Theatre,* 211–12.

84. See Cairns and Richards, "Reading a Riot," 220.

85. Yeats had deployed the police in the Antient Concert Hall for the ILT production of *The Countess Cathleen.* Such a move was unusual for that venue, but, as Gunn testified in 1892, commonplace at other Dublin theatres at the end of the nineteenth century.

86. Although the Irish were closely identified with the Draft Riots in New York City in 1863 ("A great proportion of these [conscriptees] being Irish, it naturally became an Irish question, and eventually an Irish riot," J. T. Headley, *The Great Riots of New York 1712–1873* [New York: Treat, 1873], 149), they were not linked with the most celebrated American theatre riot, the Astor Place Riot on 10 May 1849. That disturbance, which took the lives of dozens of people, including a number of innocent bystanders, was characterized by many of the same features that appeared in *The Playboy* riots. Like some performances of *The Playboy,* Macready's interpretation of Macbeth triggered "a storm of hisses, yells, and a clamor that defies description. . . . [T]he play went on, but not a word could be heard by the audience. It was in dumb show" (16). Although the first performance was greeted with hissing and audience disapproval, the riot occurred only after the production's run continued despite opposition. After the disturbances that attended his first performance of *Macbeth* at the

Astor Place Opera House, William Macready quite reasonably assumed that the run would be cancelled. When more than fifty people, with Washington Irving at their head, signed a petition imploring Macready to continue and pledging that they and the public "should sustain him," the groundwork for the riot was in place.

The terminology from the Astor Place disturbance carried over to Dublin. Macready had accused his rival, the American actor Edwin Forrest, of mounting an "organized opposition" (the very phrase that the Abbey management used in their advertisements of *The Playboy*) to his performing in Boston, New York, or any American venue. And as for *The Playboy*, the conflict between supporters and detractors became emblematic of a larger cultural clash. Later that year, in *An Account of the Terrific and Fatal Riot at the New York Astor Place Opera House* (New York, 1849), an anonymous pamphleteer summed up the climate in which the Astor Place riot took place:

> The question became not only a national [in other words, British versus American] one, but a social one. It was the rich against the poor—the aristocracy against the people; and this hatred of wealth and privilege is increasing over the world, and ready to burst out whenever there is the slightest occasion. The rich and well-bred are too apt to despise the poor and ignorant, and they must not think it strange if they are hated in return (19).

Finally, in both cases publicity brought on by protests engendered a backlash by inciting Irving and his fellow petitioners to take a stand against those who would prevent Macready's performance.

87. Sara Allgood, *Memories,* 37, Berg Collection, New York Public Library (hereafter cited as Berg).

88. Arthur Griffith alleged that Mahon had called Christy "'a dirty ____ lout.' The word omitted is so obscene that no man of ordinary decency would use it" (quoted in James Kilroy, ed., *The Playboy Riots,* [Dublin: Dolmen, 1971], 67). Ambrose Power, the actor playing Mahon, wrote that he had performed the line as Synge had written it: "a dirty, stuttering lout." Fay admitted that he misspoke the play's most celebrated line, concerning "chosen females in their shifts."

89. Nic Shiubhlaigh, *The Splendid Years,* 80.

90. On 31 January 1907, Padraic Colum (Jr.) wrote to the editor of the *Irish Independent* stating that his father "is not in sympathy with an organised opposition" (5). Several of those who wrote to the press acknowledged they were disruptive but also identified themselves as Abbey supporters (James Kilroy, *The "Playboy" Riots,* 53). As Levitas notes, "Colum was particularly grateful to Robert Gregory, whose 'prompt assistance' had saved his father from a night in the cells" (*Theatre and Nation,* 128).

91. One of these students was arrested and fined for unruly conduct on Westmoreland Street. See Hogan and Kilroy, *Years of Synge,* 130.

92. "The Passing of Anglo-Irish Drama," *An Claidheamh Soluis,* 9 February 1907, 7.

93. Yeats, "Mr. Yeats' Opening Speech at the Debate on February 4th, at the Abbey Theatre," *Arrow,* 23 February 1907, 8.

94. Gregory to Shaw, 9 August 1909, in Laurence and Grene, *Shaw, Lady Gregory, and the Abbey,* 12.

95. "'The Playboy' and Others," *Republic,* 7 February 1907, 9.

96. Lord Chamberlain's Correspondence, 1907/316, British Library, London (hereafter cited as LCP Corr). The previous day, Redford offered this recommendation:

> I am sending to the L. C. O. copies of a correspondence I have had about an Irish Drama which created a protest as when first performed in Dublin. I am most anxious not to meet troubles halfway, or make a mountain out of a molehill, but I thought you would like to have the facts before you in case any difficulties should arise. If you should wish to force me on the subject, I will come up chance. On the whole I am inclined to pass the piece; drawing the attention of the Management to the endorsement on the Licence.

97. "Great Queen Street Theatre," *Times* (London), 11 June 1907, 11.

98. On 22 June 1907 the *Illustrated London News,* for instance, wrote that *The Playboy* "could only have been condemned by a person who lacked all appreciation of humour, for as given in London it is an exceedingly diverting, if rather cynical exploitation of—what is undoubted fact—the hero-worship which some men and many women are ready to lavish on the criminal." Enthoven Collection, Theatre Museum Archives, London (hereafter cited as TMA).

99. Enthoven Collection, TMA. Less graphically, the Pall Mall Gazette's "Theatrical Notes" (24 June 1907, p. 1) reported "an organized demonstration of hostility in the gallery, which rendered the last act little more than a pantomime."

100. McCormack, *Fool of the Family,* 304.

101. Dawson Byrne notes: "A well-known gentleman, the famous Burke Corcoran, who had been one of their bitterest enemies on their first visit [to America] in 1911, now became one of their staunchest supporters" (*Story of Ireland's National Theatre,* 100).

102. See *Druid: The First Ten Years,* comp. Jerome Hynes (Galway: Druid Performing Arts and Galway Arts Festival, 1985), 53.

103. James Murray, "Theatre Riots," *Irish Independent,* 31 January 1907, 4.

4. "The Boom of the Ban"

1. Andrew Davies, *Other Theatres,* 28.

2. Henry Arthur Jones, *The Censorship Muddle and a Way Out of It: A Letter Addressed to the Right Honourable Herbert Samuel* (London: Chiswick, 1909), 4.

3. Archer to Lady Mary Murray, in C. Archer, *William Archer: Life, Work, and Friendships* (New Haven, Conn.: Yale University Press, 1931), 321.

4. G.M.G., *The Stage Censor: A Historical Sketch, 1544–1907* (London: S. Low, 1908).

5. Jones, *Censorship Muddle,* 52.

6. The text of *Blanco Posnet* occupies only the final third of the 407-page edition of Shaw's play published by Constable in 1913.

7. John Galsworthy, *Justification of the Censorship of Plays* (London: W. Heinemann, 1909), 14.

8. Quoted in de Jongh, *Politics, Prudery and Perversions,* 44.

9. Palmer further documented that "in the face of these surreptitious negotiations for withdrawal, . . . a play is in effect censored without ever being officially submitted for licence" (*The Censor and the Theatres,* 77); such works were not counted among the banned plays.

10. Tydeman and Price, *Wilde— "Salome,"* 22–23.

11. See Harold C. Gardiner, *Mysteries' End: An Investigation of the Last Days of the Medieval Religious Stage* (New Haven, Conn.: Yale University Press, 1946).

12. Johnston, *The Lord Chamberlain's Blue Pencil,* 23.

13. Quoted in Palmer, *The Censor and the Theatres,* 107.

14. Father R. Goff, C.L.K., *Irish Times,* 6 April 1911, in Hogan, Burnham, and Poteet, *Rise of the Realists,* 157–58.

15. Findlater, *Banned!* 102.

16. *Beltaine* 2 (February 1900): 5.

17. Yeats to Shaw, 5 October 1904, *Collected Letters of W. B. Yeats,* 3:662.

18. Yeats to Gregory, 7 November 1904, *Collected Letters of W. B. Yeats,* 3:666.

19. George Bernard Shaw, *The Shewing-up of Blanco Posnet: A Sermon in Crude Melodrama* (London: Constable, 1913), 384. Subsequent page references given in the text.

20. Brooke's play, its banning, and its subsequent and very profitable publication occasioned Samuel Johnson's *A Complete Vindication of the Licensers of the Stage.* See Findlater, *Banned!* 49.

21. Lucy McDiarmid, "Augusta Gregory, Bernard Shaw, and the Shewing-Up of Dublin Castle," *Publications of the Modern Language Association* 109 (January 1994): 26–44.

22. "More about 'Blanco Posnet,'" *Evening Telegraph*, 23 August 1909, *The W.A. Henderson Scrapbooks, 1899–1911: From the National Library of Ireland, Dublin*, reel 2, 153, National Library of Ireland (hereafter cited as NLI).

23. See Laurence and Grene, *Shaw, Lady Gregory, and the Abbey*, 16.

24. Gregory's role is crucial because she enjoyed much happier relations with the nationalist press than did Yeats.

25. "The Castle and the Theatre," *Sinn Féin*, 21 August 1909, 2.

26. Gregory to Shaw, 15 August 1909, in Laurence and Grene, *Shaw, Lady Gregory, and the Abbey*, 26.

27. Laurence and Grene note that in 1909 "the Abbey had been considering a production of Sophocles's *Oedipus Rex*, either in a translation by John Eglington or in a version being developed by Yeats" (*Shaw, Lady Gregory, and the Abbey*, 19).

28. Laurence and Grene, *Shaw, Lady Gregory, and the Abbey*, 27.

29. Gregory to Shaw, 18 August 1909, in Laurence and Grene, *Shaw, Lady Gregory, and the Abbey*, 31.

30. Donal Dorcey, "The Big Occasions," in *The Story of the Abbey Theatre*, ed. Sean McCann (London: New English Library, 1967), 146.

31. D. P. Moran, "Current Affairs: The Playboy of the Abbey," *The Leader*, 4 September 1909, 53.

32. "As Others See Us," *Leader*, 11 September 1909, 83.

33. "Pshaw!" *Leader*, 4 September 1909, 57–58.

34. "The Censorship Committee: Text of the Report," *Times* (London), 12 November 1909, 4.

35. "The Snowing Up of Blanco Posnet," *Dublin Evening Mail*, 21 August 1909, in *The W.A. Henderson Scrapbooks*, reel 2, 152, NLI.

36. "Decency in Drama," *The Irish Catholic*, 4 September 1909, in *The W.A. Henderson Scrapbooks*, reel 2, 185, NLI.

37. "Imported 'Drama' at the Queen's Theatre," *Leader*, 13 November 1909, 298.

38. Jacques, "'A Bad Dream,'" *Irish Independent*, 5 December 1911, 4.

5. The Riot in Westport; or, George A. Birmingham at Home

1. James Owen Hannay, *Globe*, 19 November 1913, MS 3441/12, Trinity College, Dublin (hereafter cited as TCD).

2. Jacques stated that the Abbey rejected *Eleanor's Enterprise*, "giving as their reason for doing so that they had no actors or actresses capable of playing parts of people belonging to the Upper Classes." See the *Irish Independent*, 15 December 1911, 4. Birmingham's other dramatic works include "My America," a sketch performed at the Theatre Royal on 2 October 1916 (see "Theatre Royal," *Freeman's Journal*, 3 October 1916, 2), and the libretto for Sir Sydney H. Nicholson's *The Mermaid: A Romantic Light Opera* (1928).

3. Quoted in Brian Taylor, *The Life and Writings of James Owen Hannay (George A. Birmingham), 1865–1950* (Lewiston, N.Y.: Mellen Press, 1995), 101.

4. George A. Birmingham, *Irishmen All* (New York: Frederick A. Stokes, 1913), 177.

5. George A. Birmingham, *Pleasant Places* (London: W. Heinemann, 1934), 162.

6. Stephen Gwynn, *Irish Literature and Drama in the English Language: A Short History* (London: Thomas Nelson, 1936), 173.

7. *Observer*, 12 January 1913, *General John Regan*, Enthoven Collection, TMA.

8. MS 3441/12, TCD.

9. The riot in Westport may well have grown out of the student protest that the Galway Cinema Theatre manager, Phil Mace, described as "pre-arranged." See Mace's letter to the editor, *Irish Independent*, 9 February 1914, 5.

10. See "*General John Regan* Offends," *Evening Standard*, 6 February 1914, MS 3441/12, TCD.

11. George A. Birmingham, Introduction, *General John Regan* (London: George Allen and Unwin, 1933), 16. Subsequent page references given in the text.

12. "Exploiting Irish Ireland," *Leader*, 14 February 1914, 7.

13. *General John Regan* (typescript, Act 3, p. 3), 1913, Lord Chamberlain's Papers, British Library, London (hereafter cited as LCP).

14. *Weekly Freeman*, 14 February 1914, MS 3441/12, TCD.

15. Liam Ó Domnaill, "Stage Irishman: A Re-Incarnation," *Irish Independent*, 19 February 1914, 4.

16. Albert C. White, "The Business of Mr. Birmingham," *Leader*, 27 March 1915, 160.

17. See *Dublin Evening Telegraph*, "National Literary Society," 31 March 1914, MS 3441/12, TCD.

18. *Brighton Society*, 12 February 1913, MS 3441/12, TCD.

19. Quoted in *Sketch*, 18 February 1914, MS 3441/12, TCD.

20. Quoted in "Canon Hannay's Play," *Freeman's Journal*, 9 February 1914, 9.

21. MS 3441/12, TCD.

22. *Leader*, 14 February 1914, 7.

23. *Leader*, 7 March 1914, 80.

24. See *Irish Independent*, 4 March 1914, 5.

25. *Leader*, 7 March 1914, 80.

26. *Leader*, 10 June 1916, 372.

27. *Mayo News*, 14 February 1914, 7.

28. "Dublin Theatres," *Young Ireland*, 19 July 1919, 2.

29. Birmingham, *Pleasant Places,* 175–76.

30. Patterson, *Censorship and Interpretation,* 58.

6. The Freedom of the Theatre in the Irish Free State, 1922–1929

1. Robert Welch, *The Abbey Theatre, 1899–1999: Form and Pressure* (New York: Oxford University Press, 1999), 94.

2. Adams, *Censorship,* 17. See p. 53, chap. 1, n.32.

3. Quoted in Frank O'Connor, *A Short History of Irish Literature: A Backward Look* (New York: G. P. Putnam's Sons, 1967), 223. The Catholic Truth Society was a strong but not omnipotent force in the late 1920s. One measure of its relative power came in 1927 when it actively lobbied political candidates in the general election, "to give an undertaking to use his or her influence, if elected, to secure that full legislative effect will be given the Committee's findings, as soon as possible." Less than one-third of the 376 total candidates made such a commitment. Of the 112 who did, only 50 were elected. See Catholic Truth Society, *Report for Year Ended 30th June, 1927* (Dublin: Catholic Truth Society of Ireland, 1927), 7.

4. Ireland was not alone in its concern over morality in the theatre at this time. In July 1926, George Jean Nathan, the doyen of New York theatre critics and H. L. Mencken's coeditor at *The Smart Set,* wrote in *Vanity Fair:* "[T]he dirtiest lot of shows that have ever been put on view in the New York legitimate theatres—which cater to young boys and girls as well as to adults—are permitted freely to go their way." See "Master Minds of Censorship," *Vanity Fair,* July 1926, 57, 102.

5. The publications of the Catholic Truth Society included several stories and novellas by the Cork writer J. Bernard MacCarthy, whose plays *The Supplanter, Kinship* (both 1914), *Crusaders* (1917), and *Gurranabraher* (or *The Long Road to Garranbraher* [1923]) were performed by the Abbey. In 1928 the Catholic Truth Society reported that it had effectively checked the purchase by Catholics of the "anti-Catholic" *Children's Encyclopedia.* See Catholic Truth Society, *Report for Year Ended 30th June, 1928* (Dublin: Catholic Truth Society of Ireland, 1928), 6.

6. O'Reilly, *The Problem of Undesirable Printed Matter,* 50.

7. R. S. Devane, *The Committee on Evil Literature: Some Notes of Evidence* (Dublin: Browne and Nolan, 1927). Subsequent page references given in the text refer to this edition.

8. O'Reilly, *The Problem of Undesirable Printed Matter,* 45–46.

9. R. S. Devane, *Evil Literature: Some Suggestions* (Dublin: Browne and Nolan, 1927), 9.

10. Lennox Robinson, *Ireland's Abbey Theatre: A History, 1899–1951* (London: Sidgwick and Jackson, 1951), 120.

11. Robert Hogan and Richard Burnham, eds., *The Years of O'Casey, 1921–1926* (Newark: University of Delaware Press, 1992), 116.

12. Ibid., 188.

13. Lennox Robinson, *Curtain Up: An Autobiography* (London: Michael Joseph, 1942), 55.

14. Eileen Crowe, "Eileen Crowe Tells Her Story," in *The Abbey Theatre: Interviews and Recollections,* ed. E. H. Mikhail (Totowa, N.J.: Barnes and Noble, 1988), 131.

15. Gregory and Yeats to Cosgrave, 27 June 1924, in Robinson, *Ireland's Abbey Theatre,* 125.

16. Hogan and Burnham, *Years of O'Casey,* 274–75. Holloway "assured him [O'Brien] that none of these things would occur. That the worst thing that would befall the piece was a falling off in the audiences during the week" (*Holloway's Abbey Theatre,* 246).

17. George O'Brien to W. B. Yeats, 5 September 1925, *Letters of Sean O'Casey,* vol. 1:*1910–1941* (New York: Macmillan, 1975): 144.

18. O'Brien to Yeats and Robinson, 13 September 1925, *Letters of Sean O'Casey,* 1:147.

19. See Julia Carlson, *Banned in Ireland: Censorship and the Irish Writer* (Athens: University of Georgia Press, 1990), 3.

20. O'Brien to Yeats, 5 September 1925, *Letters of Sean O'Casey,* 1:145.

21. Dolan to Lady Gregory, 1 September 1925, *Years of O'Casey,* Hogan and Burnham, 282.

22. Ria Mooney, "Playing Rosie Redmond," *Journal of Irish Literature* 6 (May 1977): 21.

23. O'Casey to Lennox Robinson, 10 January 1926, *Letters of Sean O'Casey,* 1:166.

24. See Christopher Morash, "A Night at the Theatre 5," *A History of Irish Theatre, 1601–2000* (Cambridge: Cambridge University Press, 2002), 163–71.

25. R. M. Fox, "Sean O'Casey: A Worker Dramatist," *New Statesman* 26 (10 April 1926): 805.

26. *Letters of Sean O'Casey,* 1:226.

27. Mooney, "Playing Rosie Redmond," 25.

28. Margaret Ward, *Unmanageable Revolutionaries: Women and Irish Nationalism* (London: Pluto, 1983), 205.

29. Letter to the *Independent,* 23 February 1926, quoted in Holloway, *Abbey Theatre,* 260.

30. *Lady Gregory's Journals,* quoted in Robert G. Lowery, ed., *A Whirlwind in Dublin: "The Plough and the Stars" Riots* (Westport, Conn.: Greenwood, 1984), 54.

31. Kavanagh, *Story of the Abbey Theatre,* 135.

32. Arthur Griffith, "The Playboy of the West," *Sinn Féin,* 9 February 1907, 2. These are Griffith's original words, condensed and reordered by Hanna Sheehy-Skeffington in her letter to the *Independent* cited above.

33. "A Censorship over Literature," *Irish Statesman,* 12 February 1929, 543.

34. Catholic Truth Society, *Report for Year Ended 30th June, 1928,* 6.

35. Hanna Sheehy-Skeffington, "Woman's View of Censorship," *Irish Times,* 23 November 1928, 11.

36. Adams, *Censorship,* 150.

7. Irish Stage Censorship from *Salome* through *Roly Poly*

1. Quoted in Gwynn, *Irish Literature and Drama,* 232.

2. Paul Scott Stanfield, *Yeats and Politics in the 1930s* (New York: St. Martin's Press, 1988), 9. See Terence Brown, *Ireland: A Social and Cultural History, 1922 to the Present* (Ithaca, N.Y.: Cornell University Press, 1985), 55–61.

3. See Adams, *Censorship,* 71–98.

4. Robert Hogan, in *Enter Certain Players: Edwards-Mac Liammóir and the Gate, 1928–1978,* ed. Peter Luke (Dublin: Dolmen Press, 1978), 13.

5. Robinson, *Ireland's Abbey Theatre,* 121.

6. Kavanagh, *The Story of the Abbey Theatre,* 148.

7. Box 14, Gate Theatre Archive, Northwestern University (hereafter cited as GTA/NWU).

8. *The Importance of Being Oscar,* first produced as a Gate production, previewed in the Gaelic Hall of the Curragh Military Camp and then opened at the Gaiety. It was frequently revived at the Gate. See Micheál Ó hAodha, *The Importance of Being Micheál: A Portrait of Mac Liammóir* (Dingle, Kerry: Brandon, 1990), xv.

9. *Salome* had been produced in "club performances" in London as early as 1905.

10. Johnston, *The Lord Chamberlain's Blue Pencil,* 211.

11. Micheál Mac Liammóir, *All for Hecuba: An Irish Theatrical Autobiography* (London: Methuen, 1946), 71.

12. Box 14, GTA/NWU.

13. Catholic Truth Society, *Report for Year Ended 30th June, 1930* (Dublin: Catholic Truth Society of Ireland, 1930), 6.

14. Hugh Hunt, *The Abbey: Ireland's National Theatre, 1904–1979* (New York: Columbia University Press, 1979), 145.

15. The most frequent and sustained upheavals were not in Ireland but in America and in response to Synge and O'Casey in particular. See John P. Harrington, *The Irish Play on the New York Stage* (Lexington: University Press of Kentucky, 1998).

16. "De Valera as Play Censor," *Manchester Guardian Weekly,* April 1934, 296.

17. Quoted in Hunt, *The Abbey,* 146–47.

18. Susan Cannon Harris, "All That Trouble and Nothing to Show for It: Yeats's *The Herne's Egg* and the Misbirth of a Nation," *Eire-Ireland* 33 (1997–1998): 30.

19. The lectures are collected in Robinson, *The Irish Theatre: Lectures Delivered during the Abbey Theatre Festival Held in Dublin in August 1938.*

20. "Great Poet Has Warm Reception," *Irish Independent,* 11 August 1938, 10.

21. A.E.M. [Andrew E. Malone], "Abbey Theatre Festival: A New Yeats Play," *Irish Times,* 11 August 1938, 6.

22. "The Abbey," *Irish Times,* 12 August 1938, 6.

23. "The Question," *Irish Independent,* 13 August 1938, 9.

24. W. B. Yeats, "The Plot is the Meaning," *Irish Times,* 13 August 1938, 9.

25. Frank O'Connor, "Purgatory" (Letter to the Editor), *Irish Times,* 16 August 1938, 8.

26. C. Page, "Sensorship!" *Muse* (1932).

27. The eponymous character in *The Puritan* (London: Cape, 1932), Francis Ferriter, recalls that he "belonged at that time to a vigilance society and it was part of our duty to report cases of immorality"—to ferret out, as his name suggests, morally objectionable works. Ferriter is infatuated with another lodger at his boarding house who is involved in an "immoral affair" with the son of a leader of the vigilance society. Ferriter's pathological moral crusade dates back to a direct connection with theatre: "He once had an argument with the man during a riot at a theatre. Ferriter had been one of a group of young Catholics who stopped the performance of a play in which a slighting reference had been made to the Immaculate Conception" (277).

28. Mary Manning, "Bongo-Bongo," *Motley* 2 (December 1933): 13–16.

29. Seán O'Faoláin, "Preface," *She Had to Do Something* (London: Cape, 1938), 8.

30. C.C., "The Theatre," *The Bell* 7 (September 1943): 530–31. C. C., probably Con Curran, objected to the stock characters—Miss Pry, Miss Ogle, Mr. Roué—and to the author's "playing it too easily, knowing that he would have the public on his side."

31. Paul Vincent Carroll, *Shadow and Substance* (New York: Random House, 1937), 167.

32. Michael Farrell, "A Famous Country Theatre," *The Bell* 1 (November 1940): 81.

33. One of the most illuminating articles, Rex Mac Gall's "How Your Films Are Censored" (*The Bell* 10 [September 1945]: 493–501), noted that Irish film censorship always came on top of (or after) the British censorship. The criteria for British film censorship, close kin to those for plays, were explicit:

(i) Religious: Materialised figure of Christ (Green Pastures refused certificate); mockery of religion; mockery of the Bible.

(ii) Social: All nudity except negroid or half-caste; swearing; blasphemy; indecency; child-birth and its pains; marriage nights without restraint; any mention of V.D. (though some films have recently been shown in Britain on this subject by the Ministry of Health); contempt of State; indecent behaviours; drunkenness; sex relations between whites and non-whites (racialism); incitements to crime; sadism (though the Three Stooges get away with it every time); exhibitions of bad habits (drugs, sex perversions, etc.); prolonged scenes of brutality; antagonism between capital and labour; sedition; illegal operations; prostitution; incest; cruelty to children or to animals; and anything calculated to encourage or advocate a breach of the peace.

(iii) Political: Anything calculated to arouse foreign indignation which in peace might lead to war or in war might lead to insult to allied nations; or anything which is calculated to incite revolution, unrest or discontent.

The political criteria provide the basis for the censorship under which *Roly Poly* and *The Refugee* were withdrawn.

34. See Patrick J. Gannon, "Art, Morality and Censorship," *Studies: An Irish Quarterly Review* 65 (July 1937): 434–47. Gannon anticipates Reverend Peter Connolly in opposing the practices of the Censorship Board. Gannon wrote that the "censorship was not intended against native authors" (435) and advocated an appeals procedure. These clerical voices against the censorship practices raised theological and philosophical issues and were, at least in the long run, extremely influential.

35. Quoted in Adams, *Censorship,* 95.

36. See Adams, *Censorship,* 129–34.

37. Ó Drisceoil, *Censorship in Ireland,* 52.

38. Ibid., 31.

39. Ibid., 33.

40. The previous year, 1939, "Boule de Suif" provided the inspiration for John Ford's *Stagecoach,* which was adapted by the film's screenplay writer, Dudley Nichols, from Ernest Haycox's story, "Stage to Lordsburg."

41. Several scripts of *Roly Poly* survive. Page numbers given in the text refer to the prompt script, which incorporates a penultimate, twelfth scene, in the Gate Theatre Archive at Northwestern University.

42. Unless otherwise cited, the reviews of *Roly Poly* are from box 14, GTA/NWU.

43. D.S., "De Maupassant Modernised," *Irish Independent,* 20 November 1940, 6.

44. Joseph Holloway, *Joseph Holloway's Irish Theatre,* ed. Robert

Hogan and Michael J. O'Neill, vol. 3 (Dixon, Calif.: Proscenium Press, 1970), 51.

45. Ó Drisceoil, *Censorship in Ireland*, 51.

46. Christopher Fitz-Simon, *The Boys: A Double Biography of Micheál Mac Liammóir and Hilton Edwards* (London: Nick Hern, 1994), 135.

47. Holloway, *Joseph Holloway's Irish Theatre*, 3:51.

48. Ó Drisceoil, *Censorship in Ireland*, 52.

49. "A Dublin Play Withdrawn," *Irish Independent*, 23 November 1940, 8.

50. Box 14, GTA/NWU.

51. *Irish Times*, 5 December 1940.

52. Coyne memo on Censorship, September 1945, S11445/8, p. 39, Department of the Taoiseach, S Files, National Archives, Dublin (hereafter cited as NA).

53. H. C. Game, "Reader's Report," 23 November 1942, *Roly Poly*, LCP Corr.

54. G. A. Titman to Joan Ling, 4 December 1942, *Roly Poly*, LCP Corr.

55. Peake to Thomas, 26 January 1943, *Roly Poly*, LCP Corr.

56. G. A. Titman to Joan Ling, 4 February 1943, *Roly Poly*, LCP Corr.

57. G. A. Titman to Joan Ling, 19 October 1944, *Roly Poly*, LCP Corr.

58. Sir Alexander Cadogan to Earl of Clarendon, 28 June 1945, *Roly Poly*, LCP Corr.

59. "Re/Play 'The Refugee,'" 216/303 Department of Foreign Affairs, NA.

60. Lucy Glazerbrook, "The Drama in Ireland," *New York Times*, 8 December 1940. *The Statue's Daughter* was performed by the Dublin Drama League at the Gate Theatre in December 1941.

61. James Matthews, *Voices: A Life of Frank O'Connor* (New York: Atheneum, 1983), 171.

62. Mac Liammóir, *All for Hecuba*, 376.

8. The Fifties

1. Micheál Mac Liammóir "Forward," *Theatre in Ireland* (Dublin: At the Sign of the Three Candles, 1949), 4.

2. Ibid., 44.

3. Mac Liammóir's comments were hardly unprecedented. During intermission of a performance of *The Plough and the Stars* at the Abbey in 1947, Valentine Iremonger and Roger McHugh denounced the decline in production and acting standards.

4. Eric Bentley, "Irish Theatre: Splendeurs et Misères," *Poetry* 53 (January 1952): 217.

5. Paul Vincent Carroll, "Can the Abbey Theatre Be Restored?" *Theatre Arts* 36 (January 1952): 19. Carroll blamed: "First, the unofficial

interference of the Government in Abbey policy as the price of a rather stingy subsidy. Second, the very powerful unofficial clerical censorship, and the bullying tactics of certain lay bodies. . . . Third, the deplorable policy of the Abbey Directorate to submerge criminally the Anglo-Irish achievements on which the Abbey was built, and replace them by an insane policy of purely Gaelic culture, expressed through the medium of the native language, of which the vast majority of Irish people know little and care less."

6. Gabriel Fallon, "The Future of the Irish Theatre," *Studies: An Irish Quarterly Review* 44 (Spring 1955): 99.

7. See Mary Kenny, *Goodbye to Catholic Ireland* (London: Sinclair-Stevenson, 1997), 248–54. Like many commentators, Kenny places great emphasis on the 1959 election of Seán Lemass as Taoiseach.

8. Alan Simpson, *Beckett and Behan and a Theatre in Dublin* (London: Routledge and Kegan Paul, 1962), 139.

9. Ernest Blythe held a series of ministerial posts before presiding for no fewer than twenty-six years as managing director of the Abbey (1941–67). Conor Cruise O'Brien, writing under the name Donat O'Donnell, was reviewing for the London publications such as the *New Statesman* while serving in the Department of External Affairs.

10. Adams, *Censorship,* 161.

11. R. S. Devane, *The Imported Press: A National Menace—Some Remedies* (Dublin: Duffy, 1950).

12. Adams, *Censorship,* 232. See also *Irish Times,* 10 March 1955, 7; *Irish Independent,* 11 July 1955; and John Cooney, *John Charles McQuaid: Ruler of Catholic Ireland* (Syracuse, N.Y.: Syracuse University Press, 2000), 239–40. Adams described this group as "ineffective," but in *Stage by Stage* (Dublin: Poolbeg, 1985) Carolyn Swift reports that the League of Decency protested the Pike's *The Rose Tattoo* to Brendan Smith. Founded in 1945 by Father Denis Fahey, Maria Duce took as its objective "strengthening the constitutional relationship between Church and State" (Cooney, *John Charles McQuaid,* 239–40).

13. "Where Stands *The Standard,*" *Maria Duce Bulletin* 2 (1952): 1, 4.

14. "Danny Kaye: Dublin's Unheard Protest," *Fiat* 29 (1952): 4. Similar protests against American performers rumored to have links with communist organizations were fomented against Larry Adler in 1950 and Orson Welles in 1951. Likewise, the film version of Arthur Miller's *Death of a Salesman* saw picketing outside the Metropole Cinema in Dublin. See Cooney, *John Charles McQuaid,* 234–43. Similarly, when a production of Sartre's *No Exit* by the Belfast Arts Theatre toured Dublin in August 1951, the title was blacked out on the placard outside the Royal Irish Academy.

15. Paul Blanshard, *The Irish and Catholic Power: An American Interpretation* (London: Derek Verschoyle, 1954), 27.

16. Paul Blanshard, *Personal and Confidential* (Boston: Beacon Press, 1973), 227.

17. Adams, *Censorship*, 143–49.

18. Hubert Butler, "Portrait of a Minority," *Escape from the Anthill* (Mullingar: Lilliput, 1986), 114.

19. On the basis of prepublication advertisement of a special section on family planning, customs officials seized all the editions of the *Observer* (London), 1 April 1956. Throughout the month Owen Sheehy-Skeffington and the Irish Association of Civil Liberties sustained a campaign to learn the circumstances under which the papers were withheld from the public. As Seán O'Faoláin remarked much earlier, the censorship as carried out by customs officials had a Star Chamber quality in its lack of clearly defined criteria, procedures, and accountability. See Adams, *Censorship*, 143–44.

20. See Connolly, *No Bland Facility.*

21. Ulick O'Connor, "Dublin: Decline and Fall," *Listener*, 19 April 1956, 446.

22. See Morash, "A Night at the Theatre 6," *A History of Irish Theatre*, 199–208. Morash points out that Simpson's production "even accentuated potentially offensive lines" (205).

23. John O'Riordan, *A Guide to O'Casey's Plays: From the Plough to the Stars* (London: Macmillan, 1984), 334.

24. "Sean O'Casey Again," *Standard*, 18 February 1955, 1; "Art—For Whose Sake?" *Standard*, 25 February 1955, 1.

25. Tyrone Guthrie, *A Life in the Theatre* (London: Hamish Hamilton, 1959), 268.

26. "New O'Casey Play is Booed in Dublin," *New York Times*, 1 March 1955, 22.

27. Donat O'Donnell (Conor Cruise O'Brien), "No Bishop, No Bonfire," *New Statesman and Nation*, 5 March 1955, 320.

28. "Dublin's Mixed Reception for New O'Casey Play," *Times* (London), 1 March 1955, 8.

29. W. A. Darlington, "O'Casey's Play," *New York Times*, 6 March 1955, sec. 2: 3.

30. Harold Hobson, "O'Casey's *Bishop's Bonfire*," *Christian Science Monitor*, 12 March 1955, 8.

31. Thersites, "Private Views," *Irish Times*, 12 March 1955, 6.

32. A. J. Leventhal, "Dramatic Commentary," *Dublin Magazine* 31 (April–June 1955): 28.

33. "Students Criticize Newspaper," *Irish Times*, 10 March 1955, 7.

34. Sean O'Casey, "Bonfire Under a Black Sun," in *The Green Crow* (New York: George Braziller, 1956), 132. Subsequent page references in the text are to this edition.

35. "Final Curtain?" *Irish Times*, 16 February 1958, 5.

36. *Dublin Evening Mail,* 3 April 1954, 3. The evening festivities on 17 April featured "The lighting of the Paschal Fire in defiance of Paganism" and on 18 March "Patrick, Champion of Christianity, confronts the High King of Ireland, the Druids and the Brehons at the Royal Court of Tara and confounds Paganism, symbolised by his destruction of Crom Cruach and his 'sub Gods twelve.'"

37. A. J. Leventhal, "Dramatic Commentary," *Dublin Magazine* 32 (July–September 1957): 52.

38. Quoted in *Irish Independent,* 15 May 1957, 1.

39. Quoted in *Letters of Sean O'Casey,* vol. 3: *1955–1958,* ed. David Krause (New York: Macmillan, and Washington, D.C.: Catholic University of America Press, 1975–1992), 66.

40. Phyllis Ryan, *The Company I Kept* (Dublin: Town House, 1996), 140.

41. Donald Spoto, *The Kindness of Strangers: The Life of Tennessee Williams* (Boston: Little, Brown, 1985), 200.

42. "Decision in 'Rose Tattoo' Case Next Monday," *Irish Times,* 6 June 1958, 7.

43. "Garda Action on American Play," *Irish Press,* 24 May 1957, 7.

44. Desmond Reid, "Tennessee Williams," *Studies: An Irish Quarterly Review* 46 (Winter 1957): 431. Subsequent page references given in the text.

45. Carolyn Swift, *Stage by Stage* (Dublin: Poolbeg, 1985), 241.

46. Tennessee Williams, *The Rose Tattoo,* in *Three Plays of Tennessee Williams* (Norfolk, Conn.: New Directions, 1959), 126.

47. Anna Manahan, "The Rose Tattoo: Arrest and Trial," in *Flight from the Celtic Twilight,* ed. Des Hickey and Gus Smith (New York: Bobbs-Merrill, 1973), 131.

48. Quoted in Swift, *Stage by Stage,* 243.

49. Review of *The Rose Tattoo, Irish Press,* 13 May 1957, 5.

50. Review of *The Rose Tattoo, Irish Independent,* 14 May 1957, 8.

51. "Anna Manahan's Triumph in 'Rose Tattoo,'" *Dublin Evening Mail,* 13 May 1957, 6.

52. Swift, *Stage by Stage,* 251, 254.

53. "'The Rose Tattoo' Producer Charged in Dublin Court," *Irish Times,* 25 May 1957, 5.

54. *Irish Times,* 18 June 1957, 1.

55. "Irish Writers," *Irish Times,* 30 May 1957, 7. See also *Letters of Sean O'Casey,* 3:437–38, 440–42, 515–16, 539–42, 556–58.

56. "Play Producer Acquitted," *Irish Times,* 10 June 1958, 4.

57. *Pike Newsletter* 16 (1957): 2.

58. Quoted in Gerard Whelan with Carolyn Swift, *Spiked: Church-State Intrigue and The Rose Tattoo* (Dublin: New Island, 2002), 150.

59. "Dublin Play Booking 'Cancelled,'" *Irish Times,* 6 June 1957, 7.

60. Brendan Smith, "*The Drums of Father Ned:* O'Casey and the Archbishop," in Hickey and Smith, *Flight from the Celtic Twilight,* 150.

61. Brown, *Ireland,* 176.

62. Phyllis Ryan, *The Company I Kept,* 141.

63. Brendan Smith to Hilton Edwards, 18 October 1957, Tóstal file, GTA/NWU.

64. Brendan Smith to Hilton Edwards, 28 November 1957, and Brendan Smith to Micheál Mac Liammóir, 28 November 1957, Tóstal file, GTA/NWU.

65. Christopher Murray, "O'Casey's *The Drums of Father Ned* in Context," in *A Century of Irish Drama: Widening the Stage,* ed. Stephen Watt, et al. (Bloomington: Indiana University Press, 2000), 118.

66. O'Casey to Brendan Smith, 19 July 1957, *Letters of Sean O'Casey,* 3:445.

67. Notes, Sean Martin, 2.25 P.M., 6 January 1957 [*sic,* 1958], "Arts and Culture," McQuaid Papers, Dublin Diocesan Archives (hereafter cited as DDA).

68. See Murray, "O'Casey's *The Drums,*" 125.

69. Quoted in *Letters of Sean O'Casey,* 3:523. These circumstances recall Cardinal Logue's qualified denunciation of Yeats's *The Countess Cathleen,* which he had not read, in 1899.

70. John C. McQuaid, *Wellsprings of the Faith* (Dublin: Clonmore and Reynolds, 1956), 226.

71. Notes, 6 January 1958, "Arts and Culture," McQuaid Papers, DDA.

72. Brendan Smith, "O'Casey and the Archbishop," in Hickey and Smith, *Flight from the Celtic Twilight,* 150–51.

73. Robert Hogan, "O'Casey and the Archbishop," *New Republic,* 19 May 1958, 29. Similarly, the memoir of the actor and producer Peter Daubeny, *My World of Theatre* (London: Jonathan Cape, 1971), reported that "the Bishop of Dublin had banned *The Drums of Father Ned*" (287).

74. Quoted in *Letters of Sean O'Casey,* 3:529.

75. "The Festival Committee of An Tóstal," 5 February 1958, "Arts and Culture," McQuaid Papers, DDA.

76. Anthony Cronin, *Samuel Beckett: The Last Modernist* (London: HarperCollins, 1996), 56.

77. James Knowlson, *Damned to Fame: The Life of Samuel Beckett* (New York: Simon and Schuster, 1996), 156.

78. Originally written for *Bookman* in 1935, "Censorship in the Saorstat" was first published in *Disjecta: Miscellaneous Writings and a Dramatic Fragment,* ed. Ruby Cohn (New York: Grove, 1983), 84–88.

79. *Endgame,* Enthoven Collection, TMA.

80. Alan Simpson to Samuel Beckett, 21 August 1957, MS 10731/54, TCD.

81. *Pike Newsletter,* 13 (1955): 1. Swift recalls that Beckett "kindly offered to reduce his normal fee of 12½% of gross receipts to 7½%" (*Stage by Stage,* 178). She also notes that considerable publicity was generated by the performance of *Godot* uncut. See Swift, *Stage by Stage,* 176–201.

82. Quoted in Knowlson, *Damned to Fame,* 401–02.

83. Padraic Colum, "Colum: Life in a World of Writers," in Hickey and Smith, *Flight from the Celtic Twilight,* 20.

84. Samuel Beckett to Alan Simpson, 7 May 1960, MS 10731/85, TCD.

85. McQuaid to Rev. O' Grady, S. J., 14 January 1958, "Arts and Culture," McQuaid Papers, DDA.

86. Quoted in Gabriel Fallon, "Dublin International Theatre Festival, 1959," *Threshold* 3 (Autumn 1959): 75.

87. Ibid., 63.

88. J. P. Donleavy, *The Plays of J. P. Donleavy with a Preface by the Author* (New York: Dell, 1972), 94. Subsequent page references given in the text.

89. "The Ginger Man," Hickey and Smith, *Flight from the Celtic Twilight,* 153.

90. "Irish Look Back in Anger," *Times* (London), 16 September 1959, 14.

91. Donleavy, "What They Did in Dublin with *The Ginger Man,*" *The Plays of J. P. Donleavy,* 20–29.

92. J. P. Donleavy, Introduction to *The Plays of J. P.l Donleavy,* vii.

93. *The Ginger Man,* 1959/1939, Lord Chamberlain's Papers, LCP.

94. In the 1950s, both in America and in Europe, playwrights often expressed anxiety about the threat of mob action. In France, Eugene Ionesco's *Rhinoceros* (1959) imagined humanity transformed into a herd of thundering beasts; in America Arthur Miller's *The Crucible* (1953) drew a parallel between the Salem witch hunts of the 1690s and the congressional investigations of communists in the 1940s and 1950s.

95. "Second Annual Report," CEMA: 1944–45, British Theatre Archive, Linen Hall Library, Belfast (hereafter cited as BTA/LNL).

96. "CEMA Report for 1949–50," BTA/LNL.

97. Mary O'Malley, "Letter to PEN Delegates," 11 June 1953, in *A Poets' Theatre,* Conor O'Malley (Dublin: Elo Press, 1988), 143.

98. Gerard McLarnon, *The Bonefire,* Ulster Group Theatre, BTA/LNL.

99. Quoted in "The Bonefire Spreads to Canada," *Belfast Telegraph,* September 1958, Ulster Group Theatre, BTA/LNL.

100. Quoted in Sam Hanna Bell, *The Theatre in Ulster: A Survey of the Dramatic Movement in Ulster from 1902 until the Present Day* (Dublin: Gill and Macmillan, 1972), 91.

101. O'Malley, *A Poet's Theatre*, 73.

102. Ophelia Byrne, *The Stage in Ulster from the Eighteenth Century* (Belfast: Linen Hall Library, 1997), 47. The actress is not to be confused with the playwright Margaretta D'Arcy.

103. Sam Thompson, *Over the Bridge,* ed. Stewart Parker (Dublin: Gill and Macmillan, 1970), 43. Subsequent page references given in the text.

104. After playing for six weeks in Belfast and four weeks in Dublin, *Over the Bridge* was submitted to the Lord Chamberlain for a license for its performance at the King's Theatre in Glasgow in April 1960. Thompson was resigned to the deletion of two words, "arse" and "bugger," and was quoted in the *Scotsman* (Edinburgh) as saying, "I can't really complain too much about what he has taken out. After all, my play is about tolerance, and it would be a bit hypocritical if I came to another country and showed complete intolerance of the rules of beliefs of society here" (*Over the Bridge*, 1960/744, LCP).

105. Lionel Pilkington in "Theatre and Cultural Politics in Northern Ireland: The *Over the Bridge* Controversy," *Eire/Ireland*, 30, no. 4 (Winter 1996): 83–87, argues that Thompson's revisions to the rehearsal version of *Over the Bridge* read by McKee in May 1959 for the performed and published version mark a change from the "dogmatic Unionism of Lord Brookborough to the superficially more progressive variety of Unionism" (86). Elements of both versions, specifically the character of Ephraim Smart, challenge the assertion that *Over the Bridge* depicts "sectarianism as arising from Catholic, nationalistic grievance" (87).

106. *Belfast Telegraph,* 7 May 1959, Ulster Group Theatre, BTA/LNL. "Siobhanitis" was the anxiety caused when the actress Siobhan McKenna commented on the IRA and Harold Macmillan on Edward R. Murrow's "Small World," which was broadcast without cuts by the BBC in the last week of April 1959. The decision to broadcast McKenna's remarks was publicly protested by Brian Faulkner's resignation from the BBC Northern Ireland Advisory Council on 26 April 1959. McKenna refused to retract or apologize for her remarks. The BBC decision to ban the second installment of the program was largely punitive since that broadcast was apolitical and inoffensive. The press was still reporting further rumblings over the cancellation of that second segment of "Small World" when the withdrawal of *Over the Bridge* was announced.

107. "Why 'Over the Bridge,' Was Withdrawn," *Belfast Telegraph,* 13 May 1959, Ulster Group Theatre, BTA/LNL.

108. "Stage—or Screen?" *Belfast Telegraph,* 13 May 1959, 1, Ulster Group Theatre, BTA/LNL.

109. "Lord Mayor on Sectarian Plays," *Belfast Telegraph,* 19 May 1959, BTA/LNL. Analogous situations in Ireland are found much earlier in the century and reappear in the 1970s. Then, too, subsidy meant

board representation and with that representation the possibility of the politicization of artistic decisions. In the 1930s, the Irish government had cut the Abbey subsidy, but the Abbey withstood the threat to appoint a hostile government representative to the Abbey Board and the threat of further cuts unless O'Casey and Synge were withdrawn from the upcoming American tours.

110. Roy McFadden, "Belfast Theatre Controversy," *Threshold* 3 (Autumn 1959): 26.

111. Ibid., 26.

112. Philip B. Ryan, *Lost Theatres,* 98.

113. Simpson, *Beckett and Behan,* 146–47.

9. New Theatrical Economies

1. John Ryan, *Remembering How We Stood: Bohemian Dublin at Mid-Century* (New York: Taplinger, 1975), 17.

2. Benedict Kiely, in Carlson, *Banned in Ireland,* 23.

3. John McGahern, in Carlson, *Banned in Ireland,* 55.

4. Murray, "O'Casey's *The Drums of Father Ned* in Context," in *A Century of Irish Drama,* 127.

5. *Report of the Joint Committee on Censorship of the Theatre, Together with the Proceedings of the Committee, Minutes of Evidence, Appendices and Index.* (London: Her Majesty's Stationery Office, 1967), 25.

6. Mary Maher, "The Challenge of the Project," *Irish Times,* 26 January 1977, 8.

7. Frank Kilfeather, "Lease Main Issue in Grant Refusal," *Irish Times,* 19 January 1977, 4.

8. A subversive quality of Mac Liammóir's one-man play was more evident to its first audiences than today's. The green carnation was an emblem of homosexuality as in the lyrics from Noel Coward's 1929 operetta *Bitter Sweet:* "Art is our inspiration / And as we are the reason / for the "nineties" being gay / We all wear a green carnation."

9. Lyric Theatre-O'Malley Archive, National University of Ireland, Galway (hereafter cited as LTOA/NUIG).

10. O'Malley, *A Poet's Theatre,* 76.

11. Lucy Bryson and Clem McCartney, *Clashing Symbols? A Report on the Use of Flags, Anthems and Other National Symbols in Northern Ireland* (Belfast: Institute for Irish Studies, 1994), 92.

12. Mary and Pearse O'Malley to Kenneth Darwin, 29 October 1968, LTOA/NUIG.

13. W. Brian Boyd to Pearce [*sic*] O'Malley, 15 December 1969, LTOA/NUIG.

14. Rev. Alan Cairns to Manager, Lyric Theatre, 10 January 1974, LTOA/NUIG.

15. Carol Moore and Eleanor Methven, "Charabanc Theatre Company on Irish Women's Theatres," in *Feminist Stages: Interviews with Women in Contemporary British Theatre,* ed. Lizbeth Goodman and Jane de Gay (Amsterdam: Harwood, 1996), 280.

16. Paul Hadfield, "Field Day, Over but Not Out," *Theatre Ireland* 31 (1993): 47.

17. John Sutton, quoted in Roddy Doyle, *War* (Dublin: Passion Machine, 1989), i.

18. Byrne, *The Stage in Ulster,* 75.

19. Ibid., 70.

20. *Playing the Wild Card,* www.artscoucil-ni.org/review/content.pdf, p. 61.

21. *Views of Theatre in Ireland, 1995: Report of the Arts Council Theatre Review* (Dublin: Arts Council, 1995), 126.

22. *Playing the Wild Card,* 56.

23. "Féile Funds Threatened," *An Phoblacht,* 15 May 1997.

24. Mic Moroney, "Just a Play," *The Irish Times,* 29 July 1999, and Amelia Gentleman, "Dubbel Trouble," *Guardian,* 5 August 1999, 14.

25. Murphy was incarcerated in Castlereagh.

26. "Robert Ballagh Interview" by Mic Moloney, *Ovidart,* http://www.ovidart.com/artists/rba-interview.htm.

27. Damian Smyth, quoted in Victoria White, "New Start for the Arts in the North, *Irish Times,* in www.artscouncil-ni.org/news/new31012001.htm.

28. Quoted in Pól Ó Muiri, "'I'm Here to Listen,'" *Irish Times,* 23 August 2000.

29. Moroney, "Just a Play."

30. Gentleman, "Dubbel Trouble," *Guardian,* 5 August 1999, 14.

31. Quoted in Gentleman, "Dubbel Trouble," *Guardian,* 5 August 1999, 14.

32. "Double Trouble for Dubbeljoint," *Andersontown News,* 7 August 1999, 12.

33. Eoin O'Brien, "A Clear Case of Political Censorship," *Fortnight,* September 1999, 22.

34. Malachi O'Doherty, "Play-acting of the Wrong Kind for an Audience in West Belfast," *Belfast Telegraph,* 3 August 1999, 10.

35. Gentleman, "Dubbel Trouble," *Guardian,* 5 August 1999, 14.

36. Mary Preston Silver, "Emotive Version of State's Origin," *Irish News,* 5 August 1999, www.irishnews.com/archives.

37. Malachi O'Doherty, "This Isn't Art," *Fortnight,* September 1999, 22.

38. *Private Eye,* 3 September 1999, BTA/LHL.

39. David Nowlan, *"Forced Upon Us,"* Irish Times, 7 September 2000, 12.

40. Gerry Adams, "Adams Criticises Arts Council Decisions," Sinn Féin Press Release, 5–7 Conway Street, Belfast, 30 July 1999.

41. "Forced Upon Us" (Letter to the Editor), *Irish Times,* 30 July 1999.

42. "Over to You, Mr. McFall," *Andersontown News,* 7 August 1999, 6. John McFall was the minister charged with responsibility for the ACNI.

43. Quoted in "Arts Council in Funding Bias Row," *An Phoblacht,* 25 February 1999, Irlnet.com/apm/archive/1999/February25/25/arts.html.

44. See www.parliament.the-stationery-office.co.uk/pa/cm199899/cmhansrd/vo991101/text/91101w11.htm.

45. Ian Hill, "Diary," *Belfast Newsletter,* 5 February 2001, BTA/LHL.

46. "Opening Up the Arts to Everyone," *Belfast Newsletter,* 15 February 2001, BTA/LHL.

47. Martin McDonagh, *The Lieutenant of Inishmore* (London: Methuen, 2001), 29.

48. Martin McDonagh, quoted in Jillian Edelstein, "The Wild West," *Guardian Weekend Magazine,* 24 March 2001, 35.

49. Quoted in Penelope Dening, "The Scribe of Kilburn," *Irish Times,* 18 April 2001, 12.

Conclusion

1. Annabel Patterson, "Censorship," *The Encyclopedia of Literature and Criticism,* ed. Martin Coyle, et al. (Detroit: Gale, 1991), 907.

2. Christopher Murray, "O'Casey's *The Drums of Father Ned* in Context," in *A Century of Irish Drama,* 128.

Selected Bibliography

Archival Sources

Berg Collection, New York Public Library
British Theatre Archive, Linen Hall Library, Belfast
Dublin Diocesan Archives, Dublin
Gate Theatre Archive, Northwestern University, Evanston, Illinois
Lord Chamberlain's Papers, British Library, London
Lord Chamberlain's Correspondence, British Library, London
Lyric Theatre-O'Malley Archive, National University of Ireland, Galway
National Archives, Dublin
National Library of Ireland, Dublin
P. S. O'Hegarty Collection, University of Kansas, Lawrence, Kansas
Trinity College, Dublin
Enthoven Collection, Theatre Museum Archives, London

Newspapers and Periodicals

Andersontown News
The Arrow
Belfast Newsletter
The Bell
Beltaine
Christian Science Monitor
Christus Rex
An Claidheamh Soluis
Daily Telegraph
Denvir's Monthly
Dublin Evening Mail
Dublin Magazine
Fiat
Fortnight
Freeman's Journal
Gentleman's Magazine
The Guardian
Honesty
Illustrated London News
Irish News

Irish Playgoer
Irish Press
Irish Times
Irish Independent
The Leader
The Listener
Manchester Guardian
Maria Duce Bulletin
Mayo News
Motley
Muse
New Ireland Review
New Republic
New York Times
Ovidart
Pall Mall Gazette
An Phoblacht
Pike Newsletter
Samhain
Sinn Féin
The Standard
Theatre Arts
Theatre Ireland
Threshold
The Times (London)
United Irishman
Young Ireland

Books, Articles, and Manuscripts

Account of the Terrific and Fatal Riot at the New York Astor Place Opera House, on the Night of May 10th 1849; with the Quarrels of Forrest and Macready, Including All the Causes which Led to that Awful Tragedy. New York: H. M. Ranney, 1849.

AE [George Russell]. *The Living Torch.* Ed. Monk Gibbon. London: Macmillan, 1937.

Adams, Michael. *Censorship: The Irish Experience.* Tuscaloosa: University of Alabama Press, 1968.

Aldgate, Anthony. *Censorship and the Permissive Society: British Cinema and Theatre, 1955–1965.* Oxford: Clarendon Press, 1995.

Allgood, Sara. "Memories" (unpublished manuscript). Berg.

Archer, C. *William Archer: Life, Work and Friendships.* New Haven, Conn.: Yale University Press, 1931.

Arden, John. *To Present the Pretense: Essays on the Theatre and Its Public.* London: Eyre Methuen, 1977.

Baer, Marc. *Theatre and Disorder in Late Georgian London.* Oxford: Clarendon Press, 1992.

Bailey, Peter. "Custom, Capital and Culture in the Victorian Music Hall." In *Popular Culture and Custom in Nineteenth-Century England.* Ed. Robert D. Storch. New York: St. Martin's Press, 1982.

Barrett, William. "Irish Drama?" *New Ireland Review* 3 (1895): 38–41.

Barthes, Roland. *Critical Essays.* Trans. Richard Howard. Evanston, Ill.: Northwestern University Press, 1972.

Beckett, Samuel. *Disjecta: Miscellaneous Writings and a Dramatic Fragment.* Ed. Ruby Cohn. New York: Grove, 1983.

Bell, Sam Hanna. *The Theatre in Ulster: A Survey of the Dramatic Movement in Ulster from 1902 until the Present Day.* Dublin: Gill and Macmillan, 1972.

Bennett, Susan. *Theatre Audiences: A Theory of Production and Reception.* New York: Routledge, 1990.

Bentley, Eric. "Irish Theatre: Splendeurs et Misères." *Poetry* 53 (January 1952): 216–32. Reprinted in *In Search of Theater.* Eric Bentley. New York: Vintage, 1953.

Bickley, Francis. *J. M. Synge and the Irish Dramatic Movement.* London: Constable, 1912.

Birmingham, George A. *Irishmen All.* New York: Frederick A. Stokes, 1913.

———. *General John Regan.* London: George Allen and Unwin, 1933.

———. *Pleasant Places.* London: W. Heinemann, 1934.

Blanshard, Paul. *The Irish and Catholic Power: An American Interpretation.* London: Derek Verschoyle, 1954.

———. *Personal and Confidential.* Boston: Beacon, 1973.

Blythe, Ernest. *The Abbey Theatre.* Dublin: National Theatre Society, 1965.

Books Prohibited in Eire Under the Censorship of Publications Act, 1929. Dublin: Eason, 1940.

Bourgeois, Maurice. *John Millington Synge and the Irish Theatre.* London: Constable, 1913.

Boyd, Ernest A. *The Contemporary Drama of Ireland.* Dublin: Talbot Press, 1917.

Brown, Malcolm. *The Politics of Irish Literature: From Thomas Davis to W. B. Yeats.* Seattle: University of Washington Press, 1972.

Brown, Terence. *Ireland: A Social and Cultural History, 1922 to the Present.* Ithaca, N.Y.: Cornell University Press, 1985.

Browne, Alan, ed. *Masters, Midwives and Ladies-in-Waiting: The Rotunda Hospital, 1745–1995.* Dublin: A. & A. Farmar, 1995.

Bryson, Lucy, and Clem McCartney. *Clashing Symbols? A Report on the Use of Flags, Anthems and Other National Symbols in Northern Ireland.* Belfast: Institute of Irish Studies, 1994.

Burke, Helen M. *Riotous Performances: The Struggle for Hegemony in the Irish Theatre, 1712–1784.* Notre Dame, Ind.: University of Notre Dame Press, 2003.

Burns-Bisogno, Louisa. *Censoring Irish Nationalism: The British, Irish, and American Suppression of Republican Images in Film and Television, 1909–1995.* Jefferson, N.C.: McFarland, 1997.

Burt, Richard. *Licensed by Authority: Ben Jonson and the Discourses of Censorship.* Ithaca, N.Y.: Cornell University Press, 1993.

Butler, Hubert. *Escape from the Anthill.* Mullingar: Lilliput, 1985.

Byrne, Dawson. *The Story of Ireland's National Theatre: The Abbey Theatre, Dublin.* Dublin: Talbot Press, 1929.

Byrne, Ophelia. *The Stage in Ulster from the Eighteenth Century.* Belfast: Linen Hall Library, 1997.

Cairns, David, and Shaun Richards. "Reading a Riot: The 'Reading Formation' of Synge's Abbey Audience." *Literature and History* 13 (1987): 219–37.

Carlson, Julia. *Banned in Ireland: Censorship and the Irish Writer.* Athens: University of Georgia Press, 1990.

Carlson, Marvin. *Places of Performance: The Semiotics of Theatre Architecture.* Ithaca, N.Y.: Cornell University Press, 1989.

Carroll, Paul Vincent. "Can the Abbey Theatre Be Restored?" *Theatre Arts* 36 (January 1952): 18–19, 79.

———. *Shadow and Substance.* New York: Random House, 1937.

Carty, Ciaran. *Confessions of a Sewer Rat: A Personal History of Censorship and the Irish Cinema.* Dublin: New Island Books, 1995.

Cave, Richard Allen. "Staging the Irishman." In *Acts of Supremacy: The British Empire and the Stage, 1790–1930.* Ed. J. S. Bratton, et al. New York: Manchester University Press, 1991.

Chapman, Wayne K. "'The Countess Cathleen' Row of 1899 and the Revisions of 1901 and 1911." *Yeats Annual.* No. 11. Ed. Warwick Gould, 105–23. London: Macmillan, 1995.

Chaudhuri, Una. *Staging Place: The Geography of Modern Drama.* Ann Arbor: University of Michigan Press, 1995.

Clare, Janet. *"Art Made Tongue-Tied by Authority": Elizabethan and Jacobean Dramatic Censorship.* 2d ed. Manchester: Manchester University Press, 1999.

Clark, William Smith. *The Early Irish Stage: The Beginnings to 1720.* Oxford: Clarendon Press, 1955.

Clarke, Brenna Katz. *The Emergence of the Irish Peasant Play at the Abbey Theatre.* Ann Arbor: UMI Research Press, 1982.

Colum, Mary. *The Life and the Dream.* Rev. ed. Garden City, N.Y.: Doubleday, 1968.

Colum, Padraic. "Early Days of the Irish Theatre." *Dublin Magazine* 24 (1949): 11–17.

————. "The Early Days of the Irish Theatre (Continued)." *Dublin Magazine* 25 (1950): 18–25.

————. *The Road Round Ireland.* New York: Macmillan, 1926.

Condon, Mary D. "The Dublin Riot of 1822 and Catholic Emancipation." Master's thesis, University of Southern California, 1950.

Connolly, Peter. *No Bland Facility: Selected Writings on Literature, Religion and Censorship.* Ed. James H. Murphy. Gerrards Cross: Colin Smythe, 1991.

Cooney, John. *John Charles McQuaid: Ruler of Catholic Ireland.* Syracuse, N.Y.: Syracuse University Press, 2000.

Corkery, Daniel. *Synge and Anglo-Irish Literature.* Cork: Cork University Press, 1931.

Costello, Peter. *The Heart Grown Brutal: The Irish Revolution in Literature, from Parnell to the Death of Yeats, 1891–1939.* Dublin: Gill and Macmillan, 1977.

Cousins, James, and Margaret Cousins. *We Two Together.* Madras: Ganesh, 1950.

Cowasjee, Saros. *O'Casey.* New York: Barnes and Noble, 1967.

Craig, Alec. *The Banned Books of England and Other Countries: A Study of the Conception of Literary Obscenity.* Westport, Conn.: Greenwood Press, 1977.

Cronin, Anthony. *Samuel Beckett: The Last Modernist.* London: HarperCollins, 1996.

Curran, C. P. *Under the Receding Wave.* Dublin: Gill and Macmillan, 1970.

Davies, Andrew. *Other Theatres: The Development of Alternative and Experimental Theatre in Britain.* Totowa, N.J.: Barnes and Noble, 1987.

Daubeny, Peter. *My World of Theatre.* London: Jonathan Cape, 1971.

Deane, Seamus, ed. *The Field Day Anthology of Irish Writing.* 3 vols. Derry: Field Day, 1996.

De Búrca, Séamus. *The Queen's Royal Theatre Dublin, 1829–1969.* Dublin: de Búrca, 1983.

De Jongh, Nicholas. *Politics, Prudery and Perversions: The Censoring of the English Stage, 1901–1968.* London: Methuen, 2000.

Dickson, Page Lawrence. *The Abbey Row: NOT Edited by W. B. Yeats.* Dublin: Maunsel, 1907.

Devane, R. S. *The Committee on Evil Literature: Some Notes of Evidence.* Dublin: Browne and Nolan, 1927.

————. *Evil Literature: Some Suggestions.* Dublin: Browne and Nolan, 1927.

————. *The Imported Press: A National Menace—Some Remedies.* Dublin: Duffy, 1950.

Donleavy, J. P. *The Plays of J. P. Donleavy.* New York: Dell, 1972.

————. *The History of The Ginger Man.* New York: Houghton Mifflin, 1994.

Doyle, Roddy. *War.* Dublin: Passion Machine, 1989.

Duggan, G. C. *The Stage Irishman: A History of the Irish Play and Stage Characters from the Earliest Times.* London: Longmans, 1937.

Dutton, Richard. *Mastering the Revels: The Regulation and Censorship of English Renaissance Drama.* Iowa City: University of Iowa Press, 1991.

Edwards, Hilton. "The Irish Theatre." In *A History of the Theatre.* Ed. George Freedley and John A. Reeves. 3d rev. ed. New York: Crown, 1968.

————. *The Mantle of Harlequin.* Dublin: Progress House, 1958.

Edwards, Philip. *Threshold of a Nation: A Study in English and Irish Drama.* Cambridge: Cambridge University Press, 1980.

Empson, William. *Faustus and the Censor: The English Faust-book and Marlowe's Doctor Faustus.* London: Basil Blackwell, 1987.

Ervine, St. John G. *Mixed Marriage.* London: George Allen and Unwin, 1920.

————. *The Organized Theatre: A Plea in Civics.* New York: Macmillan, 1924.

————. *The Theatre in My Time.* London: Rich and Cowan, 1933.

Eyre, Richard. *Changing Stages: A History of Twentieth-Century British Theatre.* Episode 2. British Broadcasting Corporation broadcast, 12 October 2000.

Fallon, Brian. *An Age of Innocence: Irish Culture, 1930–1960.* New York: St. Martin's Press, 1998.

Fallon, Gabriel. "Dublin International Theatre Festival, 1959." *Threshold* 3 (Autumn 1959): 63–75.

————. "Dublin's Theatre Festival." *Threshold* 1 (Autumn 1957): 75–81.

————. "The Future of the Irish Theatre," *Studies: An Irish Quarterly Review* 44 (Spring 1955): 92–100.

————. *Sean O'Casey: The Man I Knew.* Boston: Little, Brown, 1965.

Fay, Gerard. *The Abbey Theatre: Cradle of Genius.* Dublin: Clonmore and Reynolds, 1958.

Fay, W. G., and Catherine Cornwell. *The Fays of the Abbey Theatre: An Autobiographical Record.* New York: Harcourt, Brace, 1935.

Feeney, John. *John Charles McQuaid: The Man and the Mask.* Dublin: Mercier Press, 1974.

Feeney, William J. *Drama in Hardwicke Street: A History of the Irish Theatre Company.* Rutherford, N.J.: Fairleigh Dickinson University Press, 1984.

————, ed. *Edward Martyn's Irish Theatre*. Newark, Del.: Proscenium Press, 1980.

Findlater, Richard. *Banned! A Review of Theatrical Censorship in Britain*. London: Macgibbon & Kee, 1967.

————. *The Unholy Trade*. London: Victor Gollancz, 1952.

Fingall, Elizabeth. *Seventy Years Young: Memories of Elizabeth, Countess of Fingall as Told to Pamela Hinkson*. New York: Dutton, 1939.

Fitz-Simon, Christopher. *The Boys: A Double Biography of Micheál Mac Liammóir and Hilton Edwards*. London: Nick Hern, 1994.

Flannery, James W. "High Ideals and the Reality of the Marketplace: A Financial Record of the Early Abbey Theatre." *Studies* 71 (Autumn 1972): 246–69.

————. *W. B. Yeats and the Idea of a Theatre: The Early Abbey Theatre in Theory and Practice*. New Haven, Conn.: Yale University Press, 1976.

Foster, Roy. *The Irish Story: Telling Tales and Making It Up in Ireland*. New York: Penguin, 2001.

————. *W. B. Yeats, A Life. I: The Apprentice Mage, 1865–1914*. Oxford: Oxford University Press, 1997.

Foucault, Michel. *Discipline and Punish: The Birth of the Prison*. Trans. Alan Sheridan. New York: Vintage, 1995.

Fowell, Frank, and Frank Palmer. *Censorship in England*. 1913. Reprint. New York: Benjamin Blom, 1969.

Fox, R. M. "Sean O'Casey: A Worker Dramatist." *New Statesman*, 10 April 1926, 805.

Frazier, Adrian. *Behind the Scenes: Yeats, Horniman, and the Struggle for the Abbey Theatre*. Berkeley: University of California Press, 1990.

————. *George Moore: 1852–1933*. New Haven, Conn.: Yale University Press, 2000.

G. M. G. *The Stage Censor: A Historical Sketch, 1544–1907*. London: S. Low, Marston, 1908.

Galsworthy, John. *Justification of the Censorship of Plays*. London: W. Heinemann, 1909.

Gannon, Patrick J. "Art, Morality and Censorship." *Studies: An Irish Quarterly Review* 65 (July 1937): 434–47.

Gardiner, Harold C. *Mysteries' End: An Investigation of the Last Days of the Medieval Religious Stage*. New Haven, Conn.: Yale University Press, 1946.

Goodman, Lizbeth, and Jane de Gay, eds. *Feminist Stages: Interviews with Women in Contemporary British Theatre*. Amsterdam: Harwood, 1996.

Gordon, Leon. *White Cargo: A Play of the Primitive*. Boston: Four Seas, 1925.

Greaves, C. Desmond. *Sean O'Casey: Politics and Art*. Lawrence, N.J.: Humanities Press, 1979.

Greene, David H., and Edward M. Stephens. *J. M. Synge: 1871–1909.* Rev. ed. New York: New York University Press, 1989.

Gregory, Augusta. *The Image and Other Plays.* New York: G. P. Putnam's Sons, 1922.

————. *Our Irish Theatre: A Chapter of Autobiography.* 1913. Reprint. Gerrards Cross: Colin Smythe, 1972.

————. *Lady Gregory's Diaries, 1892–1902.* Ed. James Pethica. Gerrards Cross: Colin Smythe, 1996.

————. *Lady Gregory's Journals, 1916–1930.* Ed. Lennox Robinson. London: Putnam, 1946.

Grene, Nicholas. *The Politics of Irish Drama: Plays in Context from Boucicault to Friel.* Cambridge: Cambridge University Press, 1999.

Guthrie, Tyrone. *A Life in the Theatre.* London: Hamish Hamilton, 1959.

Gwynn, Stephen. *Irish Literature and Drama in the English Language: A Short History.* London: Thomas Nelson, 1936.

Hackett, Francis. *The Invisible Censor.* 1921. Reprint. Freeport, N.Y.: Books for Libraries, 1968.

Harrington, John P. "Resentment, Relevance, and the Production History of *The Playboy of the Western World.*" In *Assessing the Achievement of J. M. Synge.* Ed. Alexander G. Gonzalez. Westport, Conn.: Greenwood, 1996.

————. *The Irish Play on the New York Stage: 1874–1966.* Lexington: University Press of Kentucky, 1998.

Harris, Susan Cannon. "All That Trouble and Nothing to Show for It: Yeats's *The Herne's Egg* and the Misbirth of a Nation." *Éire-Ireland* 33 (1997–1998): 29–65.

————. "More Than a Morbid, Unhealthy Mind: Public Health and the *Playboy* Riots." In *A Century of Irish Drama: Widening the Stage.* Ed. Stephen Watt, et al. 72–94. Bloomington: Indiana University Press, 2000.

Headley, J. T. *The Great Riots of New York, 1712–1873.* New York: Treat, 1873.

Henderson, W. A. "Three Centuries of the Stage Literature of Ireland." *New Ireland Review* 7 (May 1897): 168–78.

Herr, Cheryl. *For the Land They Loved: Irish Political Melodrama, 1890–1925.* Syracuse, N.Y.: Syracuse University Press, 1991.

Hickey, Des, and Gus Smith, eds. *Flight from the Celtic Twilight.* New York: Bobbs-Merrill, 1973.

Hogan, Robert. *After the Irish Renaissance: A Critical History of Irish Drama Since "The Plough and the Stars."* Minneapolis: University of Minnesota Press, 1967.

————. *The Experiments of Sean O'Casey.* New York: St. Martin's Press, 1960.

————. "O'Casey and the Archbishop." *New Republic,* 19 May 1958, 29–30.

Hogan, Robert, and Richard Burnham, eds. *The Years of O'Casey, 1921–1926.* Newark: University of Delaware Press, 1992.

Hogan, Robert, Richard Burnham, and Daniel P. Poteet, eds. *The Rise of the Realists, 1910–1915.* Vol. 4 of *The Modern Irish Drama: A Documentary History.* Dublin: Dolmen Press, 1979.

Hogan, Robert, and James Kilroy, eds. *The Irish Literary Theatre 1899–1901.* Vol. 1 of *The Modern Irish Drama: A Documentary History.* Dublin: Dolmen Press, 1975.

————, eds. *Laying the Foundations: 1902–1904.* Vol. 2 of *The Modern Irish Drama: A Documentary History.* Dublin: Dolmen Press, 1976.

————, eds. *The Abbey Theatre: The Years of Synge, 1905–1909.* Vol. 3 of *The Modern Irish Drama: A Documentary History.* Dublin: Dolmen Press, 1978.

Hogan, Robert, James Kilroy, and Liam Miller, eds. *The Art of the Amateur: 1916–1920.* Vol. 5 of *The Modern Irish Drama: A Documentary History.* Dublin: Dolmen Press, 1984.

Holloway, Joseph. *Joseph Holloway's Abbey Theatre: A Selection from His Unpublished Journal "Impressions of a Dublin Playgoer."* Ed. Robert Hogan and Michael J. O'Neill. Carbondale: Southern Illinois University Press, 1967.

————. *Joseph Holloway's Irish Theatre.* Ed. Robert Hogan and Michael J. O'Neill. 3 vols. Dixon, Calif.: Proscenium Press, 1968–70.

Howes, Marjorie. *Yeats's Nations: Gender, Class, and Irishness.* Cambridge: Cambridge University Press, 1996.

Hunt, Hugh. *The Abbey: Ireland's National Theatre, 1904–1979.* New York: Columbia University Press, 1979.

Innes, C. L. *Woman and Nation in Irish Literature and Society, 1880–1935.* Athens: University of Georgia Press, 1993.

Jackson, Russell, ed. *Victorian Theatre: The Theatre in Its Time.* New York: New Amsterdam, 1989.

Jauss, Hans Robert. *Toward an Aesthetic of Reception.* Trans. Timothy Bahti. Brighton: Harvester, 1982.

Johnston, John. *The Lord Chamberlain's Blue Pencil.* London: Hodder & Stoughton, 1990.

Jones, Henry Arthur. *The Censorship Muddle and a Way Out of It: A Letter Addressed to the Right Honourable Herbert Samuel.* London: Chiswick, 1909.

Joyce, James. *James Joyce: Occasional, Critical, and Political Writing.* Ed. Kevin Barry. Oxford: Oxford University Press, 2000.

Kavanagh, Peter. *The Story of the Abbey Theatre: From Its Origins in 1899 to the Present.* New York: Devin-Adair, 1950.

Kelly, Éamon. *The Journeyman.* Boulder, Colo.: Irish American Book Company, 1998.

Kenny, Mary. *Goodbye to Catholic Ireland.* London: Sinclair-Stevenson, 1997.

Kiberd, Declan. "The Fall of the Stage Irishman." In *Genres of the Irish Literary Revival.* Ed. Ronald Schleifer, 39–60. Dublin: Wolfhound, 1980.

Kilroy, James. *The "Playboy" Riots.* Dublin: Dolmen Press, 1971.

Kilroy, Thomas. *The Death and Resurrection of Mr. Roche.* New York: Grove, 1969.

————, ed. *Sean O'Casey: A Collection of Critical Essays.* Englewood Cliffs, N.J.: Prentice-Hall, 1975.

Knowlson, James. *Damned to Fame: The Life of Samuel Beckett.* New York: Simon and Schuster, 1996.

Krause, David. "The Playwright's Not for Burning." *Virginia Quarterly Review* 34 (Winter 1958): 60–76.

————. *Sean O'Casey and His World.* New York: Scribner's, 1976.

————. *Sean O'Casey: The Man and His Work.* New York: Macmillan, 1960.

Laurence, Dan H. and Nicholas Grene, eds. *Shaw, Lady Gregory, and the Abbey: A Correspondence and a Record.* Gerrards Cross: Colin Smythe, 1993.

Lawrence, W. J. "Irish Characters in English Dramatic Literature." *Gentleman's Magazine,* n.s., 45 (August 1890): 178–91.

Le Bon, Gustave. *The Crowd: A Study of the Popular Mind.* New York: Viking, 1960.

The Liberal Ethic. Dublin: Irish Times, 1950.

Levitas, Ben. *Theatre and Nation: Irish Drama and Cultural Nationalism, 1890–1916.* Oxford: Clarendon Press, 2002.

Liesenfeld, Vincent J. *The Licensing Act of 1737.* Madison: University of Wisconsin Press, 1984.

Lojek, Helen. "Playing Politics with Belfast's Charabanc Theatre Company." In *Politics and Performance in Contemporary Northern Ireland.* Ed. John P. Harrington and Elizabeth J. Mitchell, 82–103. Amherst: University of Massachusetts Press, 1999.

Lowery, Robert G., ed. *A Whirlwind in Dublin: "The Plough and the Stars" Riots.* Westport, Conn.: Greenwood Press, 1984.

Luke, Peter, ed. *Enter Certain Players: Edwards-Mac Liammóir and the Gate, 1928–1978.* Dublin: Dolmen Press, 1978.

Lyons, F. S. L. *Culture and Anarchy in Ireland, 1890–1939: From the Fall of Parnell to the Death of W. B. Yeats.* New York: Oxford University Press, 1979.

McCann, Sean, ed. *The Story of the Abbey Theatre.* London: New English Library, 1967.

McCormack, W. J. *Fool of the Family: A Life of J. M. Synge.* London: Weidenfeld and Nicholson, 2000.

McDiarmid, Lucy. "August Gregory, Bernard Shaw and the Shewing-Up of Dublin Castle." *Publications of the Modern Language Association* 109 (January 1994): 26–44.

McDonagh, Martin. *The Lieutenant of Inishmore.* London: Methuen, 2001.

Mac Liammóir, Micheál. *All for Hecuba: An Irish Theatrical Autobiography.* London: Methuen, 1946.

———. *Enter a Goldfish: Memoirs of an Irish Actor, Young and Old.* London: Thames and Hudson, 1977.

———. *Theatre in Ireland.* Dublin: At the Sign of the Three Candles, 1949.

McQuaid, John C. *Wellsprings of the Faith.* Dublin: Clonmore and Reynolds, 1956.

Malone, Andrew E. *The Irish Drama.* 1929. Reprint, New York: Benjamin Blom, 1965.

Manning, Mary. "Bongo-Bongo." *Motley* 2 (December 1933): 13–16.

Matthews, James. *Voices: A Life of Frank O'Connor.* New York: Atheneum, 1983.

Mercier, Vivian. *The Irish Comic Tradition.* Oxford: Clarendon Press, 1962.

Mikhail, E. H., ed. *The Abbey Theatre: Interviews and Recollections.* Totowa, N.J.: Barnes and Noble, 1988.

Miller, Jonathan. *Censorship and the Limits of Permission.* Sixth Annual Lecture under the "Thank-Offering to Britain Fund." London: Oxford University Press, 1972.

Moody, Richard. *The Astor Place Riot.* Bloomington: Indiana University Press, 1958.

Mooney, Ria. "Playing Rosie Redmond." *Journal of Irish Literature* 6 (May 1977): 21–27.

Moore, Carol, and Eleanor Methven. "Charabanc Theatre Company on Irish Women's Theatres." In *Feminist Stages: Interviews with Women in Contemporary British Theatre.* Ed. Lizbeth Goodman and Jane de Gay. Amsterdam: Harwood, 1996.

Moore, George. *Hail and Farewell.* New York: D. Appleton, 1920.

———. *Memoirs of My Dead Life.* New York: D. Appleton, 1911.

Morash, Christopher. "All Playboys Now: The Audience and the Riot." In *Interpreting Synge: Papers from the Synge Summer School.* Ed. Nicholas Grene. Dublin: Lilliput, 2000.

———. *A History of Irish Theatre, 1601–2000.* Cambridge: Cambridge University Press, 2002.

Murphy, William M. *Prodigal Father: The Life of John Butler Yeats (1839–1922).* Ithaca, N.Y.: Cornell University Press, 1978.

Murray, Christopher. *Twentieth-Century Irish Drama: Mirror Up to Nation.* New York: Manchester University Press, 1997.

————. "O'Casey's *The Drums of Father Ned* in Context." In *A Century of Irish Drama: Widening the Stage.* Ed. Stephen Watt, et al. Bloomington: Indiana University Press, 2000.

Na Gopaleen, Myles [Flann O'Brien]. "Cruiskeen Lawn: Tóstal War." *Irish Independent,* 19 February 1958, 6.

Nathan, George Jean. "Master Minds of Censorship." *Vanity Fair,* July 1926, 57, 102.

Nicholson, Watson. *The Struggle for a Free Stage in London.* 1906. Reprint. New York: Benjamin Blom, 1966.

Nic Shiubhlaigh, Maire. *The Splendid Years: Recollections of Maire Nic Shiubhlaigh as told to Edward Kenny.* Dublin: Duffy, 1955.

Norman, E. R. *Anti-Catholicism in Victorian England.* London: George Allen and Unwin, 1968.

O'Casey, Sean. *Behind the Green Curtains.* New York: St. Martin's Press, 1961.

————. *The Bishop's Bonfire.* New York: Macmillan, 1955.

————. *The Drums of Father Ned.* New York: St. Martin's Press, 1960.

————. *The Flying Wasp: Essays on the Modern Theatre.* London: Macmillan, 1937.

————. *The Green Crow.* New York: George Braziller, 1956.

————. *The Letters of Sean O'Casey.* 4 vols. Ed. David Krause. New York: Macmillan and Washington, D.C.: Catholic University of America Press, 1975–1992.

————. *Three Plays.* London: Macmillan, 1960.

O'Connor, Frank. *My Father's Son.* London: Macmillan, 1968.

————. *A Short History of Irish Literature: A Backward Look.* New York: G. P. Putnam's Sons, 1967.

O'Donnell, F. Hugh. *Souls for Gold! A Pseudo-Celtic Drama in Dublin.* London: Nassau Press, 1899.

Ó Drisceoil, Donal. *Censorship in Ireland, 1939–1945: Neutrality, Politics, and Society.* Cork: Cork University Press, 1996.

O'Faoláin, Seán. *She Had to Do Something.* London: Jonathan Cape, 1938.

O'Flaherty, Liam. *The Puritan.* London: Jonathan Cape, 1932.

Ó hAodha, Micheál. *The Importance of Being Micheál: A Portrait of Mac Liammóir.* Dingle, Kerry: Brandon, 1990.

————. *Theatre in Ireland.* Oxford: Basil Blackwell, 1974.

One Hundred Years of Gaiety: 1871–1971. N.p., n.d.

O'Malley, Conor. *A Poets' Theatre.* Dublin: Elo Press, 1988.

O'Reilly, F. *The Problem of Undesirable Printed Matter: Some Suggested Remedies.* Dublin: Catholic Truth Society of Ireland, 1926.

O'Riordan, John. *A Guide to O'Casey's Plays: From the Plough to the Stars.* London: Macmillan, 1984.

O'Sullivan, Michael. *Brendan Behan: A Life*. Boulder, Colo.: Roberts Rinehart, 1999.

O'Sullivan, Seamus. *The Rose and the Bottle and Other Essays*. Dublin: Talbot Press, 1946.

Owens, Gary. "Nationalism without Words: Symbolism and Ritual Behaviour in the Repeal 'Monster Meetings' of 1843–45." In *Irish Popular Culture, 1650–1850*. Ed. James S. Donnelly Jr. and Kerby A. Miller, 242–69. Dublin: Irish Academic Press, 1999.

Palmer, John. *The Censor and the Theatres*. London: T. Fisher Unwin, 1912.

Patterson, Annabel. "Censorship." In *The Encyclopedia of Literature and Criticism*. Ed. Martin Coyle, et al., 901–14. Detroit: Gale, 1991.

———. *Censorship and Interpretation: The Conditions of Writing and Reading in Early Modern England*. Madison: University of Wisconsin Press, 1984.

Pavis, Patrice. *Theatre at the Crossroads of Culture*. Trans. Loren Kruger. New York: Routledge, 1992.

Pilkington, Lionel. "Theatre and Cultural Politics in Northern Ireland: The 'Over the Bridge' Controversy." *Éire-Ireland* 30 (Winter 1996): 76–93.

———. *Theatre and the State in Twentieth-Century Ireland: Cultivating the People*. New York: Routledge, 2001.

Playing the Wild Card. www.artscouncil-ni.org/review/content.pdf.

Reid, Desmond. "Tennessee Williams." *Studies: An Irish Quarterly Review* 46 (Winter 1957): 431–46.

Report for Year Ended 30th June, 1927. Dublin: Catholic Truth Society of Ireland, 1927.

Report for Year Ended 30th June, 1928. Dublin: Catholic Truth Society of Ireland, 1928.

Report for Year Ended 30th June, 1930. Dublin: Catholic Truth Society of Ireland, 1930.

Report from the Joint Select Committee of the House of Lords and the House of Commons on the Stage Plays (Censorship). London: His Majesty's Stationery Office by Wyman and Sons, 1909.

Report of the Joint Committee on Censorship of the Theatre, Together with the Proceedings of the Committee, Minutes of Evidence, Appendices and Index. London: Her Majesty's Stationery Office, 1967.

Report of the Select Committee Appointed to Inquire into the Laws Affecting Dramatic Literature, 1832. Series of British Parliamentary Papers, Stage and Theatre 1. Introduction and index by Marilyn L. Norstedt. Shannon: Irish University Press, 1968.

Report from the Select Committee on Theatres and Places of Entertainment. London: Her Majesty's Stationery Office, 1892.

Robinson, Lennox. *Curtain Up: An Autobiography*. London: Michael Joseph, 1942.

————. *Ireland's Abbey Theatre: A History, 1899–1951.* London: Sidgwick & Jackson, 1951.

————, ed. *The Irish Theatre: Lectures Delivered during the Abbey Theatre Festival Held in Dublin in August 1938.* London: Macmillan, 1939.

Ross, Ian Campbell, ed. *Public Virtue, Public Love: The Early Years of the Dublin Lying-In Hospital, The Rotunda.* Dublin: O'Brien, 1986.

Ryan, Brendan. *Keeping Us in the Dark: Censorship and Freedom of Information in Ireland.* Dublin: Gill and Macmillan, 1995.

Ryan, John. *Remembering How We Stood: Bohemian Dublin at Mid-Century.* New York: Taplinger, 1975.

Ryan, Philip B. *The Lost Theatres of Dublin.* Westbury, Wiltshire: Badger, 1998.

Ryan, Phyllis. *The Company I Kept.* Dublin: Town House, 1996.

Ryan, William Patrick. *The Irish Literary Revival: Its History, Pioneers and Possibilities.* 1894. Reprint. New York: Lemma, 1970.

Saddlemyer, Ann, ed. *The Collected Letters of John Millington Synge.* 2 vols. London: Oxford University Press, 1983–84.

————, ed. *Theatre Business: The Correspondence of the First Abbey Theatre Directors: William Butler Yeats, Lady Gregory and J. M. Synge.* Gerrards Cross: Colin Smythe, 1982.

St. John-Stevas, Norman. *Obscenity and the Law.* London: Secker and Warburg, 1956.

Seagle, William. *Cato; or the Future of Censorship.* London: K. Paul, Trench, Trubner, 1898.

Shaw, Bernard. *The Drama Observed.* Volume 4: *1911–1950.* Ed. Bernard F. Dukore. University Park: Pennsylvania State University Press, 1993.

————. *The Shewing-up of Blanco Posnet with Preface on the Censorship.* London: Constable, 1913.

Sheldon, Esther K. *Thomas Sheridan of Smock-Alley.* Princeton, N.J.: Princeton University Press, 1967.

Sidnell, Michael J. "'The Countess Cathleen' as a Study in Theatrical Genre," *South Carolina Review* 32 (Fall 1999): 38–48.

Sidnell, Michael J., and Wayne K. Chapman, eds. *"The Countess Cathleen" Manuscript Materials.* Ithaca, N.Y.: Cornell University Press, 1999.

Simpson, Alan. *Beckett and Behan and a Theatre in Dublin.* London: Routledge and Kegan Paul, 1962.

Smyth, Patrick, and Ellen Hazelkorn, eds. *Let in the Light: Censorship, Secrecy, and Democracy.* Dingle, Kerry: Brandon, 1993.

Spoto, Donald. *The Kindness of Strangers: The Life of Tennessee Williams.* Boston: Little, Brown, 1985.

Stanfield, Paul Scott. *Yeats and Politics in the 1930s.* New York: St. Martin's Press, 1988.

Steiner, George. *The Death of Tragedy.* New York: Hill and Wang, 1961.

Stephens, John Russell. *The Censorship of English Drama, 1824–1901.* New York: Cambridge University Press, 1980.

Stockwell, La Tourette. *Dublin Theatres and Theatre Customs, 1637–1820.* Kingsport, Tenn.: Kingsport, 1938.

Strand, Ginger. "*The Playboy,* Critics, and the Enduring Problem of the Audience." In *Assessing the Achievement of J. M. Synge.* Ed. Alexander G. Gonzalez, 10–23. Westport, Conn.: Greenwood, 1996.

Sullivan, Megan. *Women in Northern Ireland.* Gainesville: University Press of Florida, 1999.

Sutherland, John. *Offensive Literature.* London: Junction, 1982.

Swift, Carolyn. *Stage by Stage.* Dublin: Poolbeg, 1985.

Synge, J. M. *The Collected Works: Plays.* Vols 3 and 4. Ed. Ann Saddlemyer. Oxford: Clarendon Press, 1968.

Taylor, Brian, *The Life and Writings of James Owen Hannay (George A. Birmingham) 1865–1950.* Lewiston, N.Y.: Mellen Press, 1995.

Thompson, Sam. *Over the Bridge.* Ed. Stewart Parker. Dublin: Gill and Macmillan, 1970.

Tóibín, Colm. *Lady Gregory's Toothbrush.* Dublin: Lilliput, 2002.

Trotter, Mary. *Ireland's National Theaters: Political Performance and the Origins of the Irish Dramatic Movement.* Syracuse, N.Y.: Syracuse University Press, 2001.

A Twelfth-Century Pageant Play: Portraying Scenes of Irish History. Dublin: Hodges Figgis, 1907.

Tydeman, William, and Steven Price, eds. *Wilde— "Salome": Plays in Production.* Cambridge: Cambridge University Press, 1996.

Tymoczko, Maria, ed. "Tableaux Vivants in Ireland at the Turn of the Century." *Nineteenth Century Theatre* 23 (1995): 90–110.

Ubersfeld, Anne. *Reading Theatre.* Trans. Frank Collins. Ed. Paul Perron and Patrick Debbèche. Toronto: University of Toronto Press, 1999.

Vandevelde, Karen. "Outside the Abbey: The Irish National Theatres, 1897–1913." Ph.D. diss., National University of Ireland, Galway, 2001.

Views of Theatre in Ireland 1995: Report of the Arts Council Theatre Review. Dublin: Arts Council, 1995.

H.P.W. *Sligo Theatre: A Statement of the Proceedings taken by the Rev. W. C. Armstrong.* Dublin: printed for the author, 1824.

The W. A. Henderson Scrapbooks, 1899–1911: From the National Library of Ireland. Microfilm, National Library of Ireland.

Ward, Margaret. *Unmanageable Revolutionaries: Women and Irish Nationalism.* London: Pluto, 1983.

Watson, G. J. *Irish Identity and the Literary Revival: Synge, Yeats, Joyce, and O'Casey.* London: Croon Helm, 1979.

Watt, Stephen. *Joyce, O'Casey, and the Irish Popular Theatre.* Syracuse, N.Y.: Syracuse University Press, 1991.

Watt, Stephen, et al., eds. *A Century of Irish Drama: Widening the Stage.* Bloomington: Indiana University Press, 2000.

Watters, Eugene, and Matthew Murtagh. *Infinite Variety: Dan Lowery's Music Hall, 1879–97.* Dublin: Gill and Macmillan, 1975.

Welch, Robert. *The Abbey Theatre, 1899–1999: Form and Pressure.* New York: Oxford University Press, 1999.

Wheatley, Christopher J. *Beneath Ïerne's Banners: Irish Protestant Drama of the Restoration and Eighteenth Century.* Notre Dame, Ind.: University of Notre Dame Press, 1999.

Whelan, Gerard, with Carolyn Swift. *Spiked: Church-State Intrigue and The Rose Tattoo.* Dublin: New Island, 2002.

Williams, Tennessee. *The Rose Tattoo.* In *Three Plays of Tennessee Williams.* Norfolk, Conn.: New Directions, 1959.

Wolfe, Francis R. *Theatres in Ireland.* 2d ed. Dublin: Humphrey and Armour, 1898.

Woodman, Kieran. *Media Control in Ireland, 1923–1983.* Carbondale: Southern Illinois University Press, 1985.

Yeats, W. B. *The Arrow:* 1 June 1907—"On Taking *The Playboy* to London." *The Irish Dramatic Movement.* Vol. 8 of *The Collected Works of W. B. Yeats.* Ed. Mary FitzGerald and Richard J. Finneran. New York: Palgrave Macmillan, 2003: 113–14.

———. *The Collected Letters of W. B. Yeats.* 3 vols. Ed. John Kelly, et al. Oxford: Clarendon Press, 1986–1997.

———. *The Collected Plays of W. B. Yeats.* New York: Macmillan, 1953.

———. *The Countess Kathleen and Various Legends and Lyrics.* London: T. Fisher Unwin, 1892.

———. "Dramatis Personae: 1896–1902." *Autobiographies.* Vol. 3 of *The Collected Works of W. B. Yeats.* Ed. William H. O'Donnell and Douglas N. Archibald. New York: Scribner, 1999.

———, ed. *Beltaine: The Organ of the Irish Literary Theatre.* English Little Magazines. No. 15. London: Frank Cass, 1970.

———, ed. *Samhain: October 1901–November 1908.* English Little Magazines. No. 14. London: Frank Cass, 1970.

Index

Index

Index

Gaffney, Fr. M. H., 132
Gaiety Theatre, 17, 25, 37, 40, 120, 135, 166; patent, 39, 64
Galsworthy, John, 88
Galway, 104, 128, 130, 221n.9
Gardai. *See* police
Garnett, Edward, 87
Garvey, Maire, 215n.63
Gate Theatre, 12, 128, 138, 157, 164, 179; *Motley*, 134; patent, 144–45, 158–59
Gay, John, 13
Gay Sweatshop, 181
Gielgud, Sir John, 159
Gilbert, W. S., 13, 88
Gill, T. P., 52
Giltinan, D. J., 135
Globe Theatre Company, 163, 178
Goldsmith, Oliver, 43
Gonne, Maud, 57, 61, 65, 74–75, 122–23
Gordon, Leon, 120
Granville-Barker, Harley 87, 88
Gregory, Lady Augusta 5, 18, 25, 52, 70, 76, 78, 130; as Abbey director, 76, 90, 92–94, 120–23, 220n.24; and *Blanco Posnet*, 92; *The Gaol Gate*, 214n.48, *The Image*, 104; and *Playboy*, 4, 80, 82
Griffith, Arthur, 75, 93, 101, 124, 216n.88, 223n.32; Celtic Literary Society, 46. *See also* Sinn Féin; United Irishman
Gunn, Michael, 17–19, 38, 39, 216n.85
Guthrie, Tyrone, 151–52, 170

Hall, Peter, 159
Hammond, Philip, 191
Hang all the Harpers, 186
Hannay, Reverend James O. *See* Birmingham, George
Harrington, John, 77, 216n.80, 224n.15
Harris, Richard, 166

Harris, Susan Cannon, 132
Hayes, Richard, 7, 131
Henderson, W. A., 42–44
Herr, Cheryl, 42, 50
Higgins, F. R., 132
Hill, Ian, 193
Hobson, Harold, 152, 159
Hogan, Robert, 52, 77–78, 99, 119, 153, 162–63, 211n.75
Holloway, Joseph, 42, 53, 55–56, 120, 140–41; on O'Casey, 122, 223n.16; on Synge, 76–77
Honesty, 116
Horniman, Annie Elizabeth, 7, 9, 64, 79, 215n.63; and censorship, 203n.8
Houseman, Laurence, 89
Howes, Marjorie, 73
Hugh, Hunt, 131
Humphreys, Shiela, 122
Hyde, Douglas 74, 101; *Casadh an tSugain,* 36, 57, 62

Ibsen, Henrik, 44, 57, 128; *A Doll's House,* 72; *Ghosts,* 16; *Peer Gynt,* 128
Inghinidhe Na h-Éireann (Daughters of Erin), 62, 64–66
Ionesco, Eugene, 232n.94
Irish Academy of Letters, 127
Irish Association of Civil Liberties, 149, 229n.19
Irish Ecclesiastical Review, 116
Irish Independent, 133, 139–41, 158, 166–67
Irish Literary Society (London), 46; *Gazette,* 46–47
Irish Literary Theatre, 6, 45–58, 60–62, 66, 73–74, 216n.85
Irish National Dramatic Company, 61
Irish Press, 139–40
Irish Times, 52, 130, 133, 139, 141–42, 152, 158, 166, 191
Irving, Henry, 108

Index

Index

Irish Studies in Literature and Culture

Joyce's Critics: Transitions in Reading and Culture
Joseph Brooker

Wild Colonial Girl: Essays on Edna O'Brian
Edited by Lisa Colletta and Maureen O'Connor

Locked in the Family Cell: Gender, Sexuality, and Political Agency in Irish National Discourse
Kathryn A. Conrad

How Joyce Wrote Finnegans Wake: *A Chapter-by-Chapter Genetic Guide*
Edited by Luca Crispi and Sam Slote

Riot and Great Anger: Stage Censorship in Twentieth-Century Ireland
Joan FitzPatrick Dean

The Wee Wild One: Stories of Belfast and Beyond
Ruth C. Schwertfeger